W9-AMX-198

■ ■ ■ ■ ■

THE CONCEPTS OF

DATABASE MANAGEMENT

Second Edition

Philip J. Pratt   Joseph J. Adamski

COURSE
TECHNOLOGY

ONE MAIN STREET, CAMBRIDGE, MA 02142

an International Thomson Publishing company I(T)P®

Cambridge • Albany • Bonn • Boston • Cincinnati • London • Madrid • Melbourne • Mexico City
New York • Paris • San Francisco • Singapore • Tokyo • Toronto • Washington

Credits:

Managing Editor	Kristen Duerr	**Cover Designers**	Dick Hannus/Hannus Design Associates, Efrat Reis
Product Manager	Jennifer Normandin	**Interior Designer**	Efrat Reis
Production Editor	Nancy Ray	**Marketing Manager**	Susanne Walker
Composition House	GEX, Inc.		

For more information contact:

Course Technology
One Main Street
Cambridge, MA 02142

ITP Europe
Berkshire House 168-173
High Holborn
London WC11V 7AA
England

Nelson ITP Australia
102 Dodds Street
South Melbourne, 3205
Victoria, Australia

ITP Nelson Canada
1120 Birchmount Road
Scarborough, Ontario
Canada M1K 5G4

International Thomson Editores
Seneca, 53
Colonia Polanco
11560 Mexico D.F. Mexico

ITP GmbH
Königswinterer Strasse 418
53277 Bonn
Germany

ITP Asia
60 Albert Street, #15-01
Albert Complex
Singapore 189969

ITP Japan
Hirakawacho Kyowa Building, 3F
2-2-1 Hirakawacho
Chiyoda-ku, Tokyo 102
Japan

ISBN: 0-7600-4925-4

Printed in the United States of America

4 5 6 7 8 9 BM 0100 99 98

C O N T E N T S

P R E F A C E

Since the 1970s, comprehensive database courses have been offered in leading computer science programs to students intending to become data processing professionals. In their careers, such students often become involved in the design, development, implementation, and maintenance of large, mainframe, database-oriented application systems. Some become involved in related areas such as database administration.

Until relatively recently, such professionals were the only segment of the population that had any type of direct contact with databases and database management systems. With the advent of microcomputer database management systems, however, the picture has changed dramatically. Virtually all segments of the population can now be considered potential users of such systems, including such diverse groups as home computer owners, owners of small businesses, and end-users in large organizations. Where recently the spreadsheet was the tool that the bulk of microcomputer owners felt was essential, many are now turning to database management systems as the essential tool.

The major microcomputer database systems have continually added features to increase their ease of use, making these systems accessible to more and more users. Truly effective use of such a product, however, requires more than just knowledge of the product itself, although that is obviously important. It requires a general knowledge of databases, including such topics as database design, database administration, and application development using these systems. While the depth of understanding required is certainly not as great for the majority of users as it is for the data processing professional, any lack of understanding in these areas precludes effective use of the product in all but the most limited applications.

ABOUT THIS BOOK

This book is intended for anyone who is interested in becoming familiar with the area of database management. It is appropriate for students in introductory database classes in computer science or information systems programs, as well as for students in database courses in related disciplines, such as business, at either the undergraduate or graduate level. Such students require a general understanding of the database environment. Finally, this book is a suitable introduction for individuals considering purchasing a microcomputer database package and who want to make effective use of such a package. Above all, this book is ideal for use in the courses that have become increasingly popular over the past few years introducing students of any discipline to database management.

This book assumes that students have some familiarity with personal computers. A single introductory course is all the background that is required. While students need not have any background in programming to effectively use this text, there are certain areas where students with a little programming background will be able to explore topics in more depth than those without such a background. While database management on mainframes is discussed in the book, the main thrust is on microcomputer database management.

SPECIAL FEATURES

Detailed Coverage of the Relational Model
The text features detailed coverage of the important aspects of the relational model including comprehensive coverage of SQL. It also covers Query-by-Example and the relational algebra as well as advanced aspects of the model such as views, the use of indexes, the catalog, and the relational integrity rules.

Database Design
The important process of database design is given detailed treatment. A highly useful methodology for designing databases is presented and illustrated through a variety of examples. After mastering the design methodology presented in this text, readers should be able to produce correct database designs for whatever set of requirements they encounter.

Functions Provided by a DBMS
With such a wide variation among the features included in current microcomputer database management systems, it is important for students to know the functions that such systems should provide. These functions are presented and discussed in detail.

Database Administration (DBA)
While the office of database administration (DBA) is absolutely essential in the mainframe environment, it is also important in a microcomputer environment, especially if the database is to be shared among several users. Thus, this text includes a detailed discussion of the database administration function.

DBMS Selection
The process of selecting a DBMS is important given the myriad systems that are available. Unfortunately, it is not an easy task. To prepare students to do an effective job in this area, the text includes a detailed discussion of the process, together with a comprehensive checklist that greatly assists in making such a selection.

Emerging Topics
The text contains up-to-date coverage of important emerging topics such as distributed database management systems, client/server systems, data warehouses,

object-oriented database management systems, and the impact of the Internet on database management systems.

Glossary

A glossary provides definitions of the important terms in the text.

Numerous Realistic Examples

The book contains numerous examples illustrating each of the concepts. The examples are realistic and representative of the kinds of problems that are encountered in the design, manipulation, and administration of databases.

Exercises

The book contains a wide variety of questions. At key points within the chapters, the students are asked questions to ensure that they understand the material before proceeding. The answers to these questions are given immediately following the questions. At the end of each chapter, there are exercises which test the students' recall of the important points in the chapter and the ability to apply what they have learned. The answers to the odd-numbered exercises are given at the end of the text.

Instructor's Manual

The accompanying instructor's manual contains detailed teaching tips, answers to exercises in the text, test questions (and answers), and transparency masters.

ORGANIZATION OF THE TEXTBOOK

The textbook consists of nine chapters that deal with general database topics and are not geared to any specific database management system. A brief description of the organization of topics in the chapters follows.

Introduction

Chapter 1 provides a general introduction to the field of database management.

The Relational Model

The relational model is covered in detail in chapters 2, 3, and 4. Chapter 2 covers the data definition and manipulation aspects of the model using QBE and the relational algebra. Chapter 3 is devoted exclusively to SQL. Chapter 4 covers some advanced aspects of the model such as views, the use of indexes, the catalog, and the relational integrity rules. It also includes a discussion of the question: What does it take to be relational?

Database Design

Chapters 5 and 6 are devoted to database design. Chapter 5 covers the normalization process, which enables us to find and correct bad designs. In chapter 6 a methodology for database design is presented and illustrated through a number of examples.

Functions of a Database Management System

Chapter 7 discusses the features that should be provided by a full-functioned microcomputer database management system.

Database Administration

Chapter 8 is devoted to the role of database administration. Also included in this chapter is a discussion of the process of selecting a DBMS.

Advanced Topics

Chapter 9 covers advanced database topics including distributed database management systems, client/server systems, data warehouses, and object-oriented database management systems. It also discusses the impact of the Internet and intranets on database management systems.

GENERAL NOTES TO THE STUDENT

Embedded Questions

There are a number of places in the text where special questions have been embedded. Sometimes the purpose of these questions is to ensure that you understand some crucial material before you proceed. In other cases, the questions are designed to give you the chance to consider some special concept in advance of its actual presentation. In all cases, the answers to these questions are given immediately after the questions. You could simply read the question and its answer. You will receive maximum benefit from the text, however, if you take the time to work out the answer to each question and then check your answer against the one given in the text before you proceed with your reading.

End-of-Chapter Material

The end-of-chapter material consists of a summary and exercises. The summary briefly describes the material covered in the chapter. The exercises require you to recall and apply the important material in the chapter. The answers to the odd-numbered exercises are given in the text.

ACKNOWLEDGMENTS

We would like to acknowledge the following individuals who all made contributions during the preparation of this book. We appreciate the following individuals who reviewed the text and made many helpful suggestions: Patty Santoianni, Sinclair Community College; B.J. Sineath, Forsyth Technical Community College; and LaToria Tookes, John Tyler Community College. The efforts of the following members of the staff of Course Technology have been invaluable: Kristen Duerr, managing editor; Nancy Ray, production editor; Jennifer Normandin, product manager; Efrat Reis, text and cover designer; Lisa Ayers, editorial assistant; and Patty Stephan, production manager.

CHAPTER 1

Introduction to Database Management

OBJECTIVES

- Provide a general introduction to the field of database management.

- Introduce some basic terminology.

- Describe the advantages and disadvantages of database processing.

INTRODUCTION

Henry owns a chain of four bookstores. When he took control of the bookstores several years ago, he inherited a computerized file-oriented system that organized the data he needed to run the bookstores.

The system allowed Henry to gather and organize the basic data about publishers, authors, and books. Each book has a code that uniquely identifies the book. In addition, Henry records the title, publisher, type of book, price, and whether the book is paperback. He also records the author or authors of the books along with the number of units of the book that are in stock in each of the branches.

Henry uses this information in a variety of ways. For example, a customer might be interested in books written by a certain author or of a certain type. Henry wants to be able to tell the customer which books by the author or of that type he currently has in stock. If the customer wants a book that is not in stock at one branch, Henry needs to be able to determine if any of the other branches currently have it.

Henry's computerized file-oriented system had been developed by a programmer hired by the former owner. The system proved to be difficult to use, so Henry hired a local computer consultant to assess the system and recommend what action he should take to allow him to manage his data more effectively.

Henry's problem is common to many businesses and individuals. They need to store and retrieve data in an efficient and organized way. Further, all of them are interested in more than one category of information. In database terminology these categories are referred to as **entities**. Henry is interested in entities such as books, authors, publishers, and branches. A school is interested in students, faculty, and classes; a real estate agency is interested in clients, houses, and agents; and a used car dealer is interested in vehicles, customers, and manufacturers.

Besides wanting to store data that pertains to more than one entity, Henry also is interested in relationships between the entities. For example, he is interested in relating books to the authors who wrote them, to the publishers who published them, and to the branches that have them in stock. Likewise, a real estate agency is interested not only in clients, houses, and agents but also in the relationship between clients and houses (which clients have listed which houses and which clients have expressed interest in which houses), between agents and houses (which agent sold which house), and so on.

The consultant told Henry he should switch from the file-oriented system to a database system. A **database** is a structure that contains information about many kinds of entities and about the relationships between the entities. Henry's database, for example, would contain information about books, authors, branches, and publishers. It would provide facts that relate authors to the books they wrote and branches to the books they currently have in stock. With the use of a database, Henry would be able to start with a particular book and find out who wrote it as well as which branches have it. Alternatively, he could start with an author and find all the books he or she wrote, together with the publishers of these books. Using a database, Henry not only would be able to maintain his data better, he also would be able to use the data in the database to produce a variety of reports and to answer a variety of questions.

■   ■   ■   ■   ■

HENRY'S BASIC DATA

The consultant started by reviewing the data contained in Henry's file-oriented system. The system used several files. A **file** is an organized collection of data about a single entity. One of Henry's files, called Branch, contains data about each branch bookstore Henry owns. The Branch file, shown in Figure 1.1, is represented in the form of a table. The rows in a table are called records, and the columns are called fields. That is, a **record** pertains to a specific person, place, thing, or event. Each record consists of a number of **fields** that record facts about that specific person, place, thing, or event. The Branch file contains four records, each with values for the fields of Branch Number, Branch Name, Branch Location, and # Employees.

Branch

BRANCH NUMBER	BRANCH NAME	BRANCH LOCATION	# EMPLOYEES
1	Henry's Downtown	16 Riverview	10
2	Henry's On The Hill	1289 Bedford	6
3	Henry's Brentwood	Brentwood Mall	15
4	Henry's Eastshore	Eastshore Mall	9

each row is a record

each column is a field

Figure 1.1 Branch file

Two additional files for Henry's system are shown in Figure 1.2. The files are called Publisher and Author.

Publisher

PUBLISHER CODE	NAME	CITY
AH	Arkham House Publishing	Sauk City, WI
AP	Arcade Publishing	New York
AW	Addison-Wesley	Reading, MA
BB	Bantam Books	New York
BF	boyd & fraser	Boston
JT	Jeremy P. Tarcher	Los Angeles
MP	McPherson and Co.	Kingston
PB	Pocket Books	New York
RH	Random House	New York
RZ	Rizzoli	New York
SB	Schoken Books	New York
SI	Signet	New York
TH	Thames and Hudson	New York
WN	W.W. Norton and Co.	New York

Author

AUTHOR NUMBER	NAME
1	Archer, Jeffrey
2	Christie, Agatha
3	Clarke, Arthur C.
4	Francis, Dick
5	Cussler, Clive
6	King, Stephen
7	Pratt, Philip
8	Adamski, Joseph
10	Harmon, Willis
11	Rheingold, Howard
12	Owen, Barbara
13	Williams, Peter
14	Kafka, Franz
15	Novalis
16	Lovecraft, H.P.
17	Paz, Octavio
18	Camus, Albert
19	Castleman, Riva
20	Zinbardo, Philip
21	Gimferrer, Pere
22	Southworth, Rod
23	Wray, Robert

Figure 1.2 Publisher and Author files

The Book file is shown in Figure 1.3.

Question	To check your understanding of the relationship between publishers and books, answer the following questions: Who published *Knockdown*? Which books did Signet publish?
Answer	The Publisher Code in the row in the Book file for *Knockdown* is PB. Examining the Publisher file, you see that PB is the code assigned to Pocket Books. To find the books published by Signet, you look up its code in the Publisher file and see that it is SI. Next, you look for all records in the Book file for which the publisher code is SI and find that Signet published *Cujo, The Organ, Carrie*, and *Magritte*.

The file called Book-Author in Figure 1.4 is used to relate books and authors. The Sequence field indicates the order in which the authors of a particular book should be listed. The file called Book-Branch in the same figure is used to indicate the number of units of a particular book currently on hand at a particular branch. The first row, for example, indicates there are two units of the book whose code is 0180 currently on hand at Branch 1.

Book

BOOK CODE	TITLE	PUBLISHER CODE	TYPE	PRICE	PAPER-BACK
0180	Shyness	BB	PSY	7.65	T
0189	Kane and Abel	PB	FIC	5.55	T
0200	The Stranger	BB	FIC	8.75	T
0378	The Dunwich Horror and Others	PB	HOR	19.75	F
079X	Smokescreen	PB	MYS	4.55	T
0808	Knockdown	PB	MYS	4.75	T
1351	Cujo	SI	HOR	6.65	T
1382	Marcel Duchamp	PB	ART	11.25	T
138X	Death on the Nile	BB	MYS	3.95	T
2226	Ghost from the Grand Banks	BB	SFI	19.95	F
2281	Prints of the 20th Century	PB	ART	13.25	T
2766	The Prodigal Daughter	PB	FIC	5.45	T
2908	Hymns to the Night	BB	POE	6.75	T
3350	Higher Creativity	PB	PSY	9.75	T
3743	First Among Equals	PB	FIC	3.95	T
3906	Vortex	BB	SUS	5.45	T
5163	The Organ	SI	MUS	16.95	T
5790	Database Systems	BF	CS	54.95	F
6128	Evil Under the Sun	PB	MYS	4.45	T
6328	Vixen 07	BB	SUS	5.55	T
669X	A Guide to SQL	BF	CS	23.95	T
6908	DOS Essentials	BF	CS	20.50	T
7405	Night Probe	BB	SUS	5.65	T
7443	Carrie	SI	HOR	6.75	T
7559	Risk	PB	MYS	3.95	T
7947	dBASE Programming	BF	CS	39.90	T
8092	Magritte	SI	ART	21.95	F
8720	The Castle	BB	FIC	12.15	T
9611	Amerika	BB	FIC	10.95	T

Figure 1.3 Book file

Book-Author

BOOK CODE	AUTHOR NUMBER	SEQUENCE
0180	20	1
0189	1	1
0200	18	1
0378	16	1
079X	4	1
0808	4	1
1351	6	1
1382	17	1
138X	2	1
2226	3	1
2281	19	1
2766	1	1
2908	15	1
3350	10	1
3350	11	2
3743	1	1
3906	5	1
5163	12	2
5163	13	1
5790	7	1
5790	8	2
6128	2	1
6328	5	1
669X	7	1
6908	22	1
7405	5	1
7443	6	1
7559	4	1
7947	7	1
7947	23	2
8092	21	1
8720	14	1
9611	14	1

Book-Branch

BOOK CODE	BRANCH NUMBER	ON HAND
0180	1	2
0189	2	2
0200	1	1
0200	2	3
0378	3	2
079X	2	1
079X	3	2
079X	4	3
0808	2	1
1351	2	4
1351	3	2
1382	2	1
138X	2	3
2226	1	3
2226	3	2
2226	4	1
2281	4	3
2766	3	2
2908	1	3
2908	4	1
3350	1	2
3743	2	1
3906	2	1
3906	3	2
5163	1	1
5790	4	2
6128	2	4
6128	3	3
6328	2	2
669X	1	1
6908	2	2
7405	3	2
7443	4	1
7559	2	2
7947	2	2
8092	3	1
8720	1	3
9611	1	2

Figure 1.4 Book-Author and Book-Branch files

Question	To check your understanding of the relationship between authors and books, answer the following questions: Who wrote *The Organ*? (Be sure to list the authors in the correct order.) Which books did Jeffrey Archer write?
Answer	To determine who wrote *The Organ*, you first examine the Book file to find its book code (5163). Next, you look for all rows in the Book-Author file in which the Book Code value is 5163. There are two such rows. In one of them the Author Number is 12, and in the other, it is 13. All that is left is to look in the Author file to find the authors who have been assigned the numbers 12 and 13. The answer is Barbara Owen (12) and Peter Williams (13). The sequence number for author 12 is 2, however, and the sequence number for author 13 is 1. Thus, listing the authors in the proper order, the authors are Peter Williams and Barbara Owen. To find the books written by Jeffrey Archer, you look up his number in the Author file and find that it is 1. Then, you look for all rows in the Book-Author file for which the author number is 1. There are three such rows. The corresponding Book Code values are 0189, 2766, and 3743. Looking up these codes in the Book file, you find that Jeffrey Archer wrote *Kane and Abel, The Prodigal Daughter*, and *First Among Equals*.

Question	A customer in Branch 1 wishes to purchase the book titled *Vortex*. Is it currently in stock in Branch 1?
Answer	Looking up the code for *Vortex* in the Book file, you find it is 3906. To find out how many copies are in stock in Branch 1, you look for a row in the Book-Branch file with 3906 in the Book Code column and 1 in the Branch Number column. Because there is no such row, Branch 1 doesn't have any copies of *Vortex*.

Question	You would like to obtain a copy of *Vortex* for this customer. Which other branches currently have it in stock and how many copies do they have?
Answer	You already know that the code for *Vortex* is 3906. (If you didn't, you would simply look it up in the Book file.) To find out the branches that currently have copies, you look for rows in the Book-Branch file with 3906 in the Book Code column. There are two such rows. The

Answer (cont) first one indicates that Branch 2 currently has one copy. The second indicates that Branch 3 currently has two copies.

The consultant found that Henry's system included several programs to allow him to update the data in his files. Separate programs were required to allow for the addition, correction, and deletion of branches, books, publishers, and authors. The system also included several programs to produce the reports Henry needed. Further, the logic just discussed for relating books and publishers, authors and books, and books and branches had to be built into these programs.

Using a Database Management System

Henry's file-oriented system, in effect, implemented a database. The system certainly maintained data on several entities (branches, books, publishers, and authors). It also maintained relationships between these entities. To the computer, however, Henry was dealing with nothing more than a collection of isolated files. It was only through the efforts of Henry's programs that the crucial relationships were maintained. Another way of stating this would be to say that Henry's programs managed the database; this can be a very complex task.

Fortunately, you no longer necessarily have to create your own programs, because the computer is able to assist in managing the database. The tool it uses is called a **database management system**, or **DBMS**. A DBMS is a program or collection of programs whose function is to manage a database on behalf of the people who use it. It greatly simplifies the task of manipulating and using a database. The consultant told Henry that a DBMS could be used to replace his file-oriented system without the need to write a single program.

Henry agreed with the consultant's recommendation and they decided that a microcomputer DBMS could fulfill his needs. They determined the structure of the database he needed (this is called **designing a database**). Henry's database contained the information he needed about branches, books, publishers, and authors. Then Henry communicated this design to the DBMS, created several **forms** (screen objects you use to maintain, view, and print records from a database), and began to enter data.

The form he uses to process branch data is shown in Figure 1.5. Using this form, Henry can enter a new branch; view, change, or delete an existing branch; and print the information for a branch. Henry did not write a program to create this form; instead, the DBMS created the form based on answers from him in response to its questions about the form's contents and appearance.

Field names ← → Field values

Figure 1.5 Branch form

In this same way, the DBMS created the other forms Henry needed. A more complicated form for processing book data is shown in Figure 1.6. This form uses data about books, authors, and the relationship between books and authors.

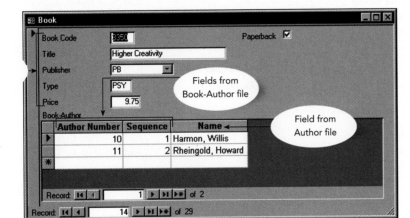

Fields from Book file

Figure 1.6 Book form

Henry was able to create the reports he needed in a similar way—the database asked him questions about the content and appearance of each report and created them automatically based on Henry's answers. The book report, listing each book title, publisher name, price, and author, is shown in Figure 1.7.

Book

Title	Publisher Name	Price	Author Name
A Guide to SQL	Boyd and Fraser	23.95	Pratt, Philip
Amerika	Bantam Books	10.95	Kafka, Franz
Carrie	Signet	6.75	King, Stephen
Cujo		6.65	King, Stephen
Database Systems	Boyd and Fraser	54.95	Pratt, Philip
			Adamski, Joseph
dBASE Programming		39.90	Pratt, Philip
			Wray, Robert
Death on the Nile	Bantam Books	3.95	Christie, Agatha
DOS Essentials	Boyd and Fraser	20.50	Southworth, Rod
Evil Under the Sun	Pocket Books	4.45	Christie, Agatha
First Among Equals		3.95	Archer, Jeffrey
Ghost from the Grand Banks	Bantam Books	19.95	Clarke, Arthur C.
Higher Creativity	Pocket Books	9.75	Harmon, Willis
			Rheingold, Howard
Hymns to the Night	Bantam Books	6.75	Novalis
Kane and Abel	Pocket Books	5.55	Archer, Jeffrey
Knockdown		4.75	Francis, Dick
Magritte	Signet	21.95	Gimferrer, Pere
Marcel Duchamp	Pocket Books	11.25	Paz, Octavio
Night Probe	Bantam Books	5.65	Cussler, Clive
Prints of the 20th Century	Pocket Books	13.25	Castleman, Riva
Risk		3.95	Francis, Dick
Shyness	Bantam Books	7.65	Zinbardo, Philip
Smokescreen	Pocket Books	4.55	Francis, Dick
The Castle	Bantam Books	12.15	Kafka, Franz
The Dunwich Horror and Others	Pocket Books	19.75	Lovecraft, H. P.
The Organ	Signet	16.95	Williams, Peter
			Owen, Barbara
The Prodigal Daughter	Pocket Books	5.45	Archer, Jeffrey
The Stranger	Bantam Books	8.75	Camus, Albert
Vixen 07		5.55	Cussler, Clive
Vortex		5.45	Cussler, Clive

Figure 1.7 Book report

Finally, Henry created several **switchboards**—special forms used to provide controlled access to the data, forms, reports, and other content of a database. The main switchboard, which appears when Henry starts work with his database, is shown in Figure 1.8.

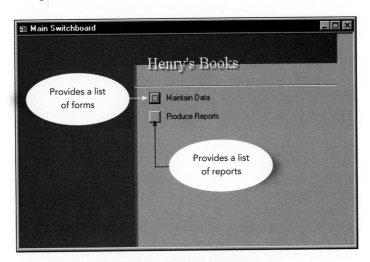

Figure 1.8 Main switchboard

When Henry chooses the "Maintain Data" option on the main switchboard, the switchboard shown in Figure 1.9 appears. Depending on which data he wants to maintain in the database, he chooses the corresponding option on this switchboard.

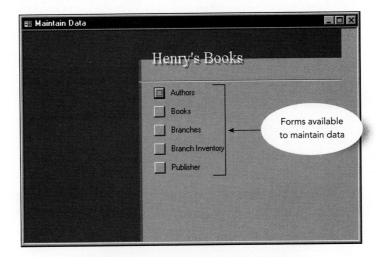

Figure 1.9 Maintain Data switchboard

Henry's interests and needs are typical of those of today's microcomputer users. Ever increasing numbers of people around the world are finding database management systems the ideal tool for solving a wide variety of simple and complex problems. Later in this text, you will learn about Henry's use of more advanced features of a DBMS such as replication (synchronizing copies of a database) and the impact of the Internet on database management.

The next section presents some background material on database management and some of the more commonly used terms. You will examine some of the advantages and disadvantages of database management systems in the last two sections of this chapter.

BACKGROUND

This section introduces some terminology and concepts that are very important in the database environment. Some of the terms will be familiar to you from the material in the preceding section.

Entities, Attributes, and Relationships

The more fundamental terms are entity, attribute, and relationship. An **entity** is really just like a noun; it is a person, place, thing, or event. The entities of interest to Henry, for example, are such things as publishers, branches, authors, and books. The entities that are of interest to a school include students, faculty, and classes; a real estate agency is interested in clients, houses, and agents; and a used car dealer is interested in vehicles, customers, and manufacturers.

An **attribute** is a property of an entity. The term is used here exactly as it is used in everyday English. For the entity **person**, for example, the list of attributes might include such things as eye color and height. For Henry, the attributes of interest for the entity **book** are such things as code, title, type of book, price, and so on.

Figure 1.10 shows two entities, Publisher and Book, and a number of attributes. The Publisher entity has three attributes: Publisher Code, Name, and City. The attributes are really just the columns or fields in the table. The Book entity has six attributes: Book Code, Title, Publisher Code, Type, Price, and Paperback. (The last attribute simply indicates whether or not the book is paperback.)

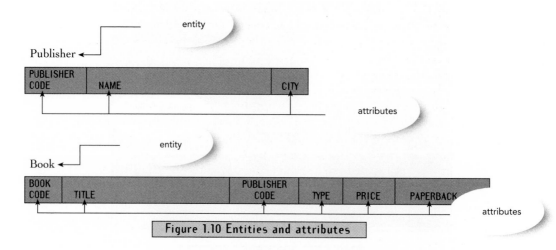

Figure 1.10 Entities and attributes

The final key term is relationship. When you speak of **relationship**, you really mean an association between entities. There is an association between publishers and books, for example. A publisher is associated with all the books that it publishes, and a book is associated with its publisher. Technically, you say that a publisher is *related to* all the books it published, and a book is *related to* its publisher.

This particular relationship is called a **one-to-many** relationship. *One* publisher is associated with *many* books, but each book is associated with only *one* publisher. (In this type of relationship, the word *many* is used differently than in everyday English; it may not always literally mean a large number. In this context, it would mean that a publisher can be associated with *any number* of books. That is, one publisher can be associated with zero, one, or more books.)

A one-to-many relationship often is represented pictorially in the fashion shown in Figure 1.11. In such a diagram, entities and attributes are represented in precisely the same way as they are shown in Figure 1.10. The relationship is represented by an arrow. The *one* part of the relationship, in this case Publisher, is indicated by a single-headed arrow, and the *many* part of the relationship, in this case Book, is indicated by a double-headed arrow.

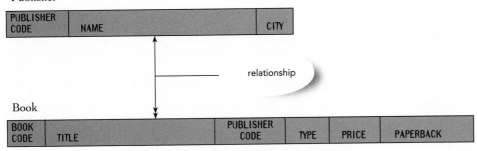

Figure 1.11 One-to-many relationship

Files and Databases

You encountered the word **file** earlier in this chapter. If you have done some programming yourself, you may be familiar with the word. Basically, a file used to store data, which often is called a **data file**, is the computer counterpart to an ordinary paper file you might keep in a filing cabinet. The crucial aspect of a data file is that it houses information on a **single entity** and the attributes of that entity. In Henry's case, an example of a single entity is book. Each record in this data file keeps information on the crucial attributes of one book.

A database, however, is much more than a file. Unlike a typical data file, a database can house information about more than one entity. There also is another difference. A database holds information about the relationships among the various entities. Not only would Henry's database have information about both books and publishers, for example, it also would hold information relating publishers to the books they had produced. Formally, the definition of a database is as follows:

Definition: A **database** is a structure that can house information about multiple types of entities, the attributes of these entities, and the relationships among the entities.

Database Management Systems (DBMS)

Managing a database is inherently a complicated task. Fortunately, software packages called **database management systems** can do the job of manipulating databases. A database management system, or **DBMS**, is a software product through which users interact with a database. The actual manipulation of the underlying database is handled by the DBMS. In some cases, users may interact with the DBMS directly, as shown in Figure 1.12a. In other cases, users may interact with programs; these programs in turn interact with the DBMS (Figure 1.12b). In either case, it is only the DBMS that actually accesses the database.

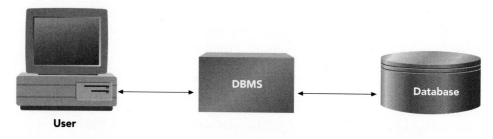

Figure 1.12a Using a database management system directly

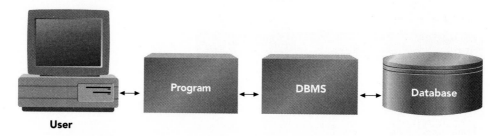

Figure 1.12b Using a database management system from a program

Using a DBMS, for example, Henry can request the system to find publisher PB and the system either will locate this publisher and give the data or tell that no such publisher exists in the database. All the work involved in this task is performed by the DBMS. If publisher PB is in the database, Henry then can ask for the books this publisher has published and again the system will perform all the work involved in locating these books. Likewise, when Henry stores a new book in the database, the DBMS performs all the tasks necessary to ensure that the book is related to the appropriate publisher.

Mainframe DBMSs have been in use since the 1960s. They continually have been enhanced over the years, gaining in selection of features and in performance. Recently, microcomputer DBMSs that possess many of the features of their mainframe counterparts have become available. The leaders in this field, such as Access from Microsoft and Paradox from Borland, also are improved on a continuous basis. They make the power of database management available to large numbers of microcomputer users. The focus of this text is microcomputer database management systems.

Database Processing

When you use the term **database processing**, you mean that the data to be processed is stored in a database and the data in the database is being manipulated by a DBMS. You have seen how database processing benefits Henry with his individual system. Still, a greater benefit is obtained by combining the activities of several users and allowing them to share a common database.

Let's first consider the nondatabase approach illustrated in Figure 1.13. Mary, Jeff, and Lucia are three separate users at the same college. Mary is involved in enrolling students in courses, in producing class lists, and so on. She has her own system of programs and files that she uses to perform this activity on the computer. Her files contain information on classes, on faculty members who teach these classes, and on the enrolled students.

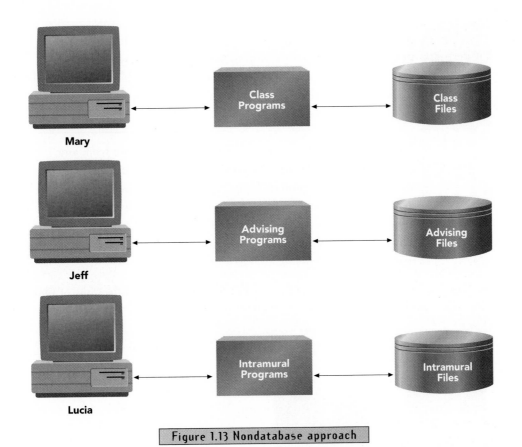

Figure 1.13 Nondatabase approach

Jeff is involved in the advising process, that is, the process of advising students about their programs and their progress toward a degree. He has his own system of programs and files. His files, which are totally separate from Mary's, contain information on faculty members, on the students who are advised by them, and on the requirements that already have been fulfilled by these students.

Lucia is in charge of maintaining information on the intramural athletic programs. She too has her own system of programs and files. Her files contain information on the various sports that are available, the teams that participate in these sports, the students who belong to these teams, and the current records of the teams.

Two major problems arise with this nondatabase approach. The first problem is duplication of data. Mary, Jeff, and Lucia all are keeping information about students, for example. Presumably, each of them will need the address of all the students. Thus the address of each student is stored in at least three separate places in the computer. Not only does this waste space, but it causes a real headache when a student moves and his or her address must be changed.

The second problem is that it is extremely difficult to fulfill requirements that involve data from more than one system. The format of the files might not even be compatible from one system to another. The following question and answer segment demonstrates such a requirement.

Question	Suppose you want to list the number, name, and address of a particular student. You also want to list the classes in which the student currently is enrolled, the name of the student's advisor, and the intramural sports in which the student participates. Where would you find the necessary data?
Answer	The student's number, name, and address could come from any one of the three systems. The classes in which the student is enrolled could be found in Mary's system. The name of the student's advisor would be found in Jeff's system. The sports in which the student participates could be found in Lucia's system. Thus, this requirement involves data from all three systems.

By contrast, in a database approach, instead of having separate collections of files, Mary, Jeff, and Lucia would share a common database managed by a DBMS (Figure 1.14).

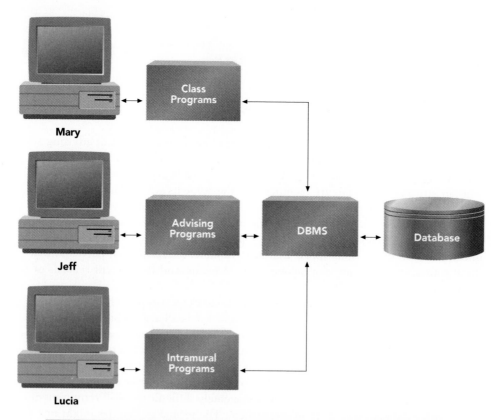

Figure 1.14 Database approach (using a database management system)

ADVANTAGES OF DATABASE PROCESSING

1.	Lower Cost
2.	Getting More Information from the Same Amount of Data
3.	Sharing of Data
4.	Balancing Conflicting Requirements
5.	Controlled or Eliminated Redundancy
6.	Consistency
7.	Integrity
8.	Security
9.	Increased Productivity
10.	Data Independence

Figure 1.15 Database processing—advantages

Each student would appear only once, so his or her address would likewise appear only once. No space would be wasted and changing a student's address would be a very simple procedure. Further, because all the data would be in a single database, listing the information on a student, the student's classes, the student's advisor, and the sports in which the student participates now would be possible. In fact, with a good DBMS, it should be a simple task.

ADVANTAGES OF DATABASE PROCESSING

The database approach to processing, using a microcomputer DBMS, offers ten clear advantages. They are listed in Figure 1.15 and are discussed on the following pages.

1. **Lower Cost**   This is an interesting advantage. In discussions about mainframe DBMSs, cost usually is listed as a disadvantage. By the time all the appropriate components have been purchased, the total price easily can run between $100,000 and $400,000. The size and complexity of a DBMS also may necessitate the use of more hardware. Purchasing, or leasing, this additional hardware represents another cost.

   On microcomputers, the opposite is true. Some of the more limited, but still very useful, systems are priced under $100. Even for the most powerful and most sophisticated of these microcomputer DBMSs, the price ranges between $500 and $800. These prices make the features of the DBMS available to a wide range of users.

2. **Getting More Information from the Same Amount of Data**   The primary goal of a computer system is to turn data—recorded facts—into information—the knowledge gained by processing these facts. In a non-database environment, data often is partitioned into several disjointed systems, each system having its own collection of files. Any request for information that would necessitate accessing data from more than one of

these collections can be extremely difficult. In many cases, for all practical purposes, it is considered impossible. Thus, the desired information is unavailable, not because it is not stored in the computer but because of the way it has been broken down into the various collections of files. When, instead, all the data for the various systems is stored in a single database, the information becomes available. Given the power of a modern DBMS, not only is the information available, but the process of getting it can be a quick and easy one.

3. **Sharing of Data**   The data of various users can be combined and shared among authorized users, allowing all users access to a greater pool of data. Several users can have access to the same piece of data, for example, a customer's address, and still use it in a variety of ways. When an address is changed, however, the new address immediately becomes available to all users. In addition, new applications can be developed through the use of the existing data in the database without the burden of having to create separate collections of files.

4. **Balancing Conflicting Requirements**   For the database approach to function adequately within an organization, a person or group should be in charge of the database itself, especially if it is to serve a number of users. This person or group often is called **Database Administration (DBA)**. By keeping the overall needs of the organization in mind, DBA can structure the database in such a way that it benefits the entire organization, not just a single group. While this may mean that an individual user group is served less well than it would have been if it had its own isolated system, the organization as a whole is better off. Ultimately, when the organization benefits, so do the individual groups of users.

5. **Controlled or Eliminated Redundancy**   With database processing, data that formerly was kept separate in a nondatabase system is integrated into a single database, so multiple copies of the same data no longer exist. With the nondatabase approach, Mary, Jeff, and Lucia each had a copy of the address of each student. With the database approach, each student's address would occur only once thus eliminating the duplication, technically called **redundancy**.

   Eliminating redundancy not only saves space but makes the process of updating much simpler. With the database approach, changing the address of a student would mean making one single change. With the nondatabase approach, in which each student happened to be stored in three different places, the same change of address would mean that three changes had to be made in the computer.

   Although eliminating redundancy is the ideal, it is not always possible. Sometimes, for reasons having to do with performance, you might choose to introduce a limited amount of redundancy into a database. But, even in these cases, you would be able to keep the redundancy under tight control, thus obtaining the same advantages. This is why it technically is better to say that you *control* redundancy rather than *eliminate* it.

6. **Consistency**   Suppose an individual student's address was to appear in more than one place. Student 176, for example, might be listed at 926 Meadowbrook at one spot within our database and 2856 Wisner at another. The data in the computer then would be inconsistent. Because the potential for this sort of problem is a direct result of redundancy, and because the

database approach eliminates (or at least controls) redundancy, there is much less potential for the occurrence of this sort of inconsistency with the database approach.

7. **Integrity**   An **integrity constraint** is a rule that must be followed by data in the database. Here is an example of an integrity constraint: The director number given for any movie must be that of a director who is already in the database. A database has **integrity** if the data in it satisfies all established integrity constraints. A good DBMS should provide an opportunity for users to articulate these integrity constraints when they describe the database. The DBMS then should ensure that these constraints never are violated. According to the integrity constraint just articulated, the DBMS should *not allow* us to store data about a given movie if the director number that you enter is not the number of a director whose name is already in the database.

8. **Security**   **Security** is the prevention of access to the database by unauthorized users. A good DBMS has a number of features that help ensure the enforcement of security measures.

9. **Increased Productivity**   A DBMS frees the programmers who are writing programs to access a database from having to engage in mundane data manipulation activities thus making the programmers more productive. A good DBMS comes with many features that allow users to gain access to data in the database without having to do any programming at all. This increases the productivity both of programmers, who may not need to write complex programs in order to perform certain tasks, and of nonprogrammers, who may be able to get the results they seek from the data in the database without waiting for a program to be written for them.

10. **Data Independence**   The structure of a database often needs to be changed. For example, new user requirements may necessitate the addition of an entity, an attribute, or a relationship, or a change may be required to improve performance. A good DBMS provides **data independence**, which is the property that the structure of a database can change without the programs that access the database having to change. Without data independence, a lot of unnecessary effort can be expended in changing programs to match the new structure of the database. The presence of many programs in the system may make this effort so prohibitive that a decision is made not to change the database. With data independence, the effort of changing all the programs is unnecessary. Thus, when the need arises to change the database, the decision to do so is more likely to be made.

DISADVANTAGES OF DATABASE PROCESSING

As you would expect, if there are advantages to doing something in a certain way, there also are disadvantages. The area of database processing is no exception. In terms of numbers alone, the advantages outweigh the disadvantages, but the latter are listed in Figure 1.16 and explained below.

DISADVANTAGES OF DATABASE PROCESSING

1.	Larger Size
2.	Greater Complexity
3.	Greater Impact of a Failure
4.	Recovery More Difficult

Figure 1.16 Database processing—disadvantages

1. **Larger Size**   In order to support all the complex functions that it provides to users, a database management system must be a large program that occupies megabytes of disk space as well as a substantial amount of internal memory.

2. **Greater Complexity**   The complexity and breadth of the functions furnished by a DBMS make it a complex product. Users of the DBMS must understand the features of the system in order to take full advantage of it, and there is a great deal for them to learn. In the design and implementation of a new system that uses a DBMS, many choices have to be made, and it is possible to make incorrect choices, especially with an insufficient understanding of the system. Unfortunately, a few incorrect choices can spell disaster for the whole project. This is especially true for a large mainframe project that serves many users, but it also can apply to microcomputer projects.

3. **Greater Impact of a Failure**   If each user has a completely separate system, the failure of any single user's system does not necessarily affect any other user. If, on the other hand, several users are sharing the same database, a failure on the part of any one user that damages the database in some way may affect all the other users.

4. **Recovery More Difficult**   Because a database inherently is more complex than a simple file, the process of recovering it in the event of a catastrophe also is more complicated than the process of recovering a simple file. This is true particularly if the database is being updated by a large number of users at the same time. It first must be restored to the condition it was in when it was last known to be correct; any updates made by users since that time must be redone. The greater the number of users involved in updating the database, the more complicated this task becomes.

SUMMARY

1. An entity is a person, place, thing, or event. An attribute is a property of an entity. A relationship is an association between entities.

2. A database is a structure that can house information about many different entities and about the relationships between these entities.

3. A database management system is a software package whose function is to manipulate a database on behalf of users.

4. Database processing offers a number of advantages, including the following:

    a. lower cost

    b. getting more information from the same amount of data

    c. sharing of data

    d. balancing conflicting requirements

    e. controlled or eliminated redundancy

    f. consistency

    g. integrity

    h. security

    i. increased productivity

    j. data independence

5. The disadvantages of database processing include the following:

    a. larger size

    b. greater complexity

    c. greater impact of a failure

    d. recovery more difficult

KEY TERMS

attribute

data independence

database

Database Administration (DBA)

database management system (DBMS)

database processing

designing a database

entity

field

file

form

integrity

integrity constraint

one-to-many

record

redundancy

relationship

security

switchboard

REVIEW QUESTIONS

1. What is a file? A record? A field?

2. What is an entity? An attribute?

3. When you speak of relationship, what exactly do you mean?

4. What is a one-to-many relationship? Give two examples of entities that have one-to-many relationships.

5. What is a database?

6. What is a DBMS?

7. Why is the cost of a DBMS listed as an advantage in the microcomputer environment and a disadvantage on mainframes?

8. How is it possible to get more information from the same amount of data through using a database approach as opposed to a file approach?

9. What is meant by sharing of data?

10. What is a DBA? What kinds of things does a DBA do in a database environment?

11. What is redundancy? What are the problems associated with redundancy?

12. How does consistency result from controlling or eliminating redundancy?

13. What is meant by integrity as it is used in this chapter?

14. What is meant by security? What does the DBMS have to do with security?

15. What is meant by data independence? Why is it desirable?

16. How can the size of a DBMS be one of its disadvantages?

17. How can the complexity of a DBMS be a disadvantage?

18. Why can a failure in a database environment be more serious than one in a file environment?

19. Why can recovery be more difficult in a database environment?

CHAPTER 2

The Relational Model 1: Introduction, QBE, and the Relational Algebra

OBJECTIVES

- Introduce Premiere Products, the company that is used as a basis for many of the examples throughout the text.

- Describe the relational model.

- Present QBE (Query-By-Example).

- Discuss the use of conditions in QBE.

- Examine the creation of calculated fields in QBE.

- Describe the use of the QBE built-in functions.

- Present the manner in which tables can be joined in QBE.

- Discuss the relational algebra.

INTRODUCTION

You begin this chapter by examining the requirements of a company called Premiere Products, which will be referred to in many examples throughout this chapter and in the rest of the text. After this examination is completed in the next section, you will move on to another section to study the relational model, the approach to database management taken by most microcomputer database management systems and many mainframe systems, as well. In the section that follows, you examine a very visual way of retrieving data from relational databases, called QBE, which stands for Query-By-Example. Finally, the last section introduces the relational algebra, one of the original ways of manipulating relational databases.

■ ■ ■ ■ ■

PREMIERE PRODUCTS

The management of Premiere Products, a distributor of appliances, housewares, and sporting goods, determined the company has grown to the point that the maintenance of customer and order data, as well as the maintenance of their inventory, no longer can be done manually. By placing the data on a computer, managed by a full-featured database management system, they will be able to ensure that the data is more current and accurate than in the present manual system. They also will be able to produce a variety of useful reports. In addition, they want to be able to ask questions concerning the data in the database and easily and rapidly obtain answers to these questions.

In deciding what data must be stored in the database, management has determined that Premiere Products must maintain the following information about its sales reps, customers, and parts inventory:

1. Premiere Products must store the sales rep number, name, address, total commission, and commission rate for each of its sales reps.

2. The company must store the customer number, name, address, current balance, and credit limit for each of its customers, as well as the number of the sales rep who represents the customer.

3. The company must store the part number, description, number of units on hand, item class, number of the warehouse where the item is stored, and unit price for each part in inventory.

Premiere Products also must store information on orders. A sample order is shown in Figure 2.1. Note that there are three components to the order: (1) The heading (top) of the order contains the order number; the date; the customer's number, name, and address; the sales rep number; and the sales rep name. (2) The body of the order contains a number of order lines, sometimes called line items. Each order line contains a part number, a part description, the number of units of the part that were ordered, and the quoted price for the part. It also contains a total, usually called an extension, which is the product of the number ordered and the quoted price. (3) Finally, the footing (bottom) of the order contains the order total. The additional items that Premiere Products must store with respect to orders are as follows:

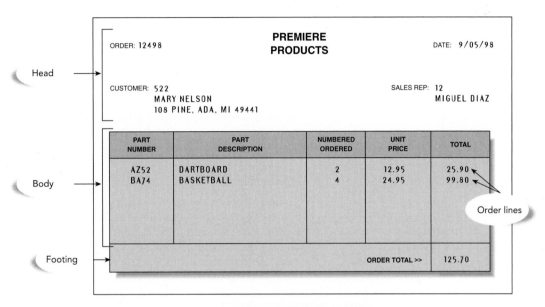

Figure 2.1 Sample order

1. For the orders: the order number, the date the order was placed, and the number of the customer who placed the order. Note that the customer's name and address and the number of the sales rep who represents the customer are stored with customer information. The name of the sales rep is stored with sales rep information.

2. For each order line: the order number, the part number, the number of units ordered, and the quoted price. Remember the part description is stored with information on parts. The product of the number of units ordered and the quoted price is not stored because it can be computed easily when needed.

3. The overall order total is not stored as part of the database. Instead, it will be computed whenever an order is printed or displayed on the screen.

Figure 2.2 shows sample data for Premiere Products. You see there are three sales reps whose numbers are 03, 06, and 12. The name of sales rep 03 is Mary Jones. Her street address is 123 Main. She lives in Grant, MI and her zip code is 49219. Her total commission is $2,150.00, and her commission rate is 5 percent (.05).

You also see there are 10 customers, numbered 124, 256, 311, 315, 405, 412, 522, 567, 587, and 622. The name of customer 124 is Sally Adams. Her street address is 481 Oak. She lives in Lansing, MI and her zip code is 49224. Her current balance is $818.75, and her credit limit is $1,000. The number 03 in the column entitled SLSREP_NUMBER indicates Sally is represented by sales rep 03 (Mary Jones).

Skipping down for a moment to the table labeled PART, you see there are 10 parts, whose part numbers are AX12, AZ52, BA74, BH22, BT04, BZ66, CA14, CB03, CX11, and CZ81. Part AX12 is an iron and the company has 104 units of this part on hand. These parts are in item class HW (housewares) and are stored in warehouse number 3. The price of an iron is $24.95.

Moving back up to the table labeled ORDERS, you see there are seven orders, numbered 12489, 12491, 12494, 12495, 12498, 12500, and 12504. Order 12489 was placed on September 2, 1998, by customer 124 (Sally Adams).

Note	In some database management systems, the word "Order" has a special purpose. Having a table with the name ORDER could cause problems in such systems. For this reason, the name is ORDERS rather than ORDER.

The table labeled ORDER_LINE may seem strange at first glance. Why do you need a separate table for the order lines? Couldn't they be included in the ORDERS table? The answer is yes, they could. The table ORDERS could be structured in the manner shown in Figure 2.3. Examining this table, you see the same orders as those shown in Figure 2.2 are present, with the same dates and the same customer numbers. In addition, each row contains all the order lines for a given order. Examining the fifth row, for example, you see order 12498 has two order lines. One of these order lines is for two AZ52s at $12.95 each; the other is for four BA74s at $24.95 each.

Question	How is the same information represented in Figure 2.2?
Answer	Take a look at the table in Figure 2.2 labeled ORDER_LINE and examine the sixth and seventh rows. The sixth row indicates there is an order line on order 12498 for two AZ52s at $12.95 each. The seventh row indicates there is an order line on order 12498 for four BA74s at $24.95 each. Thus, the same information that you find in Figure 2.3 is represented here in two separate rows rather than one.

SALES REP

SLSREP NUMBER	LAST	FIRST	STREET	CITY	STATE	ZIP CODE	TOTAL COMMISSION	COMMISSION RATE
03	Jones	Mary	123 Main	Grant	MI	49219	2150.00	.05
06	Smith	William	102 Raymond	Ada	MI	49441	4912.50	.07
12	Diaz	Miguel	419 Harper	Lansing	MI	49224	2150.00	.05

CUSTOMER

CUSTOMER NUMBER	LAST	FIRST	STREET	CITY	STATE	ZIP CODE	BALANCE	CREDIT LIMIT	SLSREP NUMBER
124	Adams	Sally	481 Oak	Lansing	MI	49224	$818.75	$1000	03
256	Samuels	Ann	215 Pete	Grant	MI	49219	$21.50	$1500	06
311	Charles	Don	48 College	Ira	MI	49034	$825.75	$1000	12
315	Daniels	Tom	914 Cherry	Kent	MI	48391	$770.75	$750	06
405	Williams	Al	519 Watson	Grant	MI	49219	$402.75	$1500	12
412	Adams	Sally	16 Elm	Lansing	MI	49224	$1817.50	$2000	03
522	Nelson	Mary	108 Pine	Ada	MI	49441	$98.75	$1500	12
567	Dinh	Tran	808 Ridge	Harper	MI	48421	$402.40	$750	06
587	Galvez	Mara	512 Pine	Ada	MI	49441	$114.60	$1000	06
622	Martin	Dan	419 Chip	Grant	MI	49219	$1045.75	$1000	03

ORDERS

ORDER NUMBER	ORDER DATE	CUSTOMER NUMBER
12489	9/02/98	124
12491	9/02/98	311
12494	9/04/98	315
12495	9/04/98	256
12498	9/05/98	522
12500	9/05/98	124
12504	9/05/98	522

ORDER LINE

ORDER NUMBER	PART NUMBER	NUMBER ORDERED	QUOTED PRICE
12489	AX12	11	$21.95
12491	BT04	1	$149.99
12491	BZ66	1	$399.99
12494	CB03	4	$279.99
12495	CX11	2	$22.95
12498	AZ52	2	$12.95
12498	BA74	4	$24.95
12500	BT04	1	$149.99
12504	CZ81	2	$325.99

PART

PART NUMBER	PART DESCRIPTION	UNITS ON HAND	ITEM CLASS	WAREHOUSE NUMBER	UNIT PRICE
AX12	Iron	104	HW	3	$24.95
AZ52	Dartboard	20	SG	2	$12.95
BA74	Basketball	40	SG	1	$29.95
BH22	Cornpopper	95	HW	3	$24.95
BT04	Gas Grill	11	AP	2	$149.99
BZ66	Washer	52	AP	3	$399.99
CA14	Griddle	78	HW	3	$39.99
CB03	Bike	44	SG	1	$299.99
CX11	Blender	112	HW	3	$22.95
CZ81	Treadmill	68	SG	2	$349.95

Figure 2.2 Sample data for Premiere Products

ORDERS

ORDER NUMBER	ORDER DATE	CUSTOMER NUMBER	PART NUMBER	NUMBER ORDERED	QUOTED PRICE
12489	9/02/98	124	AX12	11	$21.95
12491	9/02/98	311	BT04	1	$149.99
			BZ66	1	$399.99
12494	9/04/98	315	CB03	4	$279.99
12495	9/04/98	256	CX11	2	$22.95
12498	9/05/98	522	AZ52	2	$12.95
			BA74	4	$24.95
12500	9/05/98	124	BT04	1	$149.99
12504	9/05/98	522	CZ81	2	$325.99

Figure 2.3 Sample table structure

It may seem that it would be better not to take two rows to represent the same information that can be represented in one row. There is a problem, however, with the arrangement shown in Figure 2.3. The table is more complicated. In Figure 2.2, there is a single entry at each location in the table. In Figure 2.3, some of the individual positions within the table contain multiple entries, and further, there is a correspondence between these entries (in the row for order 12498, it is crucial to know that the AZ52 corresponds to the 2 in the NUMBER_ORDERED column, not the 4, and to the $12.95 in the QUOTED_PRICE column, not the $24.95). There are practical issues to worry about, such as:

1. How much room do you allow for these multiple entries?

2. What if an order has more order lines than you have allowed room for?

3. Given a part, how do you determine which orders contain order lines for that part?

Certainly, none of these problems is unsolvable. They do add a level of complexity, however, that is not present in the arrangement shown in Figure 2.2. In the structure shown in that figure, there are no multiple entries to worry about; it doesn't matter how many order lines exist for any order; and finding all the orders that contain order lines for a given part is easy (just look for all order lines with the given part number in the PART_NUMBER column). In general, this simpler structure is preferable, and that is why order lines have been placed in a separate table.

To test your understanding of the Premiere Products data, answer the following questions, using the data in Figure 2.2.

Question	Give the numbers of all the customers represented by Mary Jones.
Answer	124, 412, and 622. (Look up the number of Mary Jones in the SALES_REP table and obtain the number 03. Then find all customers in the CUSTOMER table that have number 03 in the SLSREP_NUMBER column.)

Question	Give the name of the customer who placed order 12491, then give the name of the sales rep who represents this customer.

Answer Donald Charles, Miguel Diaz. (Look up the customer number in the ORDERS table and obtain the number 311. Then find the customer in the CUSTOMER table who has customer number 311. Using this customer's sales rep number, which is 12, find the name of the sales rep in the SALES_REP table.)

Question	List all the parts that appear on order 12491. For each part, give the description, number ordered, and quoted price.

Answer PART_NUMBER: BZ66, PART_DESCRIPTION: Washer, NUMBER_ORDERED: 1, QUOTED_PRICE: $399.99. Also PART_NUMBER: BT04, PART_DESCRIPTION: Gas Grill, NUMBER_ORDERED: 1, QUOTED_PRICE: $149.99. (Look up each ORDER_LINE table row in which the order number is 12491. Each of these rows contains a part number, the number ordered, and the quoted price. The only thing missing is the description of the part. Use the part number to look up the corresponding description in the PART table.)

Question	Why is the column QUOTED_PRICE part of the ORDER_LINE table? Can't you just take the part number and look up the price in the PART table?

Answer If you don't have the QUOTED_PRICE column in the ORDER_LINE table, you must obtain the price for a part on an order line by looking up the price in the PART table. While this may not be bad, it does prevent Premiere Products from charging different prices to different customers for the same part. Because Premiere Products wants the flexibility to quote different prices to different customers, you include the QUOTED_PRICE column in the ORDER_LINE table. If you examine the ORDER_LINE table, you will see cases in which the quoted price matches the actual price in the PART table and cases in which it differs.

RELATIONAL DATABASES

You actually already have seen a relational database. A relational database is essentially just a collection of tables like the ones you just looked at for Premiere Products in Figure 2.2. A relational database is perceived by the user as being just such a collection. (The phrase "perceived by the user" simply indicates that what matters is how things appear to the user, not what the DBMS actually is doing behind the scenes.) You might wonder why this model is not called the table model, or something along that line if a database is a collection of tables. Formally, these tables are called relations, and this is where the model gets its name.

How does a DBMS that follows the relational model handle entities, attributes of entities, and relationships between entities? Entities and attributes are fairly simple. Each entity gets a table of its own. Thus, in the database for Premiere Products, there is a table for sales reps, a separate table for customers, and so on. The attributes of an entity become the columns in the table. In the table for sales reps, for example, there is a column for the sales rep number, a column for the sales rep last name, and so on.

What about relationships? At Premiere Products there is a one-to-many relationship between sales reps and customers—each sales rep is related to the many customers he or she represents, and each customer is related to the one sales rep who represents the customer. How is this relationship implemented in a relational model database? The answer is through common columns in two or more tables. Consider again Figure 2.2. The column SLSREP_NUMBER of the SALES_REP table and the column SLSREP_NUMBER of the CUSTOMER table are used to implement the relationship between sales reps and customers; that is, given a sales rep, you can use these columns to determine all the customers he or she represents, and given a customer, you can use these columns to find the sales rep who represents the customer.

Let's be more precise in our description of a relation. As previously discussed, a relation is essentially just a two-dimensional table. If you consider the tables in Figure 2.2, however, you can see there are certain restrictions you probably would want to place on relations. Each column should have a unique name, and entries within each column should all match this column name. For example, if the column name is CREDIT_LIMIT, all entries in that column should be credit limits. Also, each row should be unique. After all, if two rows absolutely are identical, the second row doesn't give any information that you already don't have. In addition, for maximum flexibility, the ordering of the columns and the rows should be immaterial. Finally, the table will be simplest if each position is restricted to a single entry, that is, if you do not allow multiple entries (often called **repeating groups**) in an individual location in the table. These ideas lead to the following definitions:

Definition: A **relation** is a two-dimensional table in which:

1. The entries in the table are single-valued, that is, each location in the table contains a single entry.

2. Each column has a distinct name (technically called the attribute name).

3. All values in a column are values of the same attribute, that is, all entries must match the column name.

4. The order of columns is immaterial.

5. Each row is distinct.

6. The order of rows is immaterial.

Definition: A **relational database** is a collection of relations.

Note	Later in the text, you will encounter situations in which a structure satisfies all the properties of a relation *except for property 1*; that is, some of the entries contain repeating groups and thus are not single-valued. Such a structure is called an **unnormalized relation**. This jargon is certainly a little strange in that an unnormalized relation is not a relation at all. It is the term used for such a structure, however. The table shown in Figure 2.3 is an example of an unnormalized relation.

Note	Rows in a table (relation) often are called **records** and columns often are called **fields**. Rows also are called **tuples** and columns are called **attributes**.

There is a commonly accepted shorthand representation of the structure of a relational database. You merely write the name of the table and then within parentheses list all of the columns (fields) in the table. Thus, this sample database consists of:

```
SALES_REP (SLSREP_NUMBER, LAST, FIRST, STREET, CITY, STATE,
      ZIP_CODE, TOTAL_COMMISSION, COMMISSION_RATE)
CUSTOMER (CUSTOMER_NUMBER, LAST, FIRST, STREET, CITY, STATE,
      ZIP_CODE, BALANCE, CREDIT_LIMIT, SLSREP_NUMBER)
PART (PART_NUMBER, PART_DESCRIPTION, UNITS_ON_HAND,
      ITEM_CLASS, WAREHOUSE_NUMBER, UNIT_PRICE)
ORDERS (ORDER_NUMBER, ORDER_DATE, CUSTOMER_NUMBER)
ORDER_LINE (ORDER_NUMBER, PART_NUMBER, NUMBER_ORDERED,
      QUOTED_PRICE)
```

Notice there is some duplication of names. The column SLSREP_NUMBER appears in both the SALES_REP table and the CUSTOMER table. Suppose a situation existed where the two might be confused. If you merely wrote SLSREP_NUMBER, how would the computer know which SLSREP_NUMBER you meant? How would a person looking at what you had written know which one you meant, for that matter? You need a mechanism for indicating the one you are referring to. One common approach to this problem is to write both the table name and the column name separated by a period. Thus, the SLSREP_NUMBER in the CUSTOMER table would be written CUSTOMER.SLSREP_NUMBER, whereas the SLSREP_NUMBER in the SALES_REP table would be written SALES_REP.SLSREP_NUMBER. Technically, when you do this you **qualify** the names. It always is acceptable to qualify data names, even if there is no possibility of confusion. If confusion may arise, however, it is *essential* to do so.

The **primary key** of a table (relation) is the column or collection of columns that uniquely identifies a given row. In the SALES_REP table, for example, the sales rep's number uniquely identifies a given row. (Sales rep 06 occurs in only one row of the table, for instance.) Thus, SLSREP_NUMBER is the primary key. Primary keys typically are indicated in the shorthand representation by underlining the column or collection of columns that comprise the primary key. Thus, the complete shorthand representation for the Premiere Products database would be:

SALES_REP (SLSREP_NUMBER, LAST, FIRST, STREET, CITY, STATE,
ZIP_CODE, TOTAL_COMMISSION, COMMISSION_RATE)

CUSTOMER (CUSTOMER_NUMBER, LAST, FIRST, STREET, CITY, STATE,
ZIP_CODE, BALANCE, CREDIT_LIMIT, SLSREP_NUMBER)

PART (PART_NUMBER, PART_DESCRIPTION, UNITS_ON_HAND,
ITEM_CLASS, WAREHOUSE_NUMBER, UNIT_PRICE)

ORDERS (ORDER_NUMBER, ORDER_DATE, CUSTOMER_NUMBER)

ORDER_LINE (ORDER_NUMBER, PART_NUMBER, NUMBER_ORDERED,
QUOTED_PRICE)

Question	Why does the primary key to the ORDER_LINE table consist of two columns, not just one?
Answer	No single column uniquely identifies a given row. It requires two: ORDER_NUMBER and PART_NUMBER.

QBE

In this section, you will investigate a visual approach to manipulating relational databases. It is called **Query-By-Example (QBE)** and was developed by M. M. Zloof at the IBM Yorktown Heights Research Laboratory. Not only are results displayed on the screen in tabular form, but users actually enter their requests by filling in portions of the displayed tables. Studies have shown that in regard to the time it takes to learn QBE, the time it takes to formulate a query using QBE, and the accuracy with which these queries are formulated, the figures for the use of QBE are as good as, if not better than, those obtained for other approaches.

> **Note**   This chapter illustrates QBE by using a particular implementation of it. The version you'll look at is found in the microcomputer DBMS called Paradox for Windows, a product of Borland International. Although the various versions of QBE certainly are not identical, the differences are relatively minor. If you have mastered one version of it, you easily should be able to learn another.

In using QBE, you first identify the table you wish to query. You then are presented with a blank form corresponding to the chosen table. You place check marks in the fields that are to be included in the answer. You also can enter conditions, such as the fact that the customer number must be 124. When you enter conditions, only the record or records on which the condition is true will be included in the answer.

You now will learn how to retrieve data, as well as update the database, using Query-By-Example.

Retrieving All Rows But Only Certain Columns

In the general QBE approach, you indicate the columns that you want to include in the query by typing the letter P followed by a period in each of the desired columns. In the Paradox version, instead of the letter, you place a check mark in the column by clicking the check box for the column. From now on you will focus on the Paradox approach. Remember other versions may differ on this point, although the basic concepts are the same.

Example 1:   List the customer number, last name, first name, balance, and credit limit of all customers in the database.

For this example, you place check marks in the CUSTOMER_NUMBER, LAST, and FIRST columns shown in the first part of Figure 2.4. You then scroll to the right so the BALANCE and CREDIT_LIMIT fields display and put check marks in those fields as well, as shown in the second part of the figure. Once you have finished, you run the query. The results are shown in the final part of Figure 2.4.

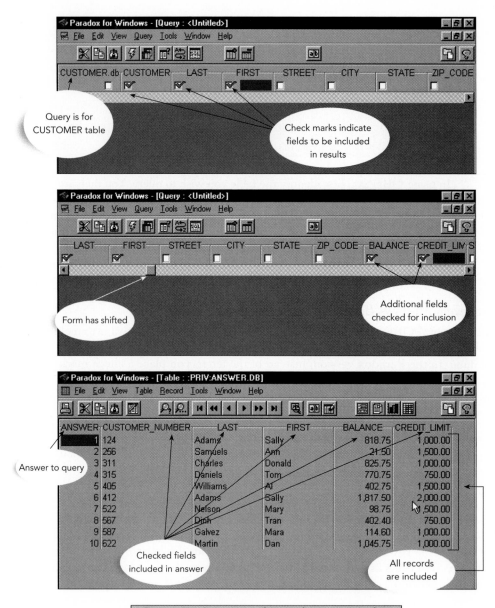

Figure 2.4 Query to select only certain fields

| Example 2: | List the complete ORDERS table. |

You certainly could put a check mark in each column in the table to obtain this result. There is, however, a simpler method. Point to the check box in the first column, the one headed by the name of the table, shown in the first part of Figure 2.5. Clicking this check box will place check marks in all columns as shown in the second part of the figure. The results of executing this query are shown in the final part of the figure.

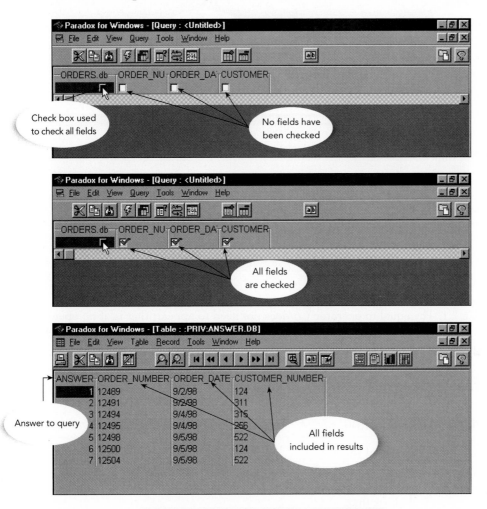

Figure 2.5 Query that includes all fields

Simple Conditions

To indicate **conditions**, that is restrictions that the records to be retrieved must satisfy, simply put the condition in the appropriate column as illustrated in the following example.

Example 3:	Find the last name and first name of customer 124.

You use the check marks, as before, to indicate the columns to be included. You also can place a specific value in a column as shown in Figure 2.6. This indicates that you only want the last name and first name for the customer whose number is 124. In other words, the condition is that the customer number must be 124. The results are shown in the second part of the figure.

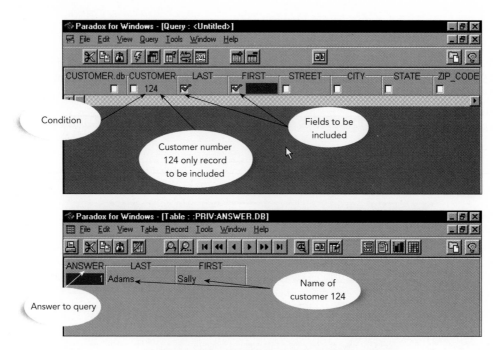

Figure 2.6 Query to find name of customer

Conditions in query images can involve any of the operators shown in Table 2.1. The equal to operator (=) does not need to appear; that is, if no operator is included, Paradox assumes you want equal to. That is why you could type the condition as 124 rather than =124.

Table 2.1 Operators Available for Conditions

OPERATOR	MEANING
=	Equal to
>	Greater than
<	Less than
>=	Greater than or equal to
<=	Less than or equal to
<>	Not equal to
..	Wildcard–stands for any series of characters
@	Wildcard–stands for any single character
like	Similar to
blank	No data in field
today	Today's date
not	Must be used before some other criterion. Then will find items that do not match the criterion

Compound Conditions

Not only can you use the operators shown in Table 2.1, but you also can combine conditions to create **compound conditions**. In many situations, you would do so by placing the word "AND" or the word "OR" between the conditions. In Query-By-Example, it is done a little differently. If you want to combine conditions with AND, place the conditions on the same line. If you want to combine conditions with OR, place the conditions on different rows in the query.

Example 4:   List the description of all parts for which there are more than 100 units on hand and which are located in warehouse number 3.

To indicate that two conditions both must be true, place the conditions on the same line as shown in Figure 2.7. In this case, you have requested those parts for which the value in the UNITS_ON_HAND field is greater than 100 and the value in the WAREHOUSE_NUMBER field is 3. The results are shown in the bottom part of the figure.

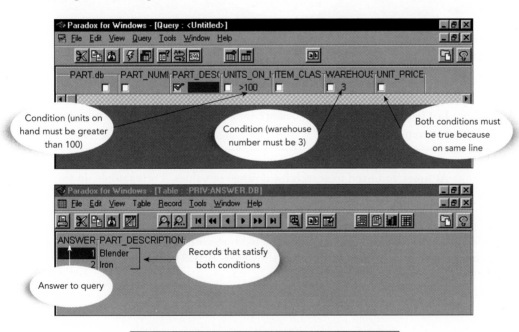

Figure 2.7 Query that involves AND condition

Example 5:   List the description of all parts for which there are more than 100 units on hand or which are located in warehouse number 3.

What you essentially have in this query is two queries. You want the descriptions of all parts for which there are more than 100 units on hand. You also want the descriptions of all parts which are located in warehouse number 3. This is effectively how you enter the request, as two queries (Figure 2.8). The first row in the query indicates you want all parts with more than 100 units on hand. The second row indicates you also want all parts in warehouse number 3. The results are shown in the bottom part of the figure.

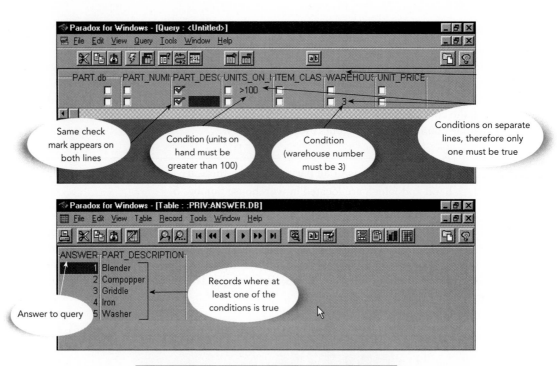

Figure 2.8 Query that involves OR condition

| Example 6: | List the number, name, and balance for each customer whose balance is between $100 and $500. |

At times you need to search for a range of values. For example, in this query you need to find all customers with balances between $100 and $500. When you ask this kind of question, you really are looking for all balances that are greater than 100 **and** less than 500. You have a compound condition in the same field. To place two conditions in the same field, separate the conditions by placing a comma (,) between them. Figure 2.9 shows the BALANCE field checked and the two conditions entered in the field.

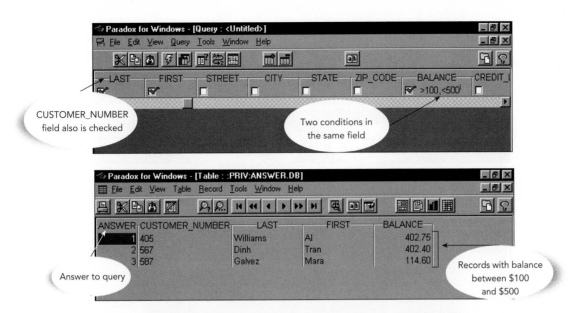

CUSTOMER_NUMBER
field also is checked

Two conditions in
the same field

Answer to query

Records with balance
between $100
and $500

Figure 2.9 Query with AND condition in a single field

Calculated Fields

You can include fields in queries that are not in the database, but that can be calculated from fields that are. Such a field is called a **calculated** or **computed field**. Their use is illustrated in the following example.

Example 7:   List the number, name, and available credit for all customers.

There is no field for available credit in the CUSTOMER table. You can calculate it from existing fields, however, because the available credit is equal to the credit limit minus the balance. To include calculated fields in queries, you need to use what QBE terms **examples**. Examples are simply a group of characters that represents a sample value in a field. You then use these examples to specify the calculation.

First you would place the normal check marks in the CUSTOMER_NUMBER, LAST, and FIRST fields. You then place examples in the BALANCE and CREDIT_LIMIT columns. In Figure 2.10, the number 100 has been entered as an example of a balance and the number 300 has been entered as an example of a credit limit.

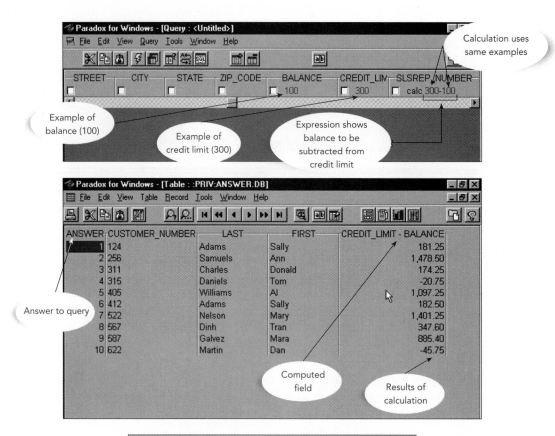

Figure 2.10 Query that involves a computed field

Once you have entered the examples in each of the fields, you place the word "calc" followed by the appropriate expression in any field. (It doesn't matter which field you choose for this purpose.) The expression will use the examples that you already created. In this case the expression would be the example you created for credit limits (300) followed by a minus sign (-), followed by the example you created for balances (100).

Note	In Paradox, you enter examples by pressing **F5** before typing the number. The example then displays in a different color. If the 300 and 100 following the word "calc" did not display differently, they would not be examples and this expression would simply instruct Paradox to subtract 100 from 300. Because they are examples, Paradox will look for other columns with similar examples in them. Because 300 is an example in the CREDIT_LIMIT column and 100 is an example in the BALANCE column, Paradox will subtract the entry in BALANCE from the entry in CREDIT_LIMIT.

Computations are not restricted to subtraction. Addition (+), multiplication (*), or division (/) also are available. You also can include parentheses in your computations.

Built-in Functions

Most database systems support the same collection of **built-in** (sometimes called **aggregate**) **functions**: Count, Sum, Average, Max, and Min. To use any of these in the Paradox version of QBE, precede it with the operator calc.

Example 8:	How many parts are in item class HW?

In this case, Count is the appropriate operation. You will place the function in the PART_NUMBER column and enter the condition in the usual manner as in Figure 2.11. The results indicate there are four such parts.

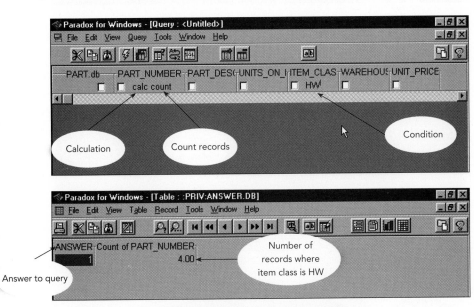

Figure 2.11 Query to count records

Using the Built-In Function Sum

Example 9:	Count the number of customers and find the total of their balances.

Here you want to use both Count and Sum. Because customer numbers are unique, you could put Count in the CUSTOMER_NUMBER column as shown in Figure 2.12. You must put Sum in the BALANCE column as in the second part of the figure, because that is the column you want totaled.

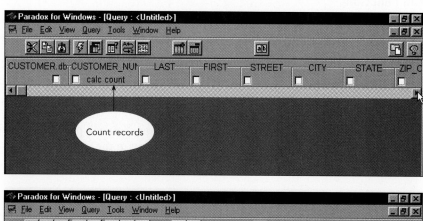

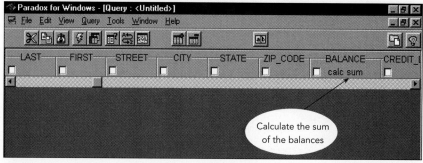

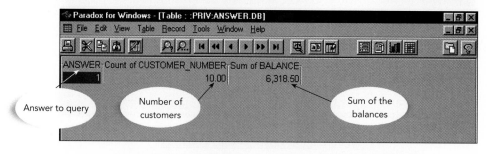

Figure 2.12 Query to perform multiple calculations

Joining Tables

So far the queries all have involved only a single table. In many cases, queries require that data be drawn from more than one table. To do so, it is necessary to **join** the tables, that is to combine tables based on matching values in corresponding columns as in the following example.

Example 10: List each customer's number and name, along with the number and name of the corresponding sales rep.

This query cannot be satisfied using a single table. The customer name is in the CUSTOMER table, whereas the sales rep name is in the SALES_REP table. You thus need to join the tables. To do so, you first need to bring query images for both tables to the screen, as shown in Figure 2.13.

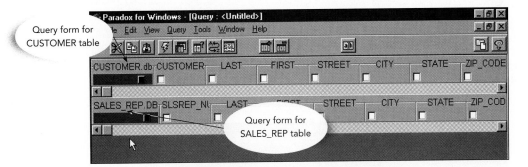

Figure 2.13 Two query forms on screen

Next put check marks in the desired fields in either query form, as shown in Figure 2.14.

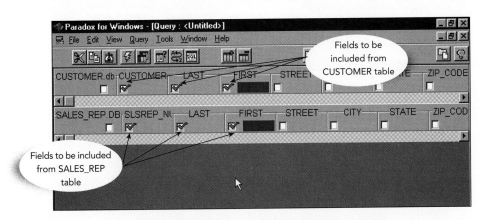

Figure 2.14 Query forms with check marks

Finally, you put the same example in the matching fields. In Figure 2.15, the example join1 has been placed in both SLSREP_NUMBER fields. The examples are necessary, and the fact that they are the same is crucial. This is what tells the system how the tables are to be joined. Note that the data from both tables is included in the results.

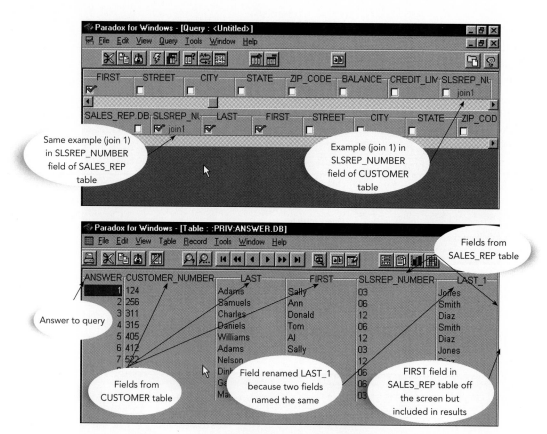

Figure 2.15 Query to join tables

Note	The **LAST** field from the SALES_REP table has been labeled LAST_1 because there is another LAST field in the results. The FIRST field from the SALES_REP table, which would be labeled FIRST_1, currently does not display, although you could scroll the fields to the left in order to see it.

Restricting the Rows in a JOIN

Example 11: For each customer whose credit limit is $1,000, list his or her number and name, along with the number and name of the corresponding sales rep.

The only special difference between this query and the previous one is that there is an extra restriction: The credit limit must be $1,000. To accommodate this, place 1000 in the CREDIT_LIMIT column as shown in Figure 2.16. Only the customers whose credit limit is $1,000 are included.

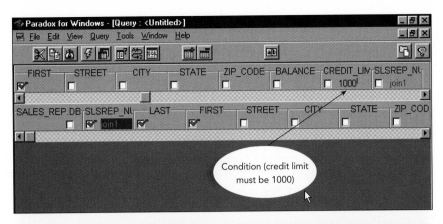

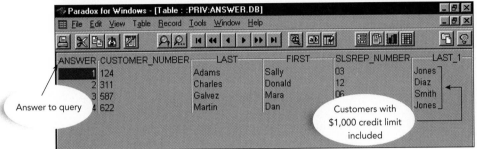

Figure 2.16 Query to restrict the records in a join

THE RELATIONAL ALGEBRA

The **relational algebra** is a theoretical way of manipulating a relational database. In the relational algebra, there are operations that act on tables to produce new tables. This is similar to the way the operations of addition and subtraction act on numbers to produce new numbers in the algebra with which you are familiar.

Retrieving data from a relational database through the use of the relational algebra involves issuing relational algebra commands to operate on existing tables to form a new table that contains the desired information. Sometimes you may need to execute a series of commands in order to obtain the final result.

As you will notice in these examples, each command ends with a clause that reads "GIVING" followed by a table name. This clause is requesting that the result of the execution of the command be placed in a table with the specified name.

Select

The **SELECT** command within the relational algebra takes a horizontal subset of a table; that is, it causes only certain rows to be included in the new table. This command causes a new table to be created, including those rows of a single table that meet some specified criteria.

Example 1: List all information from the CUSTOMER table concerning customer 256.

SELECT CUSTOMER WHERE CUSTOMER_NUMBER = 256
   GIVING ANSWER

This command will create a new table called ANSWER. The ANSWER table will contain all the columns from the CUSTOMER table, but only the single row on which the customer number is 256.

Example 2: List all information from the CUSTOMER table concerning those customers whose credit limit is $1,000.

SELECT CUSTOMER WHERE CREDIT_LIMIT = 1000
   GIVING ANSWER

This command will create a new table called ANSWER. The ANSWER table will contain all the columns from the CUSTOMER table, but only those rows on which the credit limit is $1,000.

Project

The **PROJECT** command within the relational algebra takes a vertical subset of a table; that is, it causes only certain columns to be included in the new table.

Example 3: List the number, first name, and last name of all customers.

PROJECT CUSTOMER OVER (CUSTOMER_NUMBER, FIRST, LAST)
   GIVING ANSWER

This command will create a new table called ANSWER. The ANSWER table will contain all the rows from the CUSTOMER table, but only the CUSTOMER_NUMBER, FIRST, and LAST columns.

Example 4: List the number, first name, and last name of all customers whose credit limit is $1,000.

This requires a two-step process. You first use a **SELECT** command to create a new table that contains only those customers whose credit limit is $1,000. Then you project the new table to restrict the result to only the indicated columns.

SELECT CUSTOMER WHERE CREDIT_LIMIT = 1000
   GIVING TEMP
PROJECT TEMP OVER (CUSTOMER_NUMBER, FIRST, LAST)
   GIVING ANSWER

The first command will create a new table called TEMP. The TEMP table will contain all the columns from the CUSTOMER table, but only those rows on which the credit limit is $1,000. The second command will create a new table called ANSWER. The ANSWER table will contain all the rows from the TEMP table; that is, only customers whose credit limit is $1,000, but only the CUSTOMER_NUMBER, FIRST, and LAST columns.

Join

The join operation is at the heart of the relational algebra. It is the command that allows pulling together data from more than one table. In the most usual form of the join, you join two tables together based on the values in matching columns. The join forms a new table containing the columns of both the tables that have been joined. Rows in this new table will be the concatenation of a row from the first table and a row from the second that match on the common column (often called the **join column**).

For example, suppose you wish to join the tables shown in Figure 2.17 on SLSREP_NUMBER (the join column), creating a new table called TEMP.

CUSTOMER

CUSTOMER NUMBER	LAST	FIRST	SLSREP NUMBER
124	Adams	Sally	3
256	Samuels	Ann	6
311	Charles	Don	12
315	Daniels	Tom	6
405	Williams	Al	12
412	Adams	Sally	3
522	Nelson	Mary	12
567	Dinh	Tran	6
587	Galvez	Mara	6
622	Martin	Dan	3

SALES_REP

SLSREP NUMBER	LAST	FIRST
03	Jones	Mary
06	Smith	William
12	Diaz	Miguel

Figure 2.17 CUSTOMER and SALES_REP tables

The result of the join would be the table shown in Figure 2.18. Note that the column on which the tables are joined appears only once. Other than that, all columns from both tables are present in the result. Each table contains columns labeled LAST and FIRST. To avoid any ambiguity, the names of the second column called LAST and the second column called FIRST have been changed in the TEMP table to LAST_1 and FIRST_1, respectively.

TEMP

CUSTOMER NUMBER	LAST	FIRST	SLSREP NUMB	LAST 1	FIRST 1
124	Adams	Sally	03	Jones	Mary
256	Samuels	Ann	06	Smith	William
311	Charles	Don	12	Diaz	Miguel
315	Daniels	Tom	06	Smith	William
405	Williams	Al	12	Diaz	Miguel
412	Adams	Sally	03	Jones	Mary
522	Nelson	Mary	12	Diaz	Miguel
567	Dinh	Tran	06	Smith	William
587	Galvez	Mara	06	Smith	William
622	Martin	Dan	03	Jones	Mary

Figure 2.18 Table produced by joining CUSTOMER and SALES_REP tables

You can restrict the output from the join to include only certain columns by using the **PROJECT** command, as the following example illustrates.

Example 5: List the customer number, last name, first name, sales rep number, and last name of the sales rep for each customer.

```
JOIN CUSTOMER SLSREP
      WHERE CUSTOMER.SLSREP_NUMBER =
          SALES_REP.SLSREP_NUMBER
      GIVING TEMP
PROJECT TEMP OVER (CUSTOMER_NUMBER, LAST, FIRST,
          SLSREP_NUMBER, LAST_1)
      GIVING ANSWER
```

In the **WHERE** clause in the **JOIN** command, the matching fields both are called SLSREP_NUMBER. The field in SALES_REP called SLSREP_NUMBER is supposed to match the field in CUSTOMER called SLSREP_NUMBER. In this case, if you merely mention SLSREP_NUMBER, it will not be clear which one you mean. It is necessary to qualify SLSREP_NUMBER, or to specify which field you are referring to. You do this by preceding the name of the field with the name of the table, followed by a period. The SLSREP_NUMBER field in the SALES_REP table is SALES_REP.SLSREP_NUMBER. The SLSREP_NUMBER field in the CUSTOMER table is CUSTOMER.SLSREP_NUMBER.

The JOIN command will join the two tables to create a new table called TEMP. The second command will create a new table called ANSWER. The ANSWER table will contain all the rows from the TEMP table, but only the CUSTOMER_NUMBER, FIRST, SLSREP_NUMBER, and LAST_1 columns.

SUMMARY

1. Premiere Products is an organization whose requirements include the following entities:

   a. sales reps

   b. customers

   c. orders

   d. parts

   e. order lines

2. A relation is a two-dimensional table in which:

   a. The entries are single-valued.

   b. Each field has a distinct name.

   c. All the values in a field are values of the same attribute (the one identified by the field name).

   d. The order of fields is immaterial.

   e. Each row is distinct.

   f. The order of rows is immaterial.

3. A relational database is a collection of relations.

4. An unnormalized relation is a structure in which entries need not be single-valued but which satisfies all the other properties of a relation.

5. A field name is qualified by preceding it with the table name and a period, for example, SALES_REP.SLSREP_NUMBER.

6. The primary key is the field or fields that uniquely identify a given row within the table.

7. QBE is a language used to manipulate relational databases. QBE queries are indicated by filling in forms on the screen.

8. To indicate a column is to be included in a QBE query, place a check mark in the column.

9. To indicate conditions in QBE, place the conditions in the appropriate columns.

10. To indicate AND conditions, place both conditions in the same row. To indicate OR conditions, place the conditions on separate rows.

11. To use a QBE built-in function, place it in the appropriate column and precede it with the word "Calc."

12. To create a calculated field in QBE, use examples.

13. To join tables in QBE, use the same example in both matching fields.

14. The relational algebra is another language used to manipulate relational databases.

15. The **SELECT** command in the relational algebra selects only certain rows from a table.

16. The **PROJECT** command in the relational algebra selects only certain columns from a table.

17. The **JOIN** command in the relational algebra combines data from two tables based on matching columns.

KEY TERMS

Attribute

Calculated field

Compound condition

Computed field

Condition

Example

Field

Join

Join column

Qualify

Primary key

Query-By-Example (QBE)

Record

Relation

Relational algebra

Relational database

Repeating group

Tuple

Unnormalized relation

REVIEW QUESTIONS

1. Using the data for Premiere Products as shown in Figure 2.2, give an answer for each of the following problems.

   a. Find the names of all the customers who have a credit limit of at least $1,500.

   b. Give the order numbers of those orders placed by customer 124 on September 5, 1998.

   c. Give the part number, description, and on-hand value (units on hand * price) for each part in item class AP.

   d. Find the number and name of all customers whose last name is Nelson.

   e. Find out how many customers have a credit limit of $1,000.

   f. Find the total of the balances for all the customers represented by sales rep 12.

   g. For each order, list the order number, order date, customer number, and customer name.

   h. For each order placed on September 5, 1998, list the order number, order date, customer number, and customer name.

   i. Find the number and name of all sales reps who represent any customer with a credit limit of $1,000.

   j. For each order, list the order number, order date, customer number, customer name, along with the number and name of the sales rep who represents the customer.

2. Why are order lines in the Premiere Products database in a separate table rather than being part of the ORDERS table?

3. What is a relation?

4. What is a relational database?

5. What is an unnormalized relation? Is it a relation according to the definition of the word relation?

6. How is the term attribute used in the relational model? What is a more common name for it?

7. Describe the shorthand representation of the structure of a relational database. Illustrate this technique by representing the database for Henry's Books, as shown in Chapter 1.

8. What does it mean to qualify the name of a field? How is this done?

9. What is a primary key? What is the primary key for each of the tables in Henry's database? (See Problem 7.)

Questions 10 through 19 are based on the Premiere Products database (Figure 2.2). In each case, indicate how you could use QBE to obtain the desired results.

10. List the number and name of all sales reps.

11. List the complete CUSTOMER table.

12. List the number and name of all customers represented by sales rep 03.

13. List the number and name of all customers who are represented by sales rep 03 and whose credit limit is $1,000.

14. List the number and name of all customers who are represented by sales rep 03 or whose credit limit is $1,000.

15. For each order, list the order number, order date, the number of the customer who placed the order, and the last name of the customer who placed the order.

16. List the number and name of all customers who are represented by Mary Jones.

17. Find out how many customers have a credit limit of $1,000.

18. Find the total of the balances for all the customers represented by sales rep 12.

19. Give the part number, description, and on-hand value (units on hand * price) for each part in item class AP.

Questions 20 through 22 also are based on the Premiere Products database (Figure 2.2). In each case, indicate how you could use the relational algebra to obtain the desired results.

20. List the number and name of all sales reps.

21. List all information from the PART table concerning part BT04.

22. List the order number, order date, customer number, last name, and first name for each order.

CHAPTER 3

The Relational Model 2: SQL

OBJECTIVES

- Introduce the SQL language.

- Discuss the use of simple and compound conditions in SQL.

- Present the use of calculated fields in SQL.

- Examine the use of SQL built-in functions.

- Discuss the use of nested SQL queries.

- Examine grouping in SQL.

- Examine the way tables can be joined in SQL.

- Discuss the union operator in SQL.

INTRODUCTION

In this chapter, you examine the language called **SQL (Structured Query Language)**. Like QBE, SQL provides users with a way of querying relational databases. In SQL, you must type commands to obtain the desired results, however, rather than filling in form entries on the screen, as you do in QBE.

SQL was developed under the name SEQUEL at the IBM San Jose research facilities. SQL was the data manipulation language for IBM's prototype relational model DBMS, System R, in the mid-1970s. In 1980, it was renamed SQL to avoid confusion with an unrelated hardware product called SEQUEL. It is used as the data manipulation language for IBM's current production offerings in the relational DBMS arena, SQL/DS and DB2. Most relational DBMSs use a version of SQL as a data manipulation language.

The next section reviews the way databases are created in SQL. You then examine simple retrieval in the following section and look at compound conditions in the next section. The sections that follow cover: the use of calculated fields in SQL; sorting; built-in functions, nesting queries, and grouping; how tables are joined in SQL; the union operator; and how SQL can be used to update data in a database, respectively.

■　■　■　■　■

DATABASE CREATION

The SQL statement used to describe the layout of a table is CREATE TABLE. The word "TABLE" is followed by the name of the table to be created and then by the names and data types of the columns that comprise the table. The rules for naming tables and columns vary slightly from one version of SQL to another. If you have any doubts about the validity of any of the names you have chosen, you should consult a manual. Typical restrictions are:

1. The name can be no longer than 18 characters.

2. The name must start with a letter.

3. The name can contain letters, numbers, and underscores (_).

4. The name cannot contain spaces.

The names used in this text should work on any SQL implementation.

For each field, you must enter the type of data that can be stored in the field. While the actual data types will vary somewhat from one implementation of SQL to another, the following list indicates the types that often are encountered:

1. **INTEGER**—Integers, or numbers, without a decimal part. Range is -2147483648 to 2147483647. The contents of integer fields can be used for arithmetic.

2. **SMALLINT**—Like INTEGER but does not occupy as much space. Range is -32768 to 32767. This is a better choice than INTEGER if you are certain that numbers will be in the indicated range. The contents of SMALLINT fields can be used for arithmetic.

3. **DECIMAL (p,q)**—Decimal number p digits long with q of these being decimal places. For example, DECIMAL (5,2) represents a number with three places to the left of the decimal and two to the right. The contents of decimal fields can be used for arithmetic.

4. **CHAR (n)**—Character string n characters long. This type should be used for fields that contain letters or any other special characters. It also often is used for fields that contain numbers, but will not be used for arithmetic. Because neither sales rep numbers nor customer numbers will be used in any arithmetic operations, for example, they both are assigned CHAR as the data type.

5. **DATE**—Dates in the form DD-MON-YY or MM/DD/YYYY. For example, May 12, 1998 could be stored as 12-MAY-98 or 5/12/1998.

Example 1:	Describe the layout of the SALES_REP table to the DBMS.

The CREATE TABLE statement for the SALES_REP table is:

```
CREATE TABLE SALES_REP
(SLSREP_NUMBER          CHAR(2),
LAST,                   CHAR(15),
FIRST                   CHAR(15),
STREET,                 CHAR(15),
CITY,                   CHAR(15),
STATE,                  CHAR(2),
ZIP_CODE                CHAR(5),
TOTAL_COMMISSION        DECIMAL(7,2),
COMMISSION_RATE         DECIMAL(3,2) )
```

In this SQL statement, which uses the data definition features of SQL, you're describing a table that will be called SALES_REP. It contains nine fields (columns): SLSREP_NUMBER, LAST, FIRST, STREET, CITY, STATE, ZIP_CODE, TOTAL_COMMISSION, and COMMISSION_RATE. SLSREP_NUMBER is a character field, two positions in length. LAST is a character field fifteen positions in length. TOTAL_COMMISSION is numeric and is seven digits long, including two decimal places. Similarly, COMMISSION_RATE is three digits long, and two of those are decimal places.

Note	In SQL, commands are free-format. No rule says that a particular word must begin in a particular position on the line. The previous SQL command could have been written:

```
CREATE TABLE SALES_REP (SLSREP_NUMBER CHAR(2), LAST CHAR(15), FIRST CHAR(15), STREET CHAR(15),
CITY CHAR(15), STATE CHAR(2), ZIP_CODE CHAR(5), TOTAL_COMMISSION DECIMAL(7,2),
COMMISSION_RATE DECIMAL(3,2) )
```

The manner in which it actually was written simply makes the command more readable. Throughout the text, you will strive for such readability when you write SQL commands.

SIMPLE RETRIEVAL

The basic form of an SQL retrieval expression is quite simple: SELECT-FROM-WHERE. After the SELECT, you list those fields you wish to display. The fields will appear in the results in the order listed in the expression. After the FROM, you list the table or tables involved in the query. Finally, after the WHERE, you list any conditions that apply to the data you want to retrieve.

There are no special format rules in SQL. In this text, you place the word "FROM" on a new line indented slightly, then place the word "WHERE" (when it is used) on the next line indented the same amount. This makes the commands more readable.

Note 1	Just as we did with QBE, we will use Paradox for Windows to illustrate SQL. Other versions are very similar.

Note 2	In the Paradox version, words that are part of the SQL language automatically display in boldface. This is not the case with other systems.

Example 2:	List the number, last name, first name, and balance of all customers.

Because you want all customers listed, there is no need for the WHERE clause (you have no restrictions). The query and results are shown in Figure 3.1.

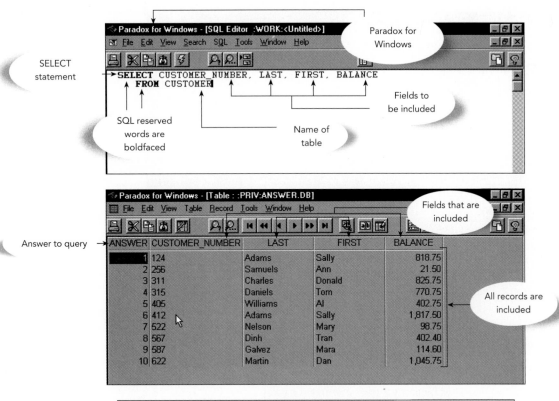

Figure 3.1 Query to list number, name, and balance of all customers

Example 3:   List the complete PART table.

You certainly could use the same approach as in Example 2, that is, list each field in the PART table after the word "SELECT." There is, however, a shortcut. Instead of listing all the field names after SELECT, you can use the * symbol. This indicates that you want all fields listed (in the order described to the system during data definition). If you want all the fields, but in a different order, you would have to type the names of the fields in the order you want them to appear. In this case, assuming the normal order is appropriate, the query and results would be as shown in Figure 3.2.

| Note | Not all fields fit on the screen. They are all included, however, and you could scroll the display to view the remaining fields. |

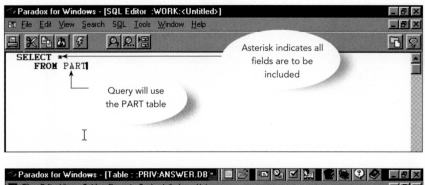

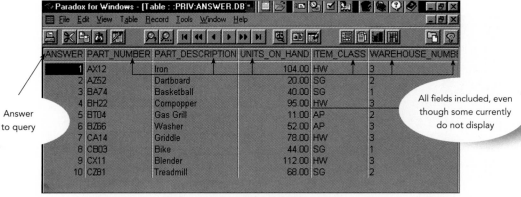

Figure 3.2 Query to list parts

Example 4:   What is the name (last and first) of any customer with a $1,000 credit limit?

You include the following condition in the WHERE clause to restrict the output of the query to those customers with the appropriate credit limit:

WHERE CREDIT_LIMIT = 1000

The query and results are shown in Figure 3.3.

The condition in the preceding WHERE clause is called a simple condition. A **simple condition** has the form: field name, comparison operator, and then either another field name or a value. The possible comparison operators are shown in Table 3.1. Note that there are two different versions for not equal to (<> and !=). You must use the one that is right for your particular implementation of SQL. (If you use the wrong one, your system instantly will let you know. Simply use the other.)

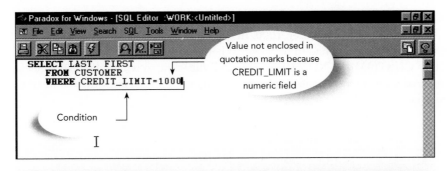

Figure 3.3 Query to list customers with given credit limit

Table 3.1 Comparison operators

COMPARISON OPERATOR	MEANING
=	Equal to
<	Less than
>	Greater than
<=	Less than or equal to
>=	Greater than or equal to
<>	Not equal to (used by most implementations of SQL)
!=	Not equal to (used by most implementations of SQL)

In Example 4, the WHERE clause compared a numeric field, CREDIT_LIMIT, to a number, 1000. In that command, you simply used the number 1000. No special action had to be taken. When the query involves a character field, such as CUSTOMER_NUMBER, or LAST, the value to which the field is being compared must be surrounded by single quotation marks, as illustrated in the next two examples.

Example 5: Find the name (last and first) for customer 124.

The query and result are shown in Figure 3.4. Notice there are single quotation marks around the 124. Notice also there is only a single record in the answer, because the CUSTOMER_NUMBER field is the primary key for the CUSTOMER table.

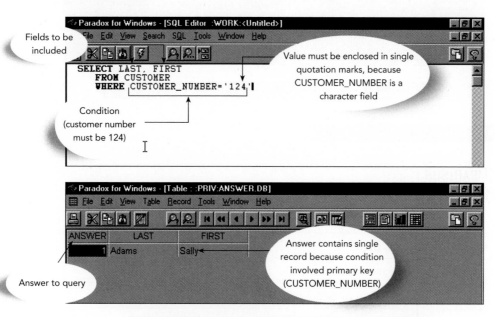

Figure 3.4 Query to list name of specific customer

Example 6: Find the customer number for any customer whose last name is Adams.

The query and results are shown in Figure 3.5. Notice there are multiple records in the answer to the query.

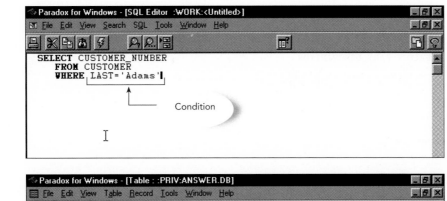

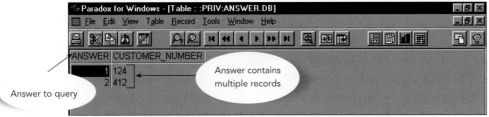

Figure 3.5 Query to list customers with given name

COMPOUND CONDITIONS

The conditions you've seen so far are called simple conditions. The next examples require compound conditions. **Compound conditions** are formed by connecting two or more simple conditions using AND, OR, and NOT. When simple conditions are connected by the word "AND," all the simple conditions must be true in order for the compound condition to be true. When simple conditions are connected by the word "OR," the compound condition will be true whenever any of the simple conditions are true. Preceding a condition by NOT reverses the truth or falsity of the original condition. That is, if the original condition is true, the new condition will be false; if the original condition is false, the new one will be true.

Example 7:	List the descriptions of all parts in warehouse number 3 that have more than 100 units on hand.

In this example, you want those parts for which *both* the warehouse number is equal to 3 *and* the number of units on hand is greater than 100. Thus, you form a compound condition using the word "AND" as shown in Figure 3.6.

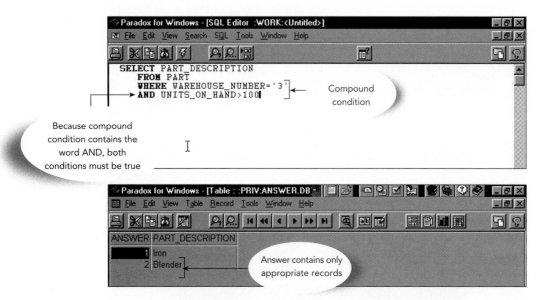

Figure 3.6 Query that includes compound condition

As you would expect, you form compound conditions involving OR in the same fashion. Simply use the word "OR" instead of the word "AND." In that case, the results would contain those records that satisfied either condition.

| Example 8: | List the descriptions of all parts that are not in warehouse number 3. |

For this example, you could use a simple condition with the condition operator not equal to. As an alternative, you could use equals in the condition, but precede the whole condition with the word "NOT," as shown in Figure 3.7.

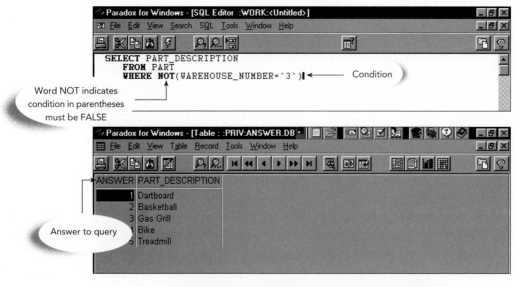

Figure 3.7 Query that includes the word NOT

CALCULATED FIELDS

Just as with QBE, you can include fields in queries that are not in the database, but that can be calculated from fields that are. Such a field is called a **calculated** or **computed field**. Such computations can involve addition (+), subtraction (-), multiplication (*), or division (/). The query in Example 9, for example, uses subtraction.

Example 9: Find the available credit for all customers who have a credit limit of at least $1,500.

There is no field for available credit in our database. It is, however, computable from two fields that are present, CREDIT_LIMIT and **BALANCE** (AVAILABLE_CREDIT = CREDIT_LIMIT - BALANCE). The query shown in Figure 3.8 includes this computation.

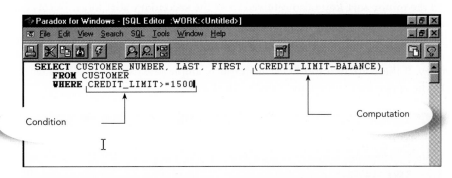

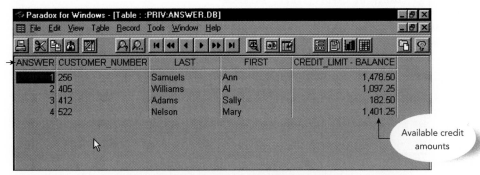

Figure 3.8 Query to find available credit

The parentheses around the calculation (CREDIT_LIMIT - BALANCE) are not essential but improve readability.

SORTING

Recall that the order of rows in a table is considered to be immaterial. From a practical standpoint, this means that in querying a relational database, there are no guarantees concerning the order in which the results will be displayed. It may be in the order in which the data was originally entered, but even this is not certain. Thus, if the order in which the data is displayed is important, you should *specifically* request that the results be displayed in the desired order. In SQL, this is done with the ORDER BY clause, as shown in Example 10.

Example 10: List the number, last name, first name, credit limit, and balance of all customers. Order the customers by balance within credit limit. (This means to order the customers by credit limit. It also means that within each group of customers that have a common credit limit, the customers are to be ordered by balance.)

The field on which data is to be sorted is called a **sort key**, or simply a **key**. If the data is to be sorted on two fields, the more important key is called the **major sort key** (also referred to as the **primary sort key**) and the less important key is called the **minor sort key** (also referred to as the **secondary sort key**). In this case, because the output is to be ordered (sorted) by balance within credit limit, the CREDIT_LIMIT field is the major sort key and the BALANCE field is the minor sort key. To sort the output, you include the words "ORDER BY," followed by the sort key. If there are two sort keys, as in this example, the major sort key is listed first. The appropriate query and results are shown in Figure 3.9.

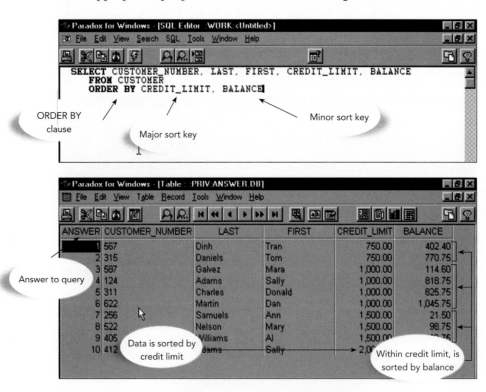

Figure 3.9 Query to sort records

BUILT-IN FUNCTIONS

SQL has **built-in functions** (sometimes called **aggregate functions**) to calculate the number of entries, the sum or average of all the entries in a given column, and the largest or smallest of the entries in a given column. In SQL, these functions are called Count, Sum, Avg, Max, and Min, respectively.

Example 11:	How many parts are in item class HW?

In this query, you're interested in the number of rows in the table produced by selecting only those parts that are in item class HW. You could count the number of part numbers in this table, the number of descriptions, or the number of entries in any other field. It doesn't make any difference. Rather than requiring you to pick one of these arbitrarily, some versions of SQL allow you to use the * symbol. In such a version, you could use the query shown in Figure 3.10.

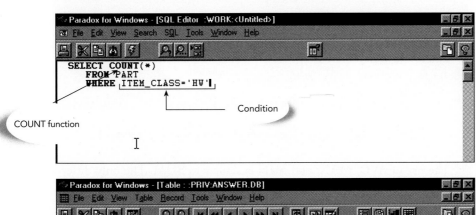

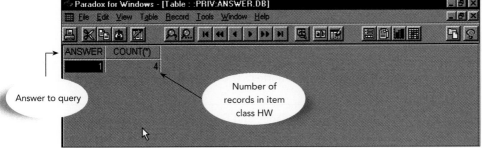

Figure 3.10 Query to count records

If this is not allowed, you would formulate it as:

```
SELECT COUNT(PART_NUMBER)
    FROM PART
    WHERE ITEM_CLASS = 'HW'
```

Example 12:	Find the number of customers and the total of their balances.

The only differences between COUNT and SUM—other than the obvious fact that they are computing different statistics—are that (1) in the case of SUM, you *must* specify the field for which you want a total, and (2) the field must be numeric. (How could you calculate a sum of names or addresses?) This query is shown in Figure 3.11.

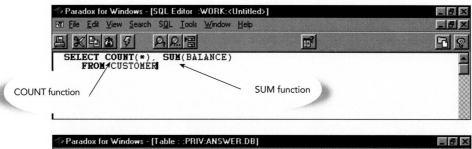

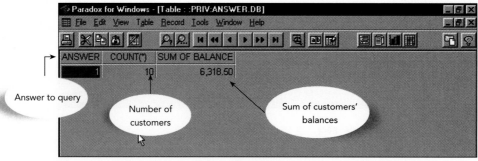

Figure 3.11 Query to count records and calculate a sum

The use of AVG, MAX, and MIN is similar to SUM. The only difference is that a different statistic is calculated.

NESTING QUERIES

It is possible to place one query inside another. The inner query is called a **subquery**.

Example 13: List the customer number, last name, and first name of all customers of Premiere Products who have a credit limit that is equal to the largest credit limit awarded to any customer of sales rep 06.

You could do this in two steps. You first could find the largest credit limit awarded to any customer of sales rep 06 as in Figure 3.12.

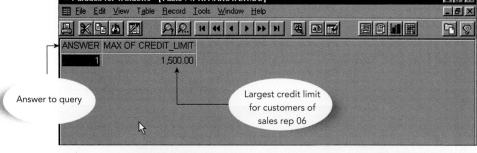

Figure 3.12 Query to find maximum credit limit

After viewing the answer (1500), you could use the query shown in Figure 3.13.

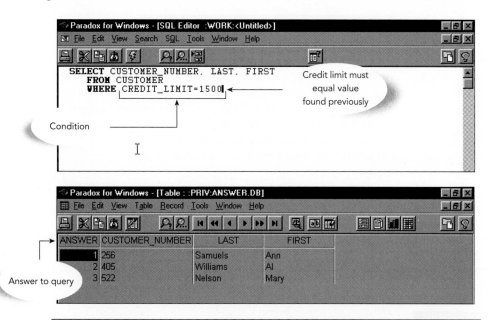

Figure 3.13 Query to find customers with credit limit from previous result

You actually can accomplish this in one step, however, by using subqueries. In this case, the query and results would be those shown in Figure 3.14. The portion in parentheses is the subquery. This subquery is evaluated first, producing a temporary table. In this case the table has one field called MAX(CREDIT_LIMIT) and a single row containing the number 1500.

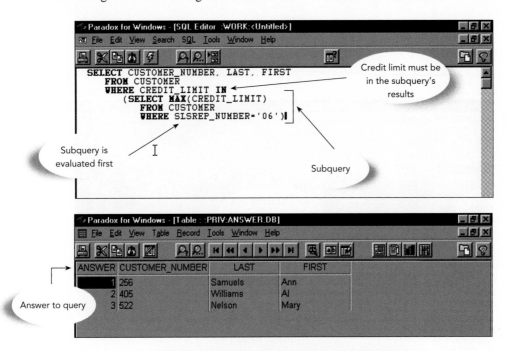

Figure 3.14 Query that includes a subquery

The outer query now can be evaluated. You only will obtain the names of customers whose credit limit is in the result produced by the subquery. Because that table contains only the maximum credit limit for the customers of sales rep 06, you will obtain the desired list of customers. Incidentally, because the subquery in this case will produce a table containing only a single value (the maximum credit limit), this query could have been formulated in another way:

```
SELECT CUSTOMER_NUMBER, LAST, FIRST
    FROM CUSTOMER
        WHERE CREDIT_LIMIT = (SELECT MAX(CREDIT_LIMIT)
            FROM CUSTOMER
            WHERE SLSREP_NUMBER = '06')
```

In this formulation, you are asking for those customers whose credit limit *is equal to* the one credit limit obtained by the subquery. In general, unless you know that the subquery *must* produce a single value, the prior formulation using IN would be the one to use.

GROUPING

Grouping is the process of creating groups (collections) of records that share some common characteristic. Grouping customers by sales rep number, for example, would create three groups. Customers of sales rep 3 would form 1 group, customers of sales rep 6 would form another, and customers of sales rep 12 would form a third. In the following example, you will use grouping to group the records in the ORDER_LINE table by order number.

Example 14:	List the order total for each order.

For each order line, you need to calculate the extension (the product of the number of units ordered and the quoted price). To calculate the order total for an order, you need to add the extensions of each of the order lines on the order. This query thus involves the sum of calculated fields (NUMBER_ORDERED times QUOTED_PRICE). There is, however, a little more to it than just including SUM(NUMBER_ORDERED * QUOTED_PRICE) in the query. This would only give the grand total over all order lines; the grand total would not be broken down by order.

To get individual totals, use the GROUP BY clause. In this case, GROUP BY ORDER_NUMBER will cause the order lines for each order to be grouped together; that is, all order lines with the same order number will form a group. Any statistics, such as totals, requested in the SELECT clause will be calculated for each of these groups. It is important to note that the GROUP BY clause does not imply that the information will be sorted. To produce the report in a particular order, the ORDER BY clause must be used. Assuming that the report is to be ordered by order number, you would have the query, and results, shown in Figure 3.15.

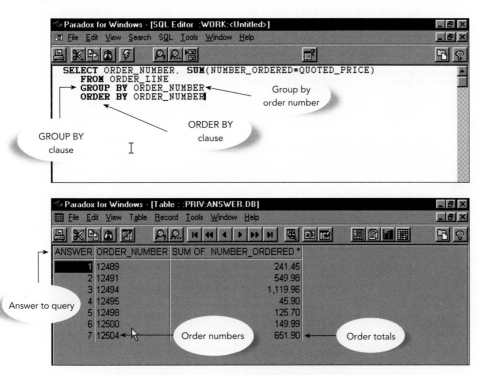

Figure 3.15 Query that involves grouping

When rows are grouped, one line of output is produced for each group. The only things that may be displayed are statistics calculated for the group or fields whose values are the same for all rows in a group.

Question	Would it be appropriate to display the order number?
Answer	Yes because the output is grouped by order number; thus, the order number on one row in a group must be the same as the order number on any other row in the group.

Question	Would it be appropriate to display a part number?
Answer	No because the part number will vary from one row in a group to another. SQL could not determine which part number to display for the group.

Example 15:　　　List the order total for those orders amounting to more than $200.

This example is like the previous one. The only difference is that there is a restriction; namely, you only want to display totals for those orders that amount to more than $200. This restriction does not apply to individual rows, but rather to *groups*. Because the WHERE clause applies only to rows, it is not the appropriate clause to accomplish the kind of selection you have here. Fortunately, there is a facility that is to groups what WHERE is to rows. It is the HAVING clause as shown in Figure 3.16.

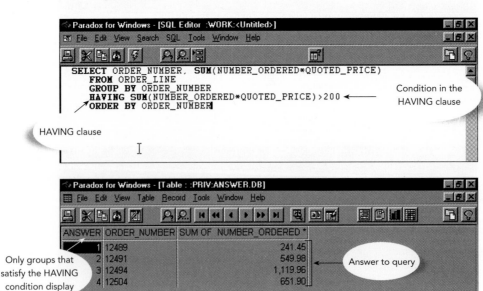

Figure 3.16 Query to restrict the groups that display

In this case, the row created for a group will be displayed only if the sum calculated for the group is larger than $200.

JOINING TABLES

Many queries require data from more than one table. Just as with QBE and the relational algebra, it is necessary to be able to **join** tables; that is, to find rows in two tables that have identical values in matching fields. In SQL, this is accomplished through appropriate conditions in the WHERE clause.

Example 16: | List the number, last name, and first name of each customer together with the number, last name, and first name of the sales rep who represents the customer.

Because the numbers and names of customers are in the CUSTOMER table, while the numbers and names of sales reps are in the SALES_REP table, you need to access both tables in your SQL command:

1. In the SELECT clause, you indicate all fields you wish displayed.

2. In the FROM clause, you list all tables involved in the query.

3. In the WHERE clause, you give the condition that will restrict the data to be retrieved to only those rows from the two tables that match; that is, to the rows that have common values in matching fields.

You have a problem, however. The matching fields are both called SLSREP_NUMBER: There is a field in the SALES_REP table called SLSREP_NUMBER, as well as a field in the CUSTOMER table called SLSREP_NUMBER. In this case, if you merely mention SLSREP_NUMBER, it will not be clear which one you mean. Just as in the relational algebra, it is necessary to **qualify** SLSREP_NUMBER, or to specify which field you are referring to. You do this by preceding the name of the field with the name of the table, followed by a period. The SLSREP_NUMBER field in the SALES_REP table is SALES_REP.SLSREP_NUMBER. The SLSREP_NUMBER field in the CUSTOMER table is CUS-TOMER.SLSREP_NUMBER. You also must qualify the LAST and FIRST fields in a similar manner. The query and results are shown in Figure 3.17.

> **Note** | Note that whenever there is potential ambiguity, you *must* qualify the fields involved. It is permissible to qualify other fields as well, even if there is no confusion. Some people prefer to qualify all fields and this certainly is not a bad approach. In this text, you only will qualify fields when it is necessary to do so.

Example 17: | List the number, last name, and first name of each customer whose credit limit is $1,000, together with the number, last name, and first name of the sales rep who represents the customer.

In Example 16, the condition in the WHERE clause served only to relate a customer to a sales rep. While relating a customer to a sales rep is essential in this example as well, you also want to restrict the output to only those customers whose credit limit is $1,000. This is accomplished by a compound condition, as shown in Figure 3.18.

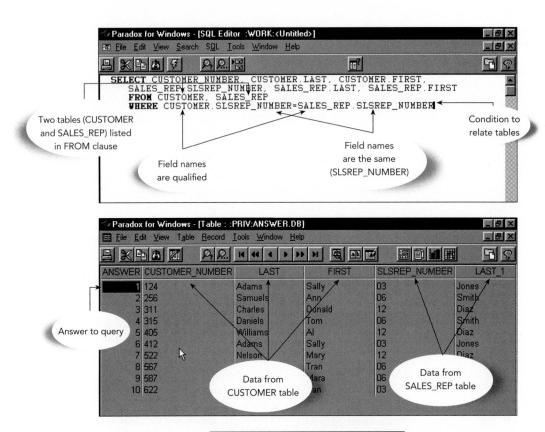

Figure 3.17 Query to join tables

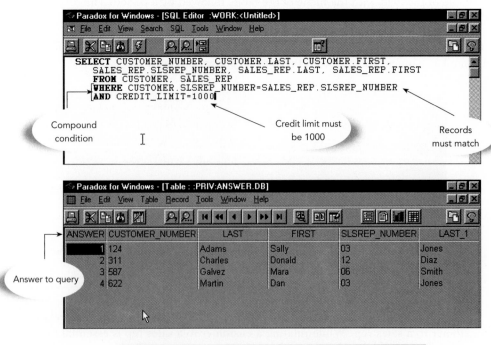

Figure 3.18 Query to restrict the records in the join

UNION

SQL supports the union operation. The **union** of two tables is a table containing all rows that are in either the first table, the second, or both. There is an obvious restriction on union. It does not make sense, for example, to talk about the union of the CUSTOMER table and the ORDERS table. What would rows in this union look like? The two tables *must* have the same structure. The formal term is union-compatible. Two tables are **union-compatible** if they have the same number of fields and if their corresponding fields have identical data types.

Note	Note that the definition does not state that the field headings of the two tables must be identical, but rather that the fields must be of the same type. Thus, if one is CHAR, the other also must be CHAR.

Example 18: List the number, last name, and first name of all customers who either are represented by sales rep 12, or who currently have orders on file, or both.

You can create a table containing the number, last name, and first name of all customers who are represented by sales rep 12 by selecting customer numbers, last names, and first names from the CUSTOMER table in which the sales rep number is 12. Then you can create another table containing the number, last name, and first name of all customers who currently have orders on file by creating a join of the CUSTOMER table and the ORDERS table. The two tables created by this process have the same structure: three fields, a customer number, a last name, and a first name. Because they are thus union-compatible, it is legitimate to take the union of these two tables. This is accomplished in SQL in the manner shown in Figure 3.19.

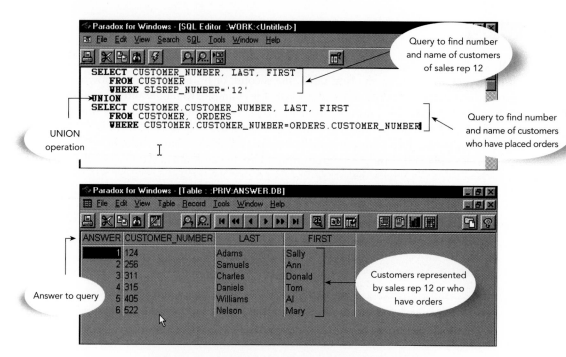

Figure 3.19 Query that involves UNION operation

If an implementation truly supports the union operation, it will remove any duplicate rows (i.e., any customers who are represented by sales rep 12 *and* who currently have orders on file will not appear twice). Some implementations of SQL have a union operation but will not remove such duplicates.

UPDATE

There are more uses to SQL than simply retrieving data from a database. SQL has several other capabilities, including the capability to update a database as demonstrated in the following examples.

Example 19:	Change the last name of customer 256 to Jones.

The SQL command to make changes to existing data is the **UPDATE** command. After the word "UPDATE," you indicate the table to be updated. After the word "SET," you indicate the field to be changed, followed by an equal sign and the new value. Finally, you can place a condition after the word "WHERE," in which case only the records that satisfy the condition will be changed. The SQL command for this example is shown in Figure 3.20.

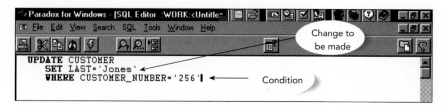

Figure 3.20 UPDATE command

| Example 20: | Add a new sales rep to the SALES_REP table. Her number is 14. Her name is Ann Crane and her address is 123 River, Ada, MI, 42411. So far, she has not earned any commission. Her commission rate is 5 percent (.05). |

Addition of new data is accomplished through the **INSERT** command. After the words "INSERT INTO," you list the name of the table, followed by the word "VALUES." You then list the values for each of the columns in parentheses as shown in Figure 3.21. Character values must be enclosed between single quotation marks.

| Example 21: | Delete from the database the customer whose last name is Williams. |

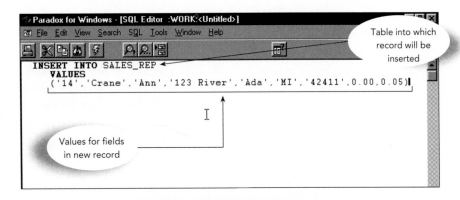

Figure 3.21 INSERT command

To delete data from the database, use the **DELETE** command, which consists of the words "DELETE FROM" followed by the name of the table. A WHERE clause is used to specify a condition. Any records satisfying the condition will be deleted. The DELETE command for this example is shown in Figure 3.22.

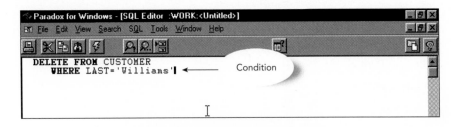

Figure 3.22 DELETE command

Note that this type of deletion can be dangerous. If there happens to be another customer whose last name also is Williams, this customer would be deleted in the process as well. The safest type of deletion occurs when the condition involves the primary key (i.e., deleting customer 124). In such a case, because the primary key is unique, you are certain not to accidentally delete other rows in the table.

SUMMARY

1. SQL (Structured Query Language) is a language used to manipulate relational databases.

2. The basic form of an SQL command is SELECT-FROM-WHERE.

3. The CREATE command is used to describe the layout of a table.

4. In SELECT commands, fields are listed after SELECT, tables are listed after FROM, and conditions are listed after WHERE.

5. In conditions, character values must be enclosed between single quotation marks.

6. Compound conditions are formed by combining simple conditions with AND or OR.

7. Sorting is accomplished through the ORDER BY clause. The field on which the records are sorted is called the sort key. If the data is sorted on more than one field, the more important is called the major sort key or primary sort key. The less important is called the minor sort key or secondary sort key.

8. SQL has the built-in (also called aggregate) functions Count, Sum, Avg, Max, and Min.

9. Joining tables is accomplished in SQL through the use of a condition that relates matching rows in the tables to be joined.

10. The INSERT command is used to add a new row to a table.

11. The UPDATE command is used to change existing data.

12. The DELETE command is used to delete records.

KEY TERMS

Aggregate functions

Built-in functions

Calculated field

CHAR (n)

Compound condition

Computed field

DATE

DECIMAL (p, q)

INTEGER

Join

Key

Major sort key

Minor sort key

Primary sort key

Qualify

Secondary sort key

Simple condition

SMALLINT

Sort key

SQL

Structured Query Language

Subquery

Union

Union-compatible

REVIEW QUESTIONS

1. Describe the process of creating a table in SQL. Describe the possible data types.

2. What is the purpose of the WHERE clause in SQL?

3. What is a compound condition in SQL? When is it true? How do you enter one in an SQL command?

4. How do you sort data in SQL? If there is more than one sort key, how do you indicate which one is the major key?

5. How do you use the SQL built-in functions?

6. When you group in SQL, are there any restrictions on the items that may be listed in the SELECT clause?

7. How do you join tables in SQL?

8. How can you take the union of two tables in SQL? What must be true of the two tables?

9. Describe the three update commands in SQL.

Questions 10 through 25 are based on the Premiere Products database (Figure 2.2 in Chapter 2). In each case, give the SQL command and the results that would be produced for each of the following:

X 10. Find the part number and description of all parts.

X 11. List the complete SALES REP table.

12. Find the names of all the customers who have a credit limit of at least $1,500.

13. Give the order numbers of those orders placed by customer 124 on September 5, 1998. (**Hint**: When you enter a condition in a DATE field, enclose the date in single quotation marks. For example, to search for all orders placed on September 5, 1998, enter '9/5/98' in the ORDER_DATE column.)

14. Give the part number, description, and on-hand value (units on hand * price) for each part in item class AP. (Remember that the AP must be enclosed in quotation marks.)

15. Find the number and name of all customers whose last name is Nelson.

16. List all details about parts. The output should be sorted by unit price.

17. Find how many customers have a credit limit of $1,000.

18. Find the total of the balances for all the customers represented by sales rep 12.

19. For each order, list the order number, order date, customer number, and customer name.

20. For each order placed on September 5, 1998, list the order number, customer number, and customer name.

21. Find the number and name of all sales reps who represent any customer with a credit limit of $1,000.

22. For each order, list the order number, order date, customer number, customer name, along with the number and name of the sales rep who represents the customer.

23. Change the description of part BT04 to Gas Stove.

24. Add order 12600 to the database. The date of the order is September 6, 1998. The order was placed by customer 311.

25. Delete all customers whose balance is under $100.00 and who are represented by sales rep 12.

CHAPTER 4

The Relational Model 3: Advanced Topics

OBJECTIVES

- Discuss views: what they are, how they are described, and how they are used.

- Discuss the use of indexes for improving performance.

- Examine the security features of a DBMS.

- Explain entity and referential integrity.

- Discuss the manner in which the structure of a relational database can be changed.

- Define the catalog and explain its use.

- Describe the characteristics a system must possess in order to be relational.

INTRODUCTION

In the last chapter, you examined data definition and manipulation within the relational model. In this chapter, you will investigate some other aspects of the model. You will look at views, which represent a way of giving each user his or her own picture of what the database looks like. You will look at indexes and their use in improving performance. The features of a DBMS that relate to security will be covered. Two critical integrity rules will be presented. One of the real strengths of the relational model, the ease with which a database structure can be changed, will be covered. You will examine the catalog that is furnished by many relational DBMSs to provide users with access to information about the structure of a database. Finally, in the last section, you will look at a very important question: How can you tell whether a system truly is relational?

In the discussion that follows, you often will use SQL as a mechanism for illustrating the concepts. It should be emphasized, however, that many systems which do not support the SQL language still provide the features discussed. Although the manner in which this is accomplished varies slightly from one system to another, the basic concepts are the same, and it should be easy for you to transfer the knowledge you gain in this chapter to a non-SQL system.

■　■　■　■　■

VIEWS

Most relational mainframe DBMSs and many of the microcomputer DBMSs support the concept of a view. A **view** is basically an individual user's picture of the database. In many cases, a user can interact with the database via a view. Because a view usually is much less involved than the full database, its use can represent a great simplification. Views also provide a measure of security, because omitting sensitive tables or columns from a view will render them unavailable to anyone who is accessing the database via the view.

To illustrate the idea of a view, let's suppose that Juan is interested in the part number, part description, units on hand, and unit price of those parts that are in item class HW. He is not interested in any of the other columns in the PART table. Nor is he interested in any of the rows that correspond to parts in other item classes. Life certainly would be simpler for Juan if the other rows and columns were not even present. While you cannot change the structure of the PART table and omit some of its rows just for Juan, you can do the next best thing. You can provide him a view that consists of precisely the rows and columns in which he is interested. Using SQL, you do this as follows:

```
CREATE VIEW HOUSEWARES AS
    SELECT PART_NUMBER, PART_DESCRIPTION,
        UNITS_ON_HAND, UNIT_PRICE
    FROM PART
    WHERE ITEM_CLASS = 'HW'
```

The **SELECT** command, which is called the **defining query**, indicates precisely what is to be included in the view. Notice it is exactly what Juan wants. Conceptually, given the current data in the Premiere Products database, this view will contain the data shown in Figure 4.1. The data does not really exist in this form, however, nor will it *ever* exist in this form. It is tempting to think that when this view is used, the query is executed and will produce some sort of temporary table, called HOUSEWARES, which Juan then could access. This is *not* what happens.

HOUSEWARES

PART NUMBER	PART DESCRIPTION	UNITS ON HAND	UNIT PRICE
AX12	Iron	104	$24.95
BH22	Cornpopper	95	$24.95
CA14	Griddle	78	$39.99
CX11	Blender	112	$22.95

Figure 4.1 HOUSEWARES view

Instead, the query acts as a sort of window into the database (Figure 4.2). As far as Juan is concerned, the whole database is just the darker portion. Any change that affects the darker portion of the PART table is seen by Juan. He is totally unaware, however, of a change that affects any other part of the database.

SALES REP

SLSREP NUMBER	LAST	FIRST	STREET	CITY	STATE	ZIP CODE	TOTAL COMMISSION	COMMISSION RATE
03	Jones	Mary	123 Main	Grant	MI	49219	2150.00	.05
06	Smith	William	102 Raymond	Ada	MI	49441	4912.50	.07
12	Diaz	Miguel	419 Harper	Lansing	MI	49224	2150.00	.05

CUSTOMER

CUSTOMER NUMBER	LAST	FIRST	STREET	CITY	STATE	ZIP CODE	BALANCE	CREDIT LIMIT	SLSREP NUMBER
124	Adams	Sally	481 Oak	Lansing	MI	49224	$818.75	$1000	03
256	Samuels	Ann	215 Pete	Grant	MI	49219	$21.50	$1500	06
311	Charles	Don	48 College	Ira	MI	49034	$825.75	$1000	12
315	Daniels	Tom	914 Cherry	Kent	MI	48391	$770.75	$750	06
405	Williams	Al	519 Watson	Grant	MI	49219	$402.75	$1500	12
412	Adams	Sally	16 Elm	Lansing	MI	49224	$1817.50	$2000	03
522	Nelson	Mary	108 Pine	Ada	MI	49441	$98.75	$1500	12
567	Dinh	Tran	808 Ridge	Harper	MI	48421	$402.40	$750	06
587	Galvez	Mara	512 Pine	Ada	MI	49441	$114.60	$1000	06
622	Martin	Dan	419 Chip	Grant	MI	49219	$1045.75	$1000	03

ORDERS

ORDER NUMBER	ORDER DATE	CUSTOMER NUMBER
12489	9/02/98	124
12491	9/02/98	311
12494	9/04/98	315
12495	9/04/98	256
12498	9/05/98	522
12500	9/05/98	124
12504	9/05/98	522

ORDER LINE

ORDER NUMBER	PART NUMBER	NUMBER ORDERED	QUOTED PRICE
12489	AX12	11	$21.95
12491	BT04	1	$149.99
12491	BZ66	1	$399.99
12494	CB03	4	$279.99
12495	CX11	2	$22.95
12498	AZ52	2	$12.95
12498	BA74	4	$24.95
12500	BT04	1	$149.99
12504	CZ81	2	$325.99

PART

PART NUMBER	PART DESCRIPTION	UNITS ON HAND	ITEM CLASS	WAREHOUSE NUMBER	UNIT PRICE
AX12	Iron	104	HW	3	$24.95
AZ52	Dartboard	20	SG	2	$12.95
BA74	Basketball	40	SG	1	$29.95
BH22	Cornpopper	95	HW	3	$24.95
BT04	Gas Grill	11	AP	2	$149.99
BZ66	Washer	52	AP	3	$399.99
CA14	Griddle	78	HW	3	$39.99
CB03	Bike	44	SG	1	$299.99
CX11	Blender	112	HW	3	$22.95
CZ81	Treadmill	68	SG	2	$349.95

Figure 4.2 Premiere Products sample data

When a user enters a query that involves a view, the DBMS changes the query to one that instead involves the tables in the database. Suppose, for example, that Juan were to type the following query:

```
SELECT *
    FROM HOUSEWARES
    WHERE UNITS_ON_HAND > 100
```

The query would *not* be executed in this form. Instead, it would be merged with the query that defines the view, forming the query that actually is executed. In this case, the merging of the two would form:

```
SELECT PART_NUMBER, PART_DESCRIPTION, UNITS_ON_HAND,
    UNIT_PRICE
    FROM PART
    WHERE ITEM_CLASS = 'HW'
        AND UNITS_ON_HAND > 100
```

Notice the following three things: the selection is from the PART table rather than the HOUSEWARES view; the * is replaced by those columns that are in the HOUSEWARES view; and the condition involves the condition in the query entered by Juan together with the condition stated in the view definition. This new query is the one that actually is executed.

Juan, however, is unaware that this kind of activity is taking place. It seems to him that there really is a table called HOUSEWARES that is being accessed. One advantage of this approach is that because HOUSEWARES never exists in its own right, any update to the PART table is available *immediately* to someone accessing the database through the view. If HOUSEWARES were an actual stored table, this would not be the case.

What if Juan wanted different names for the columns? This could be accomplished by including the desired names in the **CREATE VIEW** statement. For example, if Juan wanted the names of the Part Number, Part Description, Units On Hand, and Unit Price columns to be PNUM, DESC, ONHAND, and PRICE, respectively, the CREATE VIEW statement would be:

```
CREATE VIEW HOUSEWARES (PNUM, DESC, ONHAND, PRICE) AS
    SELECT PART_NUMBER, PART_DESCRIPTION,
    UNITS_ON_HAND, UNIT_PRICE
    FROM PART
    WHERE ITEM_CLASS = 'HW'
```

In this case, when Juan accessed the HOUSEWARES view, he would refer to PNUM, DESC, ONHAND, and PRICE rather than PART_NUMBER, PART_DESCRIPTION, UNITS_ON_HAND, and UNIT_PRICE.

The HOUSEWARES view is an example of a row-and-column subset view; that is, it consists of a subset of the rows and columns in some individual table, in this case the PART table. Because the query can be any SQL query, a view also could involve the join of two or more tables.

Suppose, for example, that Francesca needed to know the number and name of each sales rep, along with the number and name of the customers represented by each sales rep. It would be much simpler for her if this information were in a single table instead of two tables that had to be joined together. She really would like a single table that contained a sales rep number, sales rep name, customer number, and customer name. Suppose she also would like these columns to be named SNUM, SLAST, SFIRST, CNUM, CLAST, and CFIRST, respectively. This could be accomplished by using a join in the **CREATE VIEW** statement, as follows:

```
CREATE VIEW SALES_CUST (SNUM, SLAST, SFIRST, CNUM, CLAST, CFIRST) AS
    SELECT SALES_REP.SLSREP_NUMBER, SALES_REP.LAST,
    SALES_REP.FIRST, CUSTOMER.CUSTOMER_NUMBER,
    CUSTOMER.LAST, CUSTOMER.FIRST
    FROM SALES_REP, CUSTOMER
    WHERE SALES_REP.SLSREP_NUMBER =
        CUSTOMER.SLSREP_NUMBER
```

Given the current data in the Premiere Products database, this view is conceptually the table shown in Figure 4.3.

SALES_CUST

SNUMB	SLAST	SFIRST	CNUMB	CLAST	CFIRST
03	Jones	Mary	124	Adams	Sally
03	Jones	Mary	412	Adams	Sally
03	Jones	Mary	622	Martin	Dan
06	Smith	William	256	Samuels	Ann
06	Smith	William	315	Daniels	Tom
06	Smith	William	567	Dinh	Tran
06	Smith	William	587	Galvez	Mara
12	Diaz	Miguel	311	Charles	Don
12	Diaz	Miguel	405	Williams	Al
12	Diaz	Miguel	522	Nelson	Mary

Figure 4.3 SALES_CUST view

As far as Francesca is concerned, this is a real table; she does not need to know what goes on behind the scenes in order to use it. She could find the number and name of the sales rep who represents customer 256, for example, merely by entering:

```
SELECT SNUM, SLAST, SFIRST
    FROM SALES_CUST
    WHERE CNUM = 256
```

She is completely unaware that, behind the scenes, her query actually is converted to:

```
SELECT SALES_REP.SLSREP_NUMBER, SALES_REP.LAST,
    SALES_REP.FIRST
    FROM SALES_REP, CUSTOMER
    WHERE SALES_REP.SLSREP_NUMBER =
        CUSTOMER.SLSREP_NUMBER
        AND CUSTOMER_NUMBER = 256
```

The use of views furnishes several advantages:

1. Views provide data independence. If the database structure is changed (columns added, relationships changed, etc.) in such a way that the view still can be derived from existing data, the user still can access the same view. If adding extra columns to tables in the database is the only change, and these columns are not required by this user, the defining query may not even need to be changed. If relationships are changed, the defining query may be different, but because users need not even be aware of the defining query, this difference is unknown to them. They continue to access the database through the same view, as though nothing has changed.

2. Because each user has his or her own view, the same data can be viewed by different users in different ways.

3. A view should contain only those columns required by a given user. This practice accomplishes two things. First, because the view will, in all probability, contain far fewer columns than the overall database and because the view is effectively a single table, rather than a collection of tables, it greatly simplifies the user's perception of the database. Second, it furnishes a measure of security. Columns that are not included in the view are not accessible to this user. Omitting the Balance field from the view will ensure that a user of this view cannot access any customer's balance. Likewise, rows that are not included in the view are not accessible. A user of the HOUSEWARES view, for example, cannot obtain any information about parts in the AP or SG item classes.

INDEXES

If you wanted to find a discussion of a given topic in a book, you could scan the entire book from start to finish, looking for references to the topic you had in mind. More than likely, however, you wouldn't have to resort to this technique. If the book had a good index, you could use it to rapidly locate the pages on which your topic was discussed.

Within relational model systems on both mainframes and microcomputers, the main mechanism for increasing the efficiency with which data is retrieved from the database is the use of **indexes**. Conceptually, these indexes are very much like the index in a book. Consider Figure 4.4, for example, which shows the CUSTOMER table for Premiere Products together with one extra column, Record Number. This extra column gives the number of each record within the file. (Customer 124 is on record one; customer 256 is on record two; and so on.) These record numbers are used by the DBMS, not by the users, and that is why you normally do not show them. Here, however, you are dealing with the manner in which the DBMS works, so you do need to be aware of them.

CUSTOMER

RECORD NUMBER	CUSTOMER NUMBER	LAST	FIRST	. . .	BALANCE	CREDIT LIMIT	SLSREP NUMBER
1	124	Adams	Sally	. . .	$818.75	$1000	03
2	256	Samuels	Ann	. . .	$21.50	$1500	06
3	311	Charles	Don	. . .	$825.75	$1000	12
4	315	Daniels	Tom	. . .	$770.75	$750	06
5	405	Williams	Al	. . .	$402.75	$1500	12
6	412	Adams	Sally	. . .	$1817.50	$2000	03
7	522	Nelson	Mary	. . .	$98.75	$1500	12
8	567	Dinh	Tran	. . .	$402.40	$750	06
9	587	Galvez	Mara	. . .	$114.60	$1000	06
10	622	Martin	Dan	. . .	$1045.75	$1000	03

Figure 4.4 CUSTOMER table with record numbers

In order to rapidly access a customer on the basis of his or her number, you might choose to create and use an index as shown in Figure 4.5.

CUSTOMER_NUMBER INDEX

CUSTOMER NUMBER	RECORD NUMBER
124	1
256	2
311	3
315	4
405	5
412	6
522	7
567	8
587	9
622	10

Figure 4.5 Index for CUSTOMER table on Customer Number field

The index has two columns. The first column contains a customer number, and the second column contains the number of the record on which the customer is found. Because customer numbers are unique, there is only a single record number. This is not always the case, however. Suppose, for example, that you wanted rapidly to access all customers who had a given credit limit or all customers who were represented by a given sales rep. You might choose to create and use an index on credit limit as well as an index on sales rep number. These two indexes, along with the index on the customer number, are shown in Figure 4.6. In the index on credit limit, the first column contains a credit limit, and the second column contains the numbers of *all* the records on which that credit limit is found. The index on sales rep number is similar. (Actually, the structure used for an index is usually a little more complicated than these examples show. They are perfectly acceptable for these purposes, however.)

CUSTOMER_NUMBER INDEX

CUSTOMER NUMBER	RECORD NUMBER
124	1
256	2
311	3
315	4
405	5
412	6
522	7
567	8
587	9
622	10

CUSTOMER_LIMIT INDEX

CREDIT LIMIT	RECORD NUMBERS
$750	4, 8
$1000	1, 3, 9, 10
$1500	2, 5, 7
$2000	6

SLSREP_NUMBER INDEX

SLSREP NUMBER	RECORD NUMBERS
03	1, 6, 10
06	2, 4, 8, 9
12	3, 5, 7

Figure 4.6 Indexes for CUSTOMER table on Customer Number, Credit Limit, and Slsrep Number fields

Typically, an index can be created and maintained for any column or combination of columns in any table. Once an index has been created, it can be used to facilitate retrieval. In powerful mainframe relational systems, the decision concerning which index or indexes to use, if any, during a particular type of retrieval is one function of a part of the DBMS called an **optimizer**. (No reference is made to any index by the user; rather, the system makes the decision behind the scenes.) In less powerful systems and, in particular, in some microcomputer systems, the user may have to indicate specifically in some fashion that a given index should be used.

As you would expect, the use of any index is not purely advantageous or disadvantageous. The advantage already was mentioned: an index makes certain types of retrieval more efficient. There are two disadvantages. First, an index occupies space that could be used for something else. Any retrieval that can be made using an index also can be made without the index. The process may be less efficient, but it still is possible. So an index, while it occupies space, technically is not necessary. The other disadvantage is that the index must be updated whenever corresponding data in the database is updated. Without the index, these updates would not have to be performed. The main question that you must ask when considering whether or not to create a given index is: Do the benefits derived during retrieval outweigh the additional storage required and the extra processing involved in update operations?

Indexes can be added and dropped at will. The final decision concerning the columns or combination of columns on which indexes should be built does not have to be made at the time the database first is implemented. If the pattern of access to the database later indicates that overall performance would benefit from the creation of a new index, it easily can be added. Likewise, if it appears that an existing index is unnecessary, it easily can be dropped.

The exact process for creating an index varies from one DBMS to another. Figure 4.7 shows the creation of an index on the Last Name field in Microsoft Access. As illustrated in the figure, there are three choices: No, Yes (Duplicates OK), and Yes (No Duplicates).

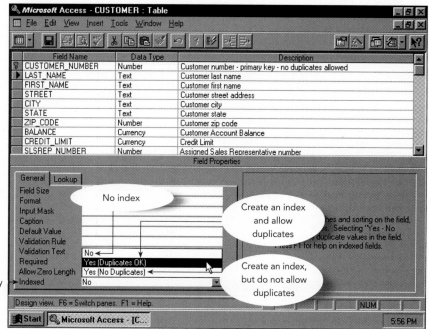

Figure 4.7 Options for creating an index

You would select No if you did not wish to create an index on the Last Name field or if you wished to remove a previously created index. You would select Yes (Duplicates OK) to create an index and to allow duplicates. In that case, Access would allow more than one customer with the same last name. If you selected Yes (No Duplicates), on the other hand, Access would create the index but you would not be able to add a customer whose last name was the same as the last name of a customer already in the database.

SECURITY

Security is the prevention of unauthorized access to the database. Within an organization, some person or group will determine the types of access various users can have to the database. Some users might be able to retrieve and update anything in the database. Other users may be able to retrieve any data from the database but not make any changes to the data. Still other users only may be able to access a portion of the database. For example, Bill may be able to retrieve and update sales rep and customer data, but not retrieve data about parts and orders. Mary may be able to retrieve data on parts and nothing else. Kyung may be able to retrieve and update data on parts of type HW, but no others.

Once these rules have been determined, it's up to the DBMS to enforce them. In particular, it's up to whatever security mechanism the DBMS provides. In SQL systems, there are two security mechanisms. You already have seen that views furnish a certain amount of security. (If someone is accessing the database through a view, they cannot access any data that is not part of the view.) The main mechanism, however, is the **GRANT** facility.

The basic idea is that different types of privileges can be granted to users and, if necessary, later revoked. These privileges include such things as the right to select rows from a table, the right to insert new rows, the right to update existing rows, and so on. Granting and revoking these privileges is accomplished through **GRANT** and **REVOKE** statements. Following are some examples of these statements.

GRANT SELECT ON CUSTOMER TO JONES

Jones is able to retrieve customer data, but will not be able to take any other action.

GRANT INSERT ON PART TO SMITH, RIVERA

Smith and Rivera are able to add new parts.

REVOKE SELECT ON CUSTOMER FROM JONES

Jones no longer has the right to retrieve customer data.

INTEGRITY RULES

There are two very special rules that should be enforced by a relational DBMS. They were defined by E. F. Codd[*] and relate to two special types of keys: primary keys and foreign keys. The two integrity rules are called entity integrity and referential integrity.

Entity Integrity

In some DBMSs, when you describe a database, you can indicate that certain columns can accept a special value called **null**. Essentially, setting the value in a given column to null is similar to not filling it in at all. It is used when a value is unknown or inapplicable. It is *not* the same as blank or zero, which are actual values. For example, a value of zero in the Balance field indicates that the customer has a zero balance. A value of null, on the other hand, indicates that for whatever reason, the customer's balance is unknown.

If you indicate that the column Balance can be null, you are saying that this situation (a customer with an unknown balance) is something you want to allow. If you don't want to allow it, you indicate that Balance cannot be null.

The decision as to whether to allow nulls generally is made on a column-by-column basis. There is one type of column for which you should *never* allow nulls, however, and that is the primary key. After all, the primary key uniquely is supposed to identify a given row, and this could not happen if nulls were allowed. How, for example, could you tell two customers apart if both had a null customer number? The restriction that the primary key cannot allow null values is called entity integrity.

Definition: Entity integrity is the rule that no column that participates in the primary key may accept null values.

---

[*]E. F. Codd, "Extending the Relational Database Model to Capture More Meaning,"

ACMTODS 4.4 (1979)

This property guarantees that each record will indeed have its own identity. In other words, preventing the primary key from accepting null values ensures that one record can be distinguished from another.

Referential Integrity

In the relational model discussed until now, relationships are not explicit. They are accomplished by having common columns in two or more tables. The relationship between sales reps and customers, for example, is accomplished by including Slsrep Number, the primary key of the SALES_REP table, as a column in the CUSTOMER table.

This approach has its problems. First, relationships are not very obvious. If you were not already familiar with the relationships within the Premiere Products database, you would have to note the matching columns in separate tables in order to be aware of a relationship. Even then, you couldn't be sure. Two columns having the same name could be just a coincidence. These columns might have nothing to do with each other. Second, what if the key to the SALES_REP table were Slsrep Number but the corresponding column within the CUSTOMER table happened to be called Slsr No? Unless you were aware that these two columns were really the same, the relationship between customers and sales reps would not be clear. In a database having as few tables and columns as the Premiere Products database, these problems might not be major ones. But picture a database that has 20 tables, each one containing an average of 30 columns. As the number of tables and columns increases, so do the problems.

There is also another problem. Nothing about the model itself would prevent a user from storing a customer whose sales rep number did not correspond to any sales rep already in the database. Clearly this is not a desirable situation.

Fortunately, a solution has been found for these two problems, and involves the use of foreign keys.

Definition: A **foreign key** is a column, or collection of columns, in one table whose value is required to match the value of the primary key for some row in another table.

The Slsrep Number in the CUSTOMER table is a foreign key that must match the primary key of the SALES_REP table. In practice, this simply means that the sales rep number for any customer must be the same as the number of some sales rep already in the database.

There is one possible exception to this. Some organizations do not require a customer to have a sales rep. This situation could be indicated in the CUSTOMER table by setting such a customer's sales rep number to null. Technically, however, a null sales rep number would violate the restrictions indicated for a foreign key. So if you were to use a null sales rep number, you would have to modify the definition of foreign keys to include the possibility of nulls. You would insist, though, that if the foreign key contained a value *other than null*, it would have to match the value of the primary key in some row in the other table. (In this example, for instance, a customer's sales rep number could be null, but if it were not, then it would have to be the number of an actual sales rep.) The general property just described is called referential integrity.

Definition: Referential integrity is the rule that if table A contains a foreign key that matches the primary key of table B then values of this foreign key either must match the value of the primary key for some row in table B or must be null.

The problems mentioned above are solved through the use of foreign keys. Indicating that the Slsrep Number in the CUSTOMER table is a foreign key that must match the Slsrep Number in the SALES_REP table makes the relationship between customers and sales reps explicit. You do not need to look for common columns in several tables. Further, with foreign keys, matching columns that have different names no longer pose a problem. For example, it would not matter if the name of the foreign key in the CUSTOMER table happened to be Slsr No while the primary key in the SALES_REP table happened to be Slsrep Number, the only thing that would matter is that this column was a foreign key that matched the SALES_REP table. Finally, through referential integrity, it is possible for a customer not to have a sales rep number, but it is not possible for a customer to have *an invalid sales rep number*; that is, a customer's sales rep number *must* either be null or the number of a sales rep who is already in the database.

The manner in which you specify referential integrity depends on the DBMS you are using. In Microsoft Access, it is specified as part of the process of defining relationships. (See Figure 4.8.)

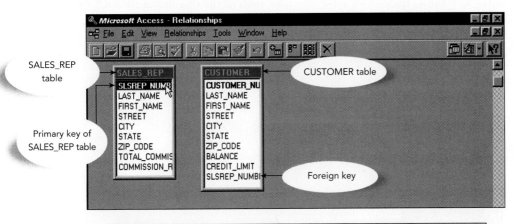

Figure 4.8 Preparing to define a relationship between two tables

Once you have indicated how two tables are to be related, you have the opportunity to request that Access enforce referential integrity (Figure 4.9). You also have the opportunity to specify whether update or delete is to "cascade." Cascade delete, for example, would mean that whenever a sales rep is deleted, all related customers also must be deleted. In the example illustrated in the figure, neither update nor delete is to cascade.

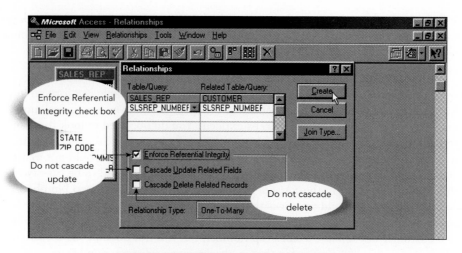

Figure 4.9 Referential integrity options

With referential integrity enforced, users would not be allowed to enter a customer whose sales rep number does not match any sales rep currently in the SALES_REP table. Instead an error message such as the one in Figure 4.10 would display.

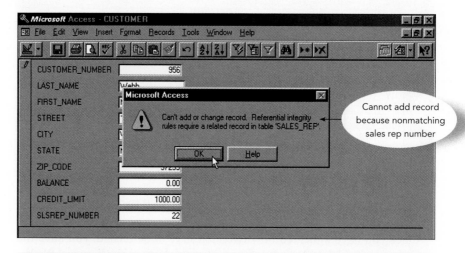

Figure 4.10 DBMS enforcing referential integrity when adding a record

Deleting a sales rep who currently has customers on file also would cause referential integrity to be violated, because the sales rep's customers would no longer match any sales rep in the SALES_REP table. The DBMS must refuse to carry out this type of deletion, instead producing an error message such as the one in Figure 4.11.

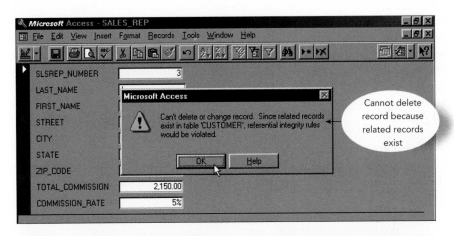

Figure 4.11 DBMS enforcing referential integrity when deleting a record

CHANGING THE STRUCTURE OF A RELATIONAL DATABASE

An important feature of relational DBMSs is the ease with which the database structure can be changed. New tables can be added and old ones removed. Columns can be added or deleted. The characteristics of columns can be changed. New indexes can be created and old ones dropped. Though the exact manner in which these changes are accomplished varies from one system to another, many systems allow all these changes to be made quickly and easily. Because SQL is so widely used, we will use it as a vehicle to illustrate the manner in which these changes may be accomplished.

Alter

Changing the table structure in SQL is accomplished through the **ALTER TABLE** command. Virtually every implementation of SQL allows new columns to be added to the end of an existing table. For example, let's suppose you now wish to maintain a customer type for each customer in the Premiere Products database. You can decide to call regular customers type R, distributors type D, and special customers type S. To implement this change, you need a new column in the CUSTOMER table. This can be added as follows:

```
ALTER TABLE CUSTOMER
    ADD CUSTTYPE     CHAR (1)
```

At this point, the CUSTOMER table contains an extra column, CustType. For rows added from this point on, the value of CustType is assigned as the row is added. For existing rows, some value of CustType must be assigned. The simplest approach (from the point of view of the DBMS, *not* the user) is to assign the value Null as a CustType on all existing rows. (This requires that CustType accept null values, and some systems do require this. This means that any column added to a table definition *will* accept nulls; the user has no choice in the matter.) A more flexible approach, and one that is supported by some systems, is to allow the user to specify an initial value. In this example, if most customers were type R, you might set all the customer types for existing customers to R and later change those customers of type D or type S to the appropriate value. To change the structure and set the value of CustType to R for all existing records, you would type:

```
ALTER TABLE CUSTOMER
    ADD CUSTTYPE      CHAR (1)   INIT = 'R'
```

Some systems allow existing columns to be deleted. The syntax for deleting the Warehouse Number column from the PART table typically would be something like this:

```
ALTER TABLE PART
    DELETE WAREHOUSE_NUMBER
```

Finally, some systems allow changes in the data types of given columns. A typical use of such a provision would be to increase the length of a character field that was found to be inadequate. Assuming that the Last column in the CUSTOMER table needed to be increased to 20 characters, the **ALTER TABLE** statement would be something like this:

```
ALTER TABLE CUSTOMER
    CHANGE COLUMN LAST TO CHAR (20)
```

Drop

A table that is no longer needed can be deleted with the **DROP TABLE** command. If the SALES REP table were no longer needed in the Premiere Products database, the command would be:

```
DROP TABLE SALES_REP
```

The table would be erased, as would all indexes and views defined on the table. References to the table would be removed from the system catalog.

THE CATALOG

Information about tables that are known to the system is kept in the system **catalog**. This section will describe the types of things kept in a catalog and the way the catalog can be queried to determine information about the database structure. (This description happens to represent the way things are done in DB2, IBM's mainframe relational DBMS.) Although catalogs in individual relational DBMSs will vary from what is shown here, the general ideas apply to most relational systems.

The catalog you will look at contains two tables, SYSTABLES (information about the tables known to SQL) and SYSCOLUMNS (information about the columns within these tables). An actual catalog contains other tables as well, such as SYSINDEXES (information about the indexes that are defined on these tables) and SYSVIEWS (information about the views that have been created). While these tables would have many columns, only a few are of concern here.

SYSTABLES contains the columns Name, Creator, and ColCount (Figure 4.12). The Name column identifies the name of a table. The Creator column contains an identification of the person or group that created the table. The ColCount column contains the number of columns within the table that is being described. If, for example, the user whose name is Brown created the SALES_REP table and the SALES_REP table had nine columns, there would be a row in the SYSTABLES table in which Name is SALES_REP, Creator is Brown, and ColCount is 9. Similar rows would exist for all tables known to the system.

SYSTABLES

NAME	CREATOR	COLCOUNT
CUSTOMER	BROWN	10
PART	BROWN	6
ORDERS	BROWN	3
ORDERS_LINE	BROWN	4
SALES_REP	BROWN	9

Figure 4.12 SYSTABLES table

SYSCOLUMNS contains columns ColName, TbName, and ColType (Figure 4.13). The ColName column identifies the name of a column in one of the tables. The table in which the column is found is stored in TbName, and the data type for the column is found in ColType. There is a row in the SYSCOLUMNS table for each column in the SALES REP table, for example. On each of these rows, TbName is SALES_REP. On one of these rows, ColName is Slsrep Number and ColType is Char (2). On another row, ColName is Last and ColType is Char (12).

SYSCOLUMNS

COLNAME	TBNAME	COLTYPE
BALANCE	CUSTOMER	DECIMAL(8,2)
CITY	CUSTOMER	CHAR(20)
CITY	SALES_REP	CHAR(20)
COMMISSION_RATE	SALES_REP	DECIMAL(4,2)
CREDIT_LIMIT	CUSTOMER	DECIMAL (5,0)
CUSTOMER_NUMBER	CUSTOMER	CHAR(4)
CUSTOMER_NUMBER	ORDERS	DECIMAL(5,0)
FIRST	CUSTOMER	CHAR(10)
FIRST	SALES_REP	CHAR(10)
ITEM_CLASS	PART	CHAR(2)
LAST	CUSTOMER	CHAR(12)
LAST	SALES_REP	CHAR(12)
NUMBER_ORDERED	ORDER_LINE	DECIMAL(4,0)
ORDER_DATE	ORDERS	DATE
ORDER_NUMBER	ORDERS	CHAR(5)
ORDER_NUMBER	ORDER_LINE	CHAR(5)
PART_DESCRIPTION	PART	CHAR(15)
PART_NUMBER	ORDER_LINE	CHAR(4)
PART_NUMBER	PART	CHAR(4)
QUOTED_PRICE	ORDER_LINE	DECIMAL(6,2)
SLSREP_NUMBER	CUSTOMER	CHAR(2)
SLSREP_NUMBER	SALES_REP	CHAR(2)
STATE	CUSTOMER	CHAR(2)
STATE	SALES_REP	CHAR(2)
STREET	CUSTOMER	CHAR(20)
STREET	SALES_REP	CHAR(20)
TOTAL_COMMISSION	SALES_REP	DECIMAL(10,3)
UNITS_ON_HAND	PART	DECIMAL(4,0)
UNIT_PRICE	PART	DECIMAL(6,2)
WAREHOUSE_NUMBER	PART	CHAR(2)
ZIP_CODE	CUSTOMER	CHAR(5)
ZIP_CODE	SALES_REP	CHAR(5)

Figure 4.13 SYSCOLUMNS table

The system catalog is a relational database of its own. Consequently, in general, the same types of queries that are used to retrieve information from relational databases can be used to retrieve information from the system catalog. The following queries illustrate this process.

1. List the name and creator of all tables known to the system.

    SELECT NAME, CREATOR
       FROM SYSTABLES

2. List all of the columns in the CUSTOMER table as well as their associated data types.

    SELECT COLNAME, COLTYPE
       FROM SYSCOLUMNS
       WHERE TBNAME = 'CUSTOMER'

3. List all tables that contain a column called SlsRep Number.

```
SELECT TBNAME
    FROM SYSCOLUMNS
    WHERE COLNAME = 'SLSREP_NUMBER'
```

Thus, information about the tables in your relational database, the columns they contain, and the indexes built on them can be obtained from the catalog by using the same SQL syntax used to query any other relational database. You don't need to worry about updating these tables; the system will do it for you automatically every time the database structure is changed.

WHAT DOES IT TAKE TO BE RELATIONAL?

This chapter concludes with a discussion of this interesting question. If you look at ads for both microcomputer and mainframe DBMSs, you rarely will find one that doesn't claim the DBMS is "relational." In order to make some sense out of all these claims, you need a yardstick to measure them with. In other words, you need to know what it really means for a system to be relational. For the answer to this question, you first turn to the person who initially proposed the relational model, Dr. E. F. Codd.

E. F. Codd[*] defines a relational system as one in which at least the following two properties hold:

1. Users perceive databases as collections of tables and are not aware of the presence of any additional structures.

2. The operations of **SELECT**, **PROJECT**, and **JOIN** from the relational algebra are supported. This support is independent of any predefined access paths; that is, it makes no difference what indexes do or do not exist. If, for example, a join can be performed only when indexes exist for the columns on which the join is to take place, the system should not be considered relational.

Codd's definition states that for a system to be relational, it must support the **SELECT**, **PROJECT**, and **JOIN** operations of the relational algebra, but the definition does *not* indicate that the system must use this terminology. SQL supports these three operations through the **SELECT** statement, which is considerably more powerful than the relational algebra **SELECT** indicated in Codd's definition. The following are examples of the manner in which SQL supports the **SELECT**, **PROJECT**, and **JOIN** operations:

SELECT (choose certain rows from a table):

```
SELECT *
    FROM CUSTOMER
    WHERE CREDIT_LIMIT = 1500
```

PROJECT (choose certain columns from a table):

```
SELECT CUSTOMER_NUMBER, LAST, FIRST, STREET, CITY,
    STATE, ZIP_CODE
    FROM CUSTOMER
```

---

[*]E. F. Codd, "Relational Database: A Practical Foundation for Productivity," Communications of the ACM 25.2 (1982).

JOIN (combine tables based on matching columns):

```
SELECT SALES_REP.SLSREP_NUMBER, SALES_REP.LAST,
       SALES_REP.FIRST, SALES_REP.STREET, SALES_REP.CITY,
       SALES_REP.STATE, SALES_REP.ZIP_CODE,
       TOTAL_COMMISSION, COMMISSION_RATE,
       CUSTOMER_NUMBER, CUSTOMER.LAST, CUSTOMER.FIRST,
       CUSTOMER.STREET, CUSTOMER.CITY, CUSTOMER.STATE,
       CUSTOMER.ZIP_CODE, BALANCE, CREDIT_LIMIT
       FROM SALES_REP, CUSTOMER
       WHERE SALES_REP.SLSREP_NUMBER =
             CUSTOMER.SLSREP_NUMBER
```

C. J. Date[*] discusses a classification scheme for systems that support at least the relational structure; that is, systems in which the only structure that the user perceives is the table. Such systems fall into one of the following four categories:

1. Tabular System. In a **tabular** system, the only structure perceived by the user is the table, but the system does not support the **SELECT**, **PROJECT**, and **JOIN** operations in the unrestricted fashion indicated by Codd. (In this case, either the system does not support **SELECT**, **PROJECT**, and **JOIN**, or, if it does, the support relies on predefined access paths.) The microcomputer file-management systems and some of the database management systems are in this category.

2. Minimally Relational. Actually, the operations **SELECT**, **PROJECT**, and **JOIN** are not the only operations in the relational algebra. There are eight operations altogether. A **minimally relational** system is one that supports the tabular structure together with the **SELECT**, **PROJECT**, and **JOIN** operations but that does not support the complete set of operations from the relational algebra. Some of the early microcomputer DBMSs fall into this category.

3. Relationally Complete. Any system that supports the tabular structure and all the operations of the relational algebra (without requiring appropriate indexes) is said to be **relationally complete**. Many relational mainframe DBMSs and some microcomputer DBMSs fall into this category. In particular, any system that supports a *full* implementation of SQL is relationally complete.

4. Fully Relational. A system that supports the tabular structure, all the operations of the relational algebra, and the two integrity rules (entity and referential integrity) described earlier in this section, is said to be **fully relational**. This is the goal for which systems are, or should be, striving. Currently, the principal failing on the part of many systems is lack of support for referential integrity. Much progress is occurring in this area, and soon you shall see a number of fully relational systems.

---

[*]C. J. Date, <u>Introduction to Database Systems</u>, 5th edition, volumn 1 (Boston: Addison-Wesley, 1990).

Finally, Codd* specified 12 rules that can be used to test whether a product is, in fact, fully relational. He actually specified a 13th rule, which he labeled "Rule Zero." This rule forms the foundation for the others. The set of rules is as follows:

Rule Zero: Relational capabilities. A relational DBMS must be able to manage data entirely through its relational capabilities. It is not acceptable to require users to use nonrelational capabilities to accomplish certain tasks. (Some systems claim this may be necessary to achieve acceptable performance. Such systems do *not* satisfy Rule Zero.)

1. Information. *All* data should be represented by values in tables. This not only includes the data in a database, but also information about the database, such as table names, column names, information on indexes, information on views, and so on.

2. Access. Users should be able to access any value in a database by giving the name of the table, the name of the column, and a value for the primary key of the table. (In nonrelational systems, users often are forced to follow linked lists or do a sequential scan of a database to find a certain value.)

3. Nulls. A relational DBMS should support null data values. (See the discussion of nulls earlier in this chapter for details of what this support should entail.)

4. Catalog. A relational DBMS should furnish a user-accessible catalog. Users must be able to access this catalog using the same relational features they use to access data in a database.

5. Data sublanguage. A relational DBMS must furnish at least one language capable of supporting all the following: data definition, view definition, data manipulation, integrity constraints, authorizations, and logical transactions. (Many nonrelational DBMSs have one language for defining the structure of a database, another for defining views, still another for manipulating data, and so on.)

6. Updatable views. Any view that is updatable in theory must be updatable by a relational DBMS.

7. High-level update. A relational DBMS should furnish facilities for retrieving, adding, updating, or deleting a set of rows with a single command. (In most nonrelational DBMSs, users are limited to accessing a single row at a time.)

8. Physical data independence. In a relational DBMS, changes to the physical storage and/or access methods used in a database should not impact users or application programs. The creation or dropping of an index, for example, would not change the way users interact with the database. Nor would it necessitate changes in application programs.

---

*E. F. Codd, <u>Relational Database: A Practical Foundation for Productivity</u>.

9. Logical data independence. In a relational DBMS, changes to the logical structure of a database should not impact users or application programs. This is provided, of course, that the user's view of data still is legitimate with the new structure. If a change invalidates a particular user's view, clearly there is no way the DBMS can prevent the user from being affected. For example, the removal from the database of a column required by the user will clearly have an impact on the user.

10. Integrity. The data sublanguage must support the definition of integrity constraints. These constraints must be stored in the system catalog and enforced by the DBMS, *not* by application programs.

11. Distribution. A **distributed database** is a database that is stored on computers at several sites of a computer network, and in which users can access data at any site in the network. A relational DBMS that manipulates a distributed database should allow users and programs to access data at a remote site in exactly the same fashion they do at the local site.

12. Nonsubversion. Any low-level (record-at-a-time) language in a relational DBMS should not be able to be used to bypass the integrity constraints that have been specified by the high-level language (i.e., the data sublanguage specified in Rule 5).

SUMMARY

1. Views are used to give each user his or her own picture of the database.

    a. A view is defined in SQL through the use of a defining query.

    b. When a query is entered that references a view, it is merged with the defining query to produce the query that actually is executed.

    c. Retrieving data through a view presents no problem, but updating the database through a view often is prohibited.

2. Indexes often are used to facilitate retrieval. Indexes may be created on any column or combination of columns.

3. Security is provided in SQL systems through the GRANT and REVOKE commands.

4. There are two special integrity rules for relational databases as follows:

    a. Entity integrity is the property that no column that is part of the primary key can accept null values.

    b. Referential integrity is the property that the value in any foreign key either must be null or must match an actual value of the primary key of another table.

5. Relational DBMSs provide facilities that allow users easily to change the structure of a database. Two examples of such facilities are as follows:

    a. ALTER TABLE allows columns to be added to a table, columns to be deleted, or characteristics of columns to be changed.

    b. DROP allows a table to be deleted from a database.

6. The catalog is a feature of many relational model DBMSs that stores information about the structure of a database. The system updates the catalog automatically. Users can retrieve data from the catalog in the same manner in which they retrieve data from the database.

7. According to Codd, a DBMS cannot be considered to be relational unless the following two conditions pertain:

    a. Users perceive a database as simply a collection of tables.

    b. The DBMS supports at least the SELECT, PROJECT, and JOIN operations of the relational algebra.

8. According to Date, DBMSs in which users perceive databases as collections of tables can be classified as:

    a. Tabular, if data is viewed as tables and if the system does not support SELECT, PROJECT, and JOIN independently of any predefined access paths.

    b. Minimally relational, if SELECT, PROJECT, and JOIN are supported but the full set of operations in the relational algebra is not.

c. Relationally complete, if the DBMS supports all operations of the relational algebra.

d. Fully relational, if the DBMS supports all operations of the relational algebra and both integrity rules (entity and referential integrity).

9. Codd presented 12 rules that a relational DBMS should follow.

KEY TERMS

Catalog

Defining query

Distributed database

Entity integrity

Foreign key

Fully relational

Index

Minimally relational

Null

Optimizer

Referential integrity

Relationally complete

Security

Tabular

View

REVIEW QUESTIONS

1. What is a view? How is it defined? Does the data described in a view definition ever exist in that form? What happens when a user accesses a database through a view?

2. Define a view called SMLCUST. It consists of the customer number, name, address, balance, and credit limit for all customers whose credit limit is $1,000 or less.

   a. Write the view definition for SMLCUST.

   b. Write an SQL query to retrieve the number and name of all customers in SMLCUST whose balance is over their credit limit.

 c. Convert the query from (b) to the query that actually will be executed.

3. Define a view called CUSTORD. It consists of the customer number, name, balance, order number, and order date for all orders currently on file.

 a. Write the view definition for CUSTORD.

 b. Write an SQL query to retrieve the customer number, name, order number, and order date for all orders in CUSTORD for customers whose balance is more than $100.

 c. Convert the query from (b) to the query that actually will be executed.

4. What are the advantages of using indexes? The disadvantages?

5. On relational mainframe DBMSs, who or what is responsible for the decision to use a particular index? What about on microcomputer DBMSs?

6. Describe the GRANT mechanism and explain how it relates to security. What types of privileges may be granted? How are they revoked?

7. What is the catalog? Name three items about which the catalog maintains information.

8. Why is it a good idea for the DBMS to update the catalog automatically when a change is made in the database structure? Could users cause problems by updating the catalog themselves?

9. What are nulls? Which column should never be allowed to be null?

10. State the two integrity rules. Indicate the reasons for enforcing each rule.

11. The ORDERS table contains a foreign key, Customer Number, that is required to match the primary key of the CUSTOMER table. What type of update to the ORDERS table would violate referential integrity? If delete does not cascade, what type of update to the CUSTOMER table would violate referential integrity? If delete cascades, what would happen when a customer is deleted?

12. How can the structure of a table be changed in SQL? What general types of changes are possible? Which commands are used to implement these changes?

13. List the two basic properties specified by Codd that a system must satisfy to be considered relational.

14. List the four categories of systems proposed by Date. Describe the characteristics of systems in each category.

15. List and briefly describe the 12 rules that a true relational DBMS should follow.

CHAPTER 5

Database Design 1: Normalization

OBJECTIVES

- Present the idea of functional dependence.

- Define the term primary key.

- Define first normal form (1NF), second normal form (2NF), and third normal form (3NF).

- Describe the problems associated with relations (tables) that are not in 1NF, 2NF, or 3NF, along with the mechanism for converting to all three.

- Discuss the problems associated with incorrect conversions to 3NF.

INTRODUCTION

You have studied the basic relational model, its structure, and the various ways of manipulating data within a relational database. In this chapter, the normalization process and its underlying concepts and features is discussed. **Normalization** enables us to identify the existence of potential problems, called **update anomalies**, in the design of a relational database. The normalization process also supplies methods for correcting these problems.

The process involves various types of **normal forms**. First normal form (1NF), second normal form (2NF), and third normal form (3NF) are three of these types. These three will be of the greatest use to you during database design. They form a progression in which a table that is in 1NF is better than a table that is not in 1NF; a table that is in 2NF is better yet; and so on. The goal of this process is to allow you to start with a table or collection of tables and produce a new collection of tables that is equivalent to the original collection (i.e., that represents the same information), but is free of problems. For practical purposes, this means that tables in the new collection will be in 3NF.

These normal forms initially were defined by Codd[*] in 1972. Subsequently, it was discovered that the definition of third normal form was inadequate for certain situations. A revised and stronger definition was provided by Boyce and Codd[**] in 1974. This more recent definition of third normal form (sometimes called **Boyce-Codd normal form (BCNF)**) will be examined later in this chapter.

This chapter discusses two crucial concepts that are fundamental to the understanding of the normalization process: functional dependence and keys. First, second, and third normal forms are discussed. Finally, the chapter covers the application of normalization to database design. You then will be ready to begin your study of the database design process in the next chapter.

■ ■ ■ ■ ■

Many of the examples in this chapter use data from the Premiere Products database (Figure 5.1).

---

[*]E. F. Codd, "Futher Normalization of the Data Base Relational Model," <u>Data Base Systems</u>, Courant Computer Science Symposia Ser. 6 (Boston: Prentice-Hall, 1972).

[**]E. F. Codd, "Proceedings of the IFIP Congress, 1974: General Session on Recent Investigations into Relational Data Base Systems:" (IFIP Congress, 1974).

SALES REP

SLSREP NUMBER	LAST	FIRST	STREET	CITY	STATE	ZIP CODE	TOTAL COMMISSION	COMMISSION RATE
03	Jones	Mary	123 Main	Grant	MI	49219	2150.00	.05
06	Smith	William	102 Raymond	Ada	MI	49441	4912.50	.07
12	Diaz	Miguel	419 Harper	Lansing	MI	49224	2150.00	.05

CUSTOMER

CUSTOMER NUMBER	LAST	FIRST	STREET	CITY	STATE	ZIP CODE	BALANCE	CREDIT LIMIT	SLSREP NUMBER
124	Adams	Sally	481 Oak	Lansing	MI	49224	$818.75	$1000	03
256	Samuels	Ann	215 Pete	Grant	MI	49219	$21.50	$1500	06
311	Charles	Don	48 College	Ira	MI	49034	$825.75	$1000	12
315	Daniels	Tom	914 Cherry	Kent	MI	48391	$770.75	$750	06
405	Williams	Al	519 Watson	Grant	MI	49219	$402.75	$1500	12
412	Adams	Sally	16 Elm	Lansing	MI	49224	$1817.50	$2000	03
522	Nelson	Mary	108 Pine	Ada	MI	49441	$98.75	$1500	12
567	Dinh	Tran	808 Ridge	Harper	MI	48421	$402.40	$750	06
587	Galvez	Mara	512 Pine	Ada	MI	49441	$114.60	$1000	06
622	Martin	Dan	419 Chip	Grant	MI	49219	$1045.75	$1000	03

ORDERS

ORDER NUMBER	ORDER DATE	CUSTOMER NUMBER
12489	9/02/98	124
12491	9/02/98	311
12494	9/04/98	315
12495	9/04/98	256
12498	9/05/98	522
12500	9/05/98	124
12504	9/05/98	522

ORDER LINE

ORDER NUMBER	PART NUMBER	NUMBER ORDERED	QUOTED PRICE
12489	AX12	11	$21.95
12491	BT04	1	$149.99
12491	BZ66	1	$399.99
12494	CB03	4	$279.99
12495	CX11	2	$22.95
12498	AZ52	2	$12.95
12498	BA74	4	$24.95
12500	BT04	1	$149.99
12504	CZ81	2	$325.99

PART

PART NUMBER	PART DESCRIPTION	UNITS ON HAND	ITEM CLASS	WAREHOUSE NUMBER	UNIT PRICE
AX12	Iron	104	HW	3	$24.95
AZ52	Dartboard	20	SG	2	$12.95
BA74	Basketball	40	SG	1	$29.95
BH22	Cornpopper	95	HW	3	$24.95
BT04	Gas Grill	11	AP	2	$149.99
BZ66	Washer	52	AP	3	$399.99
CA14	Griddle	78	HW	3	$39.99
CB03	Bike	44	SG	1	$299.99
CX11	Blender	112	HW	3	$22.95
CZ81	Treadmill	68	SG	2	$349.95

Figure 5.1 Premiere Products sample data

FUNCTIONAL DEPENDENCE

The concept of functional dependence is crucial to the material in the rest of this chapter. Functional dependence is a formal name for what is basically a simple idea. To illustrate, suppose the SALES REP table for Premiere Products is as shown in Figure 5.2. The only difference between this SALES REP table and the one you have been looking at previously is the addition of an extra column, Pay Class. Let's suppose further that one of the policies at Premiere Products is that all sales reps in any given pay class get the same commission rate. If you were asked to describe this policy in another way, you might say something like, "A sales rep's pay class *determines* his or her commission rate." Or you might say, "A sales rep's commission rate *depends on* his or her pay class." If you said either of these things, you would be using the word "determines" or the words "depends on" in exactly the fashion that you will be using them in this chapter. If you wanted to be formal, you would precede either expression with the word "functionally". Thus you might say, "A sales rep's pay class *functionally determines* his or her commission rate." Or you might say, "A sales rep's commission rate *functionally depends on* his or her pay class." The formal definition of functional dependence is as follows:

SALES REP

SLSREP NUMBER	LAST	FIRST	STREET	CITY	STATE	ZIP CODE	TOTAL COMMISSION	PAY CLASS	COMMISSION RATE
03	Jones	Mary	123 Main	Grant	MI	49219	2150.00	1	.05
06	Smith	William	102 Raymond	Ada	MI	49441	4912.50	2	.07
12	Diaz	Miguel	419 Harper	Lansing	MI	49224	2150.00	1	.05

Figure 5.2 SALES REP table with additional column, Pay Class

Definition: An attribute (column), B, is **functionally dependent** on another attribute, A (or possibly a collection of attributes), if a value for A determines a single value for B at any one time.

You can think of this as follows. If you are given a value for A, do you know that you will be able to find a single value for B? If so, B is functionally dependent on A (often written as A - -> B). If B is functionally dependent on A, you also say that A **functionally determines** B.

For example, in the CUSTOMER table, is Last functionally dependent on Customer Number? The answer is yes. If you are given customer number 124, for example, you would find a *single* last name, Adams, associated with it.

In the same CUSTOMER table, is Street functionally dependent on Last? Here the answer is no because given the last name Adams, you would not be able to find a single street address.

In the ORDER LINE table, is the Number Ordered functionally dependent on Order Number? No. Order Number does not give enough information. Is it functionally dependent on Part Number? No. Again, not enough information is given. In reality, Number Ordered is functionally dependent on the **concatenation** (combination) of Order Number and Part Number.

At this point, a question naturally arises: How do you determine functional dependencies? Can you determine them by looking at sample data, for example? The answer is no.

Consider Figure 5.3 in which last names happen to be unique. It is very tempting to say that Last functionally determines Street, City, State, and Zip Code (or equivalently that Street, City, State, and Zip Code are all functionally dependent on Last). After all, given the last name of a customer, you can find the single address.

CUSTOMER

CUSTOMER NUMBER	LAST	FIRST	STREET	CITY	STATE	ZIP CODE	BALANCE	CREDIT LIMIT	SLSREP NUMBER
124	Adams	Sally	481 Oak	Lansing	MI	49224	$818.75	$1000	03
256	Samuels	Ann	215 Pete	Grant	MI	49219	$21.50	$1500	06
311	Charles	Don	48 College	Ira	MI	49034	$825.75	$1000	12
315	Daniels	Tom	914 Cherry	Kent	MI	48391	$770.75	$750	06
405	Williams	Al	519 Watson	Grant	MI	49219	$402.75	$1500	12
522	Nelson	Mary	108 Pine	Ada	MI	49441	$98.75	$1500	12
567	Dinh	Tran	808 Ridge	Harper	MI	48421	$402.40	$750	06
587	Galvez	Mara	512 Pine	Ada	MI	49441	$114.60	$1000	06
622	Martin	Dan	419 Chip	Grant	MI	49219	$1045.75	$1000	03

Figure 5.3 CUSTOMER table

What happens when customer 412, whose last name also happens to be Adams, is added to the database? You then have the situation exhibited in Figure 5.4. If the name you are given is Sally Adams, you no longer can find a single address. Thus you were misled by your original sample data. The only way to really determine the functional dependencies that exist is to examine the user's policies.

CUSTOMER

CUSTOMER NUMBER	LAST	FIRST	STREET	CITY	STATE	ZIP CODE	BALANCE	CREDIT LIMIT	SLSREP NUMBER
124	Adams	Sally	481 Oak	Lansing	MI	49224	$818.75	$1000	03
256	Samuels	Ann	215 Pete	Grant	MI	49219	$21.50	$1500	06
311	Charles	Don	48 College	Ira	MI	49034	$825.75	$1000	12
315	Daniels	Tom	914 Cherry	Kent	MI	48391	$770.75	$750	06
405	Williams	Al	519 Watson	Grant	MI	49219	$402.75	$1500	12
412	Adams	Sally	16 Elm	Lansing	MI	49224	$1817.50	$2000	03
522	Nelson	Mary	108 Pine	Ada	MI	49441	$98.75	$1500	12
567	Dinh	Tran	808 Ridge	Harper	MI	48421	$402.40	$750	06
587	Galvez	Mara	512 Pine	Ada	MI	49441	$114.60	$1000	06
622	Martin	Dan	419 Chip	Grant	MI	49219	$1045.75	$1000	03

Figure 5.4 CUSTOMER table with second Sally Adams

KEYS

A second underlying concept of the normalization process is that of the primary key. You already encountered the basic concept of a primary key in earlier chapters. In this chapter, you need to be more precise about its definition, however.

Definition: Attribute A (or a collection of attributes) is the **primary key** for a relation (table), R, if

1. *All* attributes in R are functionally dependent on A.

2. No subcollection of the attributes in A (assuming A is a collection of attributes and not just a single attribute) also has property 1.

For example, is Last the primary key for the CUSTOMER table? No, because the other attributes are not functionally dependent on the last name. (Note that the answer would be different in an organization that had a policy enforcing uniqueness of customer names.)

Is Customer Number the primary key for the CUSTOMER table? Yes, because all attributes in the CUSTOMER table are functionally dependent on Customer Number.

Is Order Number the primary key for the ORDER LINE table? No, because it does not uniquely determine Number Ordered or Quoted Price.

Is the combination of the Order Number and the Part Number the primary key for the ORDER LINE table? Yes, because all attributes can be determined by this combination, and nothing less will do.

Is the combination of the Part Number and the Part Description the primary key for the PART table? No. Although it is true that all attributes of the PART table can be determined by this combination, something less, namely, the PART NUMBER alone, also has this property.

Occasionally, but not often, there might be more than one possibility for the primary key. For example, in an EMPLOYEE table either the Employee Number or the Soc Sec Numb (social security number) could serve as the key. In this case one of these is designated as the primary key. The other is referred to as a **candidate key**. A candidate key is a collection of attributes that has the same properties presented in the definition of the primary key. (Technically, the definition given for primary key really defines candidate key. From all the candidate keys one is chosen to be the primary key. The candidate keys that are not chosen to be the primary key often are referred to as **alternate keys**.)

> **Note** The primary key frequently is called simply the **key** in other studies on database management and the relational model. We will continue to use the term primary key in order to clearly distinguish among the several different concepts of a key that we will encounter.

FIRST NORMAL FORM

A relation (table) that contains a repeating group is called an **unnormalized relation**. Technically, it is not a relation at all. Removal of repeating groups is the starting point in our quest for relations that are as free of problems as possible. Relations without repeating groups are said to be in first normal form.

Definition: A relation (table) is in **first normal form (1NF)** if it does not contain repeating groups.

As an example, consider the following ORDERS table, in which there is a repeating group consisting of Part Number and Number Ordered. As the example shows, there is one row per order with Part Number, Number Ordered repeated as many times as is necessary.

ORDERS (<u>ORDER_NUMBER</u>, ORDER_DATE, (PART_NUMBER,

NUMBER_ORDERED))

Note	This notation indicates a table called ORDERS, consisting of an underlined primary key, Order Number, and an attribute Order Date. The inner parentheses indicate that there is a repeating group. The repeating group contains two attributes, Part Number and Number Ordered. This means that for a single order, there can be multiple combinations of a part number and a corresponding number of units ordered.

Figure 5.5 shows a sample of this table.

CUSTOMER

ORDER NUMBER	ORDER DATE	PART NUMBER	NUMBER ORDERED
12489	9/02/98	AX12	11
12491	9/02/98	BT04	1
		BZ66	1
12494	9/04/98	CB03	4
12495	9/04/98	CX11	2
12498	9/05/98	AZ52	2
		BA74	4
12500	9/05/98	BT04	1
12504	9/05/98	CZ81	2

Figure 5.5 Sample unnormalized table

To convert the table to 1NF, the repeating group is removed, giving the following:

ORDERS (<u>ORDER_NUMBER</u>, ORDER_DATE, <u>PART_NUMBER</u>,

NUMBER_ORDERED)

The corresponding example of the new table is shown in Figure 5.6.

CUSTOMER

ORDER NUMBER	ORDER DATE	PART NUMBER	NUMBER ORDERED
12489	9/02/98	AX12	11
12491	9/02/98	BT04	1
12491	9/02/98	BZ66	1
12494	9/04/98	CB03	4
12495	9/04/98	CX11	2
12498	9/05/98	AZ52	2
12498	9/05/98	BA74	4
12500	9/05/98	BT04	1
12504	9/05/98	CZ81	2

Figure 5.6 Result of normalization (conversion to 1NF)

Note that the second row of the unnormalized table indicates that part BZ66 and part BT04 both are present for order 12491. In the normalized table, this information is represented by *two* rows, the second and third. The primary key to the unnormalized ORDERS table was the Order Number alone. The primary key to the normalized table is now the combination of Order Number and Part Number.

In general it will be true that the primary key will expand in converting a non-1NF table to 1NF. It typically will include the original primary key concatenated with the key to the repeating group (i.e., the attribute that distinguishes one occurrence of the repeating group from another within a given row in the table). In this case, Part Number is the key to the repeating group and thus becomes part of the primary key of the 1NF table.

SECOND NORMAL FORM

Even though the following table is in 1NF, problems exist within the table that will cause you to want to restructure it. Consider the table:

ORDERS (<u>ORDER_NUMBER</u>, ORDER_DATE, <u>PART_NUMBER</u>,

PART_DESCRIPTION, NUMBER_ORDERED, QUOTED_PRICE)

with the functional dependencies

ORDER_NUMBER--> ORDER_DATE

PART_NUMBER--> PART_DESCRIPTION

ORDER_NUMBER, PART_NUMBER--> NUMBER_ORDERED,

QUOTED_PRICE

Thus Order Number determines Order Date, Part Number determines Part Description, and the concatenation of Order Number and Part Number determines Number Ordered and Quoted Price. Consider the sample of this table shown in Figure 5.7.

ORDERS

ORDER NUMBER	ORDER DATE	PART NUMBER	PART DESCRIPTION	NUMBER ORDERED	QUOTED PRICE
12489	9/02/98	AX12	Iron	11	$21.95
12491	9/02/98	BT04	Gas Grill	1	$149.99
12491	9/02/98	BZ66	Washer	1	$399.99
12494	9/04/98	CB03	Bike	4	$279.99
12495	9/04/98	CX11	Blender	2	$22.95
12498	9/05/98	AZ52	Dartboard	2	$12.95
12498	9/05/98	BA74	Basketball	4	$24.95
12500	9/05/98	BT04	Gas Grill	1	$149.99
12504	9/05/98	CZ81	Treadmill	2	$325.99

Figure 5.7 Sample ORDERS table

As you can see in the example, the description of a specific part, BT04 for example, occurs several times in the table. This redundancy causes several problems. It certainly is wasteful of space, but that in itself is not nearly as serious as some of the other problems. These other problems are called **update anomalies** and they fall into four categories:

1. Update. A change to the description of part BT04 requires not one change but several—you have to change each row in which BT04 appears. This certainly makes the update process much more cumbersome; it is more complicated logically and takes more time to update.

2. Inconsistent data. There is nothing about the design that would prohibit part BT04 from having two different descriptions in the database. In fact, if it occurs in 20 rows, it conceivably could have 20 *different* descriptions in the database!

3. Additions. You have a real problem when you try to add a new part and its description to the database. Because the primary key for the table consists of both Order Number and Part Number, you need values for both of these in order to add a new row. If you have a part to add but there are as yet no orders for it, what do you use for an Order Number? Your only solution would be to make up a dummy order number and then replace it with a real Order Number once an order for this part actually had been received. Certainly this is not an acceptable solution!

4. Deletions. In the example above, if you delete order 12489 from the database, you also *lose* the fact that part AX12 is an iron.

The above problems occur because you have an attribute, Part Description, that is dependent on only a portion of the primary key, Part Number, and *not* on the complete primary key. This leads to the definition of second normal form. Second normal form represents an improvement over first normal form because it eliminates these update anomalies in these situations. First, we need to define nonkey attribute.

Definition: An attribute is a **nonkey attribute** if it is not a part of the primary key.

We now can provide a definition for second normal form.

Definition: A relation (table) is in **second normal form (2NF)** if it is in first normal form and no nonkey attribute is dependent on only a portion of the primary key.

Note	If the primary key of a relation contains only a single attribute, the relation is automatically in second normal form.

For another perspective on 2NF, consider Figure 5.8. This type of diagram, sometimes called a **dependency diagram**, indicates graphically all the functional dependencies present in the ORDERS table. The arrows above the boxes indicate the normal dependencies that should be present (i.e., the primary key functionally determines all other attributes). In this case, the concatenation of Order Number and Part Number determines all other attributes. It is the arrows below the boxes that prevent the table from being in 2NF. These arrows represent what often is termed **partial dependencies**, which are dependencies on something less than the primary key. In fact, an alternative definition for 2NF is that a table is in 2NF if it is in 1NF but contains no partial dependencies.

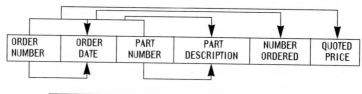

Figure 5.8 Dependencies in ORDERS table

Either way you view 2NF, you now can name the fundamental problem with the ORDERS table: it is *not* in 2NF. While it may be pleasing to have a name for the problem, what you really need, of course, is a method to *correct* it. Such a method follows.

First, for each subset of the set of attributes that make up the primary key, begin a table with this subset as its primary key. For the ORDERS table, this would give:

(ORDER NUMBER,

(PART NUMBER,

(ORDER NUMBER, PART NUMBER,

Next, place each of the other attributes with the appropriate primary key; that is, place each one with the minimal collection on which it depends. For the ORDERS table this would yield:

(ORDER NUMBER, ORDER_DATE)

(PART NUMBER, PART_DESCRIPTION)

(ORDER NUMBER, PART NUMBER, NUMBER_ORDERED, QUOTED_PRICE)

Each of these tables now can be given a name that is descriptive of the meaning of the table, such as ORDERS, PART, and ORDER LINE. Figure 5.9 shows samples of the tables involved.

ORDERS

ORDER NUMBER	ORDER DATE	PART NUMBER	PART DESCRIPTION	NUMBER ORDERED	QUOTED PRICE
12489	9/02/98	AX12	Iron	11	$21.95
12491	9/02/98	BT04	Gas Grill	1	$149.99
12491	9/02/98	BZ66	Washer	1	$399.99
12494	9/04/98	CB03	Bike	4	$279.99
12495	9/04/98	CX11	Blender	2	$22.95
12498	9/05/98	AZ52	Dartboard	2	$12.95
12498	9/05/98	BA74	Basketball	4	$24.95
12500	9/05/98	BT04	Gas Grill	1	$149.99
12504	9/05/98	CZ81	Treadmill	2	$325.99

is replaced by

ORDERS

ORDER NUMBER	ORDER DATE
12489	9/02/98
12491	9/02/98
12494	9/04/98
12495	9/04/98
12498	9/05/98
12500	9/05/98
12504	9/05/98

PART

PART NUMBER	PART DESCRIPTION
AX12	Iron
AZ52	Dartboard
BA74	Basketball
BH22	Cornpopper
BT04	Gas Grill
BZ66	Washer
CA14	Griddle
CB03	Bike
CX11	Blender
CZ81	Treadmill

ORDER LINE

ORDER NUMBER	PART NUMBER	NUMBER ORDERED	QUOTED PRICE
12489	AX12	11	$21.95
12491	BT04	1	$149.99
12491	BZ66	1	$399.99
12494	CB03	4	$279.99
12495	CX11	2	$22.95
12498	AZ52	2	$12.95
12498	BA74	4	$24.95
12500	BT04	1	$149.99
12504	CZ81	2	$325.99

Figure 5.9 Conversion to 2NF

Note that the update anomalies have been eliminated. A description appears only once, so you do not have the earlier design redundancy. Changing the description of part BT04 to Outdoor Grill is now a simple process involving a single change. Because the description for a part occurs in one single place, it is not possible to have multiple descriptions for a single part in the database at the same time.

To add a new part and its description, you create a new row in the PART table and thus there is no need to have an order exist for that part. Also, deleting order 12489 does not cause part AX12 to be deleted from the PART table, and thus you still have its description (Iron) in the database. Finally, you have not lost any information in the process. The data in the original design can be reconstructed from the data in the new design.

THIRD NORMAL FORM

Problems still can exist with tables that are in 2NF. Consider the following CUSTOMER table:

CUSTOMER (<u>CUSTOMER_NUMBER</u>, CUST_LAST, CUST_FIRST, BALANCE,
CREDIT_LIMIT, SLSREP_NUMBER, SLSREP_LAST, SLSREP_FIRST)

Note	This table contains first and last names of both customers and sales reps. To distinguish last names, the customer's last name is denoted Cust Last and the sales rep's last name is Slsrep Last. Similarly, the customer's first name is Cust First and the sales rep's first name is Slsrep First.)

The functional dependencies in this table are:

CUSTOMER_NUMBER--> CUST_LAST, CUST_FIRST, BALANCE, CREDIT_LIMIT,
SLSREP_NUMBER, SLSREP_LAST, SLSREP_FIRST

SLSREP_NUMBER--> SLSREP_LAST, SLSREP_FIRST

Customer Number determines all the other attributes. In addition Slsrep Number determines Slsrep Last and Slsrep First.

If the primary key of a table is a single column, the table is automatically in second normal form. (If the table were not in 2NF, some column would be dependent on only a *portion* of the primary key, which is impossible when the primary key is just one column.) Thus, the CUSTOMER table is in second normal form.

As the sample table shown in Figure 5.10 demonstrates, this table possesses problems similar to those encountered earlier, even though it is in second normal form. In this case it is the name of a sales rep that can occur many times in the table (e.g., sales rep 12, Miguel Diaz). This redundancy results in the same exact set of problems that was described in the previous ORDERS table. In addition to the problem of wasted space, you have similar update anomalies, as follows:

CUSTOMER

CUSTOMER NUMBER	CUST LAST	CUST FIRST	BALANCE	CREDIT LIMIT	SLSREP NUMBER	SLSREP LAST	SLSREP FIRST
124	Adams	Sally	$818.75	$1000	03	Jones	Mary
256	Samuels	Ann	$21.50	$1500	06	Smith	William
311	Charles	Don	$825.75	$1000	12	Diaz	Miguel
315	Daniels	Tom	$770.75	$750	06	Smith	William
405	Williams	Al	$402.75	$1500	12	Diaz	Miguel
412	Adams	Sally	$1817.50	$2000	03	Jones	Mary
522	Nelson	Mary	$98.75	$1500	12	Diaz	Miguel
567	Dinh	Tran	$402.40	$750	06	Smith	William
587	Galvez	Mara	$114.60	$1000	06	Smith	William
622	Martin	Dan	$1045.75	$1000	03	Jones	Mary

Figure 5.10 Sample CUSTOMER table

1. Update. A change to the name of a sales rep requires not one change but several. Again, the update process becomes very cumbersome.

2. Inconsistent data. There is nothing about the design that would prohibit a sales rep from having two different names in the database. In fact, if the same sales rep represents 20 different customers (and thus would be found on 20 different rows), he or she could have 20 different names in the database.

3. Additions. In order to add sales rep 47, whose name is Mary Daniels, to the database, you must have at least one customer whom she represents. If she has not yet been assigned any customers, then you either cannot record the fact that her name is Mary Daniels or you have to create a fictitious customer for her to represent. Again, this is not a very desirable solution to the problem.

4. Deletions. If you were to delete all the customers of sales rep 06 from the database, then you also would lose the name of sales rep 06.

These update anomalies are due to the fact that Slsrep Number determines Slsrep Last and Slsrep First but Slsrep Number is not the primary key. As a result, the same Slsrep Number and consequently the same Slsrep Last and Slsrep First can appear on many different rows.

You've seen that 2NF is an improvement over 1NF, but in order to eliminate 2NF problems, you need an even better strategy for creating tables in your database. Third normal form gives you that strategy. Before you look at third normal form, however, you need to become familiar with the special name that is given to any column that determines another column (like Slsrep Number in the CUSTOMER table).

Definition: Any attribute or collection of attributes that determine another attribute is called a **determinant**.

Certainly the primary key in a table will be a determinant. In fact, by definition any candidate key will be a determinant. (Remember that a candidate key is an attribute or collection of attributes that could have functioned as the primary key.) In this case, SlsRep Number is a determinant but it is certainly not a candidate key, and that is the problem.

Definition: A relation (table) is in **third normal form (3NF)** if it is in second normal form and if the only determinants it contains are candidate keys.

Again, for an additional perspective, you will consider a dependency diagram, as shown in Figure 5.11. As before, the arrows above the boxes represent the normal dependencies of all attributes on the primary key. It is the arrows below the boxes that cause the problem. The presence of these arrows makes Slsrep Number a determinant. If there were arrows from Slsrep Number to all the attributes, Slsrep Number would be a candidate key and you would not have a problem. The absence of these arrows indicates that this table possesses a determinant that is not a candidate key. Thus, the table is not in 3NF.

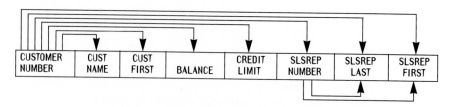

Figure 5.11 Dependencies in CUSTOMER table

You now have named the problem with the CUSTOMER table: it is not in 3NF. What you need is a scheme to correct the deficiency in the CUSTOMER table and in all tables having similar deficiencies. Such a method follows.

First, for each determinant that is not a candidate key, remove from the table the attributes that depend on this determinant. Next, create a new table containing all the attributes from the original table that depend on this determinant. Finally, make the determinant the primary key of this new table.

In the CUSTOMER table, for example, Slsrep Last and Slsrep First are removed because they depend on the determinant Slsrep Number, which is not a candidate key. A new table is formed, consisting of Slsrep Number as the primary key, Slsrep Last and Slsrep First. Specifically,

CUSTOMER (<u>CUSTOMER NUMBER</u>, CUST_LAST, CUST_FIRST, BALANCE,
   CREDIT_LIMIT, SLSREP_NUMBER, SLSREP_LAST, SLSREP_FIRST)

is replaced by

CUSTOMER (<u>CUSTOMER NUMBER</u>, CUST_LAST, CUST_FIRST, BALANCE,
   CREDIT_LIMIT, SLSREP_NUMBER)

and

SALES_REP (<u>SLSREP NUMBER</u>, SLSREP_LAST, SLSREP_FIRST)

Figure 5.12 shows samples of the tables involved.

CUSTOMER

CUSTOMER NUMBER	CUST LAST	CUST FIRST	BALANCE	CREDIT LIMIT	SLSREP NUMBER	SLSREP LAST	SLSREP FIRST
124	Adams	Sally	$818.75	$1000	03	Jones	Mary
256	Samuels	Ann	$21.50	$1500	06	Smith	William
311	Charles	Don	$825.75	$1000	12	Diaz	Miquel
315	Daniels	Tom	$770.75	$750	06	Smith	William
405	Williams	Al	$402.75	$1500	12	Diaz	Miguel
412	Adams	Sally	$1817.50	$2000	03	Jones	Mary
522	Nelson	Mary	$98.75	$1500	12	Diaz	Miguel
567	Dinh	Tran	$402.40	$750	06	Smith	William
587	Galvez	Mara	$114.60	$1000	06	Smith	William
622	Martin	Dan	$1045.75	$1000	03	Jones	Mary

is replaced by

CUSTOMER

CUSTOMER NUMBER	CUST LAST	CUST FIRST	BALANCE	CREDIT LIMIT	SLSREP NUMBER
124	Adams	Sally	$818.75	$1000	03
256	Samuels	Ann	$21.50	$1500	06
311	Charles	Don	$825.75	$1000	12
315	Daniels	Tom	$770.75	$750	06
405	Williams	Al	$402.75	$1500	12
412	Adams	Sally	$1817.50	$2000	0
522	Nelson	Mary	$98.75	$1500	12
567	Dinh	Tran	$402.40	$750	06
587	Galvez	Mara	$114.60	$1000	06
622	Martin	Dan	$1045.75	$1000	03

SALES REP

SLSREP NUMBER	SLSREP LAST	SLSREP FIRST
03	Jones	Mary
06	Smith	William
12	Diaz	Miguel

Figure 5.12 Conversion to 3NF

Note

The first and last names of customers are now in the CUSTOMER table. The first and last names of sales reps are now in the SALES REP table. Thus, there is no longer any need to have special names to distinguish between the fields. In the database design process you will see in Chapter 6, you typically would rename them at this point to simply First and Last. For the purposes of this discussion, however, you will keep the current names: Cust Last, Cust First, Slsrep Last, and Slsrep First.

Have you now corrected all previously identified problems? A sales rep's name appears only once, thus avoiding redundancy and making the process of changing a sales rep's name a very simple one. It is not possible with this design for the same sales rep to have two different names in the database. To add a new sales rep to the database, you add a row in the SALES REP table so that it is not necessary to have a customer whom the sales rep represents. Finally, deleting all the customers of a given sales rep will not remove the sales rep's record from the SALES REP table, so you do retain the sales rep's name; all the data in the original table can be reconstructed from the data in the new collection of tables. All previously mentioned problems indeed have been solved.

The three normal forms are summarized in Table 5.1.

Table 5.1 Normal Forms

NORMAL FORM	MEANING	NOTES
1NF	No repeating groups.	
2NF	1NF and no nonkey attribute dependent on only a portion of the primary key.	Automatically 2NF if the primary key contains only a single attribute.
3NF	2NF and the only determinants are candidate keys.	Actually Boyce-Codd normal form (BCNF)

INCORRECT DECOMPOSITIONS

It is important to note the decomposition of a table into two or more 3NF tables **must** be accomplished by the method indicated even though there are other seemingly legitimate possibilities. Let's examine two other decompositions of the CUSTOMER table into 3NF tables in order to understand the difficulties they pose.

What if, in the decomposition process,

CUSTOMER (<u>CUSTOMER NUMBER</u>, CUST_LAST, CUST_FIRST, BALANCE,
    CREDIT_LIMIT, SLSREP_NUMBER, SLSREP_LAST, SLSREP_FIRST)

is replaced by

CUSTOMER (<u>CUSTOMER NUMBER</u>, CUST_LAST, CUST_FIRST, BALANCE,
    CREDIT_LIMIT, SLSREP_NUMBER)

and

SALES_REP (<u>CUSTOMER NUMBER</u>, SLSREP_LAST, SLSREP_FIRST)

Samples of these tables are shown in Figure 5.13. Both new tables are in 3NF. In addition, by joining these two tables together on Customer Number, you can reconstruct the original CUSTOMER table. The result, however, still suffers from some of the same problems that the original CUSTOMER table did.

CUSTOMER

CUSTOMER NUMBER	CUST LAST	CUST FIRST	BALANCE	CREDIT LIMIT	SLSREP NUMBER	SLSREP LAST	SLSREP FIRST
124	Adams	Sally	$818.75	$1000	03	Jones	Mary
256	Samuels	Ann	$21.50	$1500	06	Smith	William
311	Charles	Don	$825.75	$1000	12	Diaz	Miguel
315	Daniels	Tom	$770.75	$750	06	Smith	William
405	Williams	Al	$402.75	$1500	12	Diaz	Miguel
412	Adams	Sally	$1817.50	$2000	03	Jones	Mary
522	Nelson	Mary	$98.75	$1500	12	Diaz	Miguel
567	Dinh	Tran	$402.40	$750	06	Smith	William
587	Galvez	Mara	$114.60	$1000	06	Smith	William
622	Martin	Dan	$1045.75	$1000	03	Jones	Mary

is replaced by

CUSTOMER

CUSTOMER NUMBER	CUST LAST	CUST FIRST	BALANCE	CREDIT LIMIT	SLSREP NUMBER
124	Adams	Sally	$818.75	$1000	03
256	Samuels	Ann	$21.50	$1500	06
311	Charles	Don	$825.75	$1000	12
315	Daniels	Tom	$770.75	$750	06
405	Williams	Al	$402.75	$1500	12
412	Adams	Sally	$1817.50	$2000	03
522	Nelson	Mary	$98.75	$1500	12
567	Dinh	Tran	$402.40	$750	06
587	Galvez	Mara	$114.60	$1000	06
622	Martin	Dan	$1045.75	$1000	03

SALES REP

CUSTOMER NUMBER	SLSREP LAST	SLSREP FIRST
124	Jones	Mary
256	Smith	William
311	Diaz	Miguel
315	Smith	William
405	Diaz	Miguel
412	Jones	Mary
522	Diaz	Miguel
567	Smith	William
587	Smith	William
622	Jones	Mary

Figure 5.13 Incorrect decomposition

Consider, for example, the redundancy in the storage of sales reps' names, the problem encountered in changing the name of sales rep 12, and the difficulty of adding a new sales rep for whom there are as yet no customers. In addition, because the sales rep number is in one table and the sales rep name is in another, you actually have *split a functional dependence across two different tables*. Thus, this decomposition, while it may appear to be valid, is definitely not a desirable way to create 3NF tables.

There is another decomposition that you might choose, and that is to replace

CUSTOMER (<u>CUSTOMER NUMBER</u>, CUST_LAST, CUST_FIRST, BALANCE,
CREDIT_LIMIT, SLSREP_NUMBER, SLSREP_LAST, SLSREP_FIRST)

by

CUSTOMER (<u>CUSTOMER NUMBER</u>, CUST_LAST, CUST_FIRST, BALANCE,
CREDIT_LIMIT, SLSREP_LAST, SLSREP_FIRST)

and

SALES_REP (<u>SLSREP NUMBER</u>, SLSREP_LAST, SLSREP_FIRST)

Samples of these tables are shown in Figure 5.14.

CUSTOMER

CUSTOMER NUMBER	CUST LAST	CUST FIRST	BALANCE	CREDIT LIMIT	SLSREP NUMBER	SLSREP LAST	SLSREP FIRST
124	Adams	Sally	$818.75	$1000	03	Jones	Mary
256	Samuels	Ann	$21.50	$1500	06	Smith	William
311	Charles	Don	$825.75	$1000	12	Diaz	Miguel
315	Daniels	Tom	$770.75	$750	06	Smith	William
405	Williams	Al	$402.75	$1500	12	Diaz	Miguel
412	Adams	Sally	$1817.50	$2000	03	Jones	Mary
522	Nelson	Mary	$98.75	$1500	12	Diaz	Miguel
567	Dinh	Tran	$402.40	$750	06	Smith	William
587	Galvez	Mara	$114.60	$1000	06	Smith	William
622	Martin	Dan	$1045.75	$1000	03	Jones	Mary

is replaced by

CUSTOMER

CUSTOMER NUMBER	CUST LAST	CUST FIRST	BALANCE	CREDIT LIMIT	SLSREP LAST	SLSREP FIRST
124	Adams	Sally	$818.75	$1000	Jones	Mary
256	Samuels	Ann	$21.50	$1500	Smith	William
311	Charles	Don	$825.75	$1000	Diaz	Miguel
315	Daniels	Tom	$770.75	$750	Smith	William
405	Williams	Al	$402.75	$1500	Diaz	Miguel
412	Adams	Sally	$1817.50	$2000	Jones	Mary
522	Nelson	Mary	$98.75	$1500	Diaz	Miguel
567	Dinh	Tran	$402.40	$750	Smith	William
587	Galvez	Mara	$114.60	$1000	Smith	William
622	Martin	Dan	$1045.75	$1000	Jones	Mary

SALES REP

SLSREP NUMBER	SLSREP LAST	SLSREP FIRST
03	Jones	Mary
06	Smith	William
12	Diaz	Miguel

Figure 5.14 Incorrect decomposition

This seems to be a possibility. Not only are both tables in 3NF, but joining them together based on Slsrep Last and Slsrep First seems to reconstruct the data in the original table. Or does it? Suppose the name of sales rep 06 is also Mary Jones. In that case, when you join the two new tables together, you will get a row in which customer 124 (Sally Adams) is associated with sales rep 03 and *another* row in which customer number 124 is associated with sales rep 06. Because you obviously want decompositions that preserve the original information, this scheme is not appropriate.

Question	Using the types of entities found in a college environment (faculty, students, departments, courses, etc.), create an example of a table that is in 1NF but not in 2NF and an example of a table that is in 2NF but not 3NF. In each case justify the answers and show how to convert to the higher forms.
Answer	There are many possible solutions. If your solution differs from the one shown, this does not mean that it is an unsatisfactory solution. To create a 1NF table that is not in 2NF, you need a table that (a) has no repeating groups and (b) has at least one attribute that is dependent on only a portion of the primary key. For an attribute to be dependent on a portion of the primary key, the key must contain at least two attributes. Following is a picture of what you need:

    (__1__, __2__, 3 , 4)

This table contains four attributes, numbered 1, 2, 3, and 4, in which attributes 1 and 2 functionally determine both attributes 3 and 4. In addition, neither attribute 1 nor attribute 2 can determine **all** other attributes, otherwise the key would contain only this one attribute. Finally, you want part of the key, say attribute 2, to determine another attribute, say attribute 4. Now that you have the pattern you need, you would like to find attributes from within the college environment to fit it. One example would be:

    (STUDENT NUMBER, COURSE NUMBER, GRADE, COURSE_DESCRIPTION)

In this example, the concatenation of Student Number and Course Number determines both Grade and Course Description. Both attributes are required to determine Grade, and thus the primary key consists of their concatenation (nothing less will do). The Course Description, however, is only dependent on the Course Number. This violates second normal form. To convert this table to 2NF, you would replace it by the two tables:

    (STUDENT NUMBER, COURSE NUMBER, GRADE)

and

    (COURSE NUMBER, COURSE_DESCRIPTION)

You would of course now give these tables appropriate names.

Answer (cont)

To create a table that is in 2NF but not in 3NF, you need a 2NF table in which there is a determinant that is *not* a candidate key. If you choose a table that has a single attribute as the primary key, it is automatically in 2NF, so the real problem is the determinant. You need a table like the following:

(__1__ , 2 , 3)

This table contains three attributes, numbered 1, 2, and 3, in which attribute 1 determines each of the others and is thus the primary key. If, in addition, attribute 2 determines attribute 3, it is a determinant. If it also does not determine attribute 1, then it is not a candidate key. One example that fits this pattern would be:

(STUDENT_NUMBER, ADVISOR_NUMBER, ADVISOR_NAME)

Here Student Number determines both the student's Advisor Number and Advisor Name. Advisor Number determines Advisor Name but Advisor Number does not determine Student Number, because one advisor can have many advisees. This table is in 2NF but not 3NF. To convert it to 3NF, you replace it by:

(STUDENT_NUMBER, ADVISOR_NUMBER)

and

(ADVISOR_NUMBER, ADVISOR_NAME)

Question

Convert the following table to 3NF:

STUDENT (STUDENT_NUMBER, STUDENT_NAME, NUMBER_CREDITS,

ADVISOR_NUMBER, ADVISOR_NAME, (COURSE_NUMBER,

COURSE_DESCRIPTION, GRADE))

In this table, Student Number determines Student Name, Number Credits, Advisor Number, and Advisor Name. Advisor Number determines Advisor Name. Course Number determines Course Description. The combination of a Student Number and a Course Number determines a Grade.

Answer

Step 1. Remove the repeating group to convert to 1NF. This yields:

STUDENT (STUDENT_NUMBER, STUDENT_NAME, NUMBER_CREDITS,

ADVISOR_NUMBER, ADVISOR_NAME, COURSE_NUMBER,

COURSE_DESCRIPTION, GRADE)

This table is now in 1NF, because it has no repeating groups. It is not, however, in 2NF, because Student Name is dependent only on Student Number, which is only a portion of the primary key.

Answer (cont)

Step 2. Convert the 1NF table to 2NF. First, for each subset of the primary key, start a table with that subset as its key yielding:

> (<u>STUDENT NUMBER</u>,
>
> (<u>COURSE NUMBER</u>,
>
> (<u>STUDENT NUMBER</u>, <u>COURSE NUMBER</u>,

Next, place the rest of the attributes with the minimal collection on which they depend, giving:

> (<u>STUDENT NUMBER</u>, STUDENT_NAME, NUMBER_CREDITS,
>
>   ADVISOR_NUMBER, ADVISOR_NAME)
>
> (<u>COURSE NUMBER</u>, COURSE_DESCRIPTION)
>
> (<u>STUDENT NUMBER</u>, <u>COURSE NUMBER</u>, GRADE)

Finally, you assign names to each of the newly created tables:

> STUDENT (<u>STUDENT NUMBER</u>, STUDENT_NAME, NUMBER_CREDITS,
>
>   ADVISOR_NUMBER, ADVISOR_NAME)
>
> COURSE (<u>COURSE NUMBER</u>, COURSE_DESCRIPTION)
>
> GRADE (<u>STUDENT NUMBER</u>, <u>COURSE NUMBER</u>, GRADE)

While these tables are all in 2NF, both COURSE and GRADE are also in 3NF. The STUDENT table is not, however, because it contains a determinant, Advisor Number, that is not a candidate key.

Step 3: Convert the 2NF STUDENT table to 3NF by removing the attribute that depends on the determinant Advisor Number and placing it in a separate table:

> (<u>STUDENT NUMBER</u>, STUDENT_NAME, NUMBER_CREDITS,
>
>   ADVISOR_NUMBER)
>
> (<u>ADVISOR NUMBER</u>, ADVISOR_NAME)

Step 4: Name these tables and put the entire collection together, giving:

> STUDENT (<u>STUDENT NUMBER</u>, STUDENT_NAME, NUMBER_CREDITS,
>
>   ADVISOR_NUMBER)
>
> ADVISOR (<u>ADVISOR NUMBER</u>, ADVISOR_NAME)
>
> COURSE (<u>COURSE NUMBER</u>, COURSE_DESCRIPTION)
>
> GRADE (<u>STUDENT NUMBER</u>, <u>COURSE NUMBER</u>, GRADE)

SUMMARY

1. Column B is functionally dependent on column (or collection of columns) A, if a value of A uniquely determines a value of B at any point in time.

2. The primary key is a column (or collection of columns) A, such that all other columns are functionally dependent on A and no subcollection of the columns in A also has this property.

3. If there is more than one possible choice for the primary key, one of the possibilities is chosen to be the primary key. The others are referred to as candidate keys.

4. A relation (table) is in first normal form (1NF) if it does not contain repeating groups.

5. A relation (table) is in second normal form (2NF) if it is in 1NF and if no column that is not a part of the primary key is dependent on only a portion of the primary key.

6. A determinant is any column that functionally determines another column.

7. A relation (table) is in third normal form (3NF) if it is in 2NF and if the only determinants it contains are candidate keys.

8. A collection of relations (tables) that is not in 3NF possesses inherent problems, called update anomalies. Replacing this collection by an equivalent collection of relations (tables) that is in 3NF removes these anomalies. This replacement must be done carefully, following a method like the one proposed in this text. If not, other problems, such as those discussed in this chapter, very well may be introduced.

KEY TERMS

Alternate key

Boyce-Codd normal form (BCNF)

Candidate key

Concatenation

Dependency diagram

Determinant

First normal form (1NF)

Functional dependent

Key

Nonkey attribute

Normal forms

Normalization

Partial dependency

Primary key

Repeating group

Second normal form (2NF)

Third normal form (3NF)

Unnormalized relation

Update anomalies

REVIEW QUESTIONS

1. Define functional dependence.

2. Give an example of an attribute, A, and another attribute, B, such that B is functionally dependent on A. Give an example of an attribute, C, and an attribute, D, such that D is not functionally dependent on C.

3. Define primary key.

4. Define candidate key.

5. Define first normal form.

6. Define second normal form. What types of problems are encountered in tables that are not in second normal form?

7. Define third normal form. What types of problems are encountered in tables that are not in third normal form?

8. Consider a student table containing a student's number, student's name, student's major department, student advisor's number, student advisor's name, student advisor's office number, student advisor's phone number, student's number of credits, and student's class standing (freshman, sophomore, and so on). List the functional dependencies that exist, along with the assumptions that would support these dependencies.

9. Using the types of entities found in the Henry's Books database system (books, authors, and publishers), create an example of a table that is in 1NF but not in 2NF and an example of a table that is in 2NF but not in 3NF. In each case, justify the answers and show how to convert to the higher forms.

10. Convert the following table to an equivalent collection of tables that is in 3NF.

PATIENT (HOUSEHOLD_NUMBER, HOUSEHOLD_NAME, HOUSEHOLD_STREET,
  HOUSEHOLD_CITY, HOUSEHOLD_STATE, HOUSEHOLD_ZIP, BALANCE,
  PATIENT NUMBER, PATIENT_NAME, (SERVICE_CODE,
  SERVICE_DESCRIPTION, SERVICE_FEE, SERVICE_DATE))

This is a table concerning information about patients of a dentist. Each patient belongs to a household. The head of the household is designated as HH in the table. The following dependencies exist in the PATIENT table:

PATIENT_NUMBER--> HOUSEHOLD_NUMBER, HOUSEHOLD_NAME,
  HOUSEHOLD_STREET, HOUSEHOLD_CITY, HOUSEHOLD_STATE,
  HOUSEHOLD_ZIP, BALANCE, PATIENT_NAME
HOUSEHOLD_NUMBER--> HOUSEHOLD_NAME, HOUSEHOLD_STREET,
  HOUSEHOLD_CITY, HOUSEHOLD_STATE, HOUSEHOLD_ZIP, BALANCE
SERVICE_CODE--> SERVICE_DESCRIPTION, SERVICE_FEE
PATIENT_NUMBER, SERVICE_CODE--> SERVICE_DATE

11. List the functional dependencies in the following table, subject to the specified conditions. Convert this table to an equivalent collection of tables that are in 3NF.

INVOICE (INVOICE NUMBER, CUSTOMER_NUMBER, LAST, FIRST, STREET, CITY, STATE,
  ZIP_CODE, INVOICE_DATE, (PART_NUMBER,
  PART_DESCRIPTION, UNIT_PRICE, NUMBER_SHIPPED))

This table concerns invoice information. For a given invoice (identified by the invoice number) there will be a single customer. The customer's number, name, and address appear on the invoice as well as the invoice date. Also, there may be several different parts appearing on the invoice. For each part that appears, the Part Number, Part Description, Unit Price, and Number Shipped will be displayed. The price is from the current master price list.

12. Using your knowledge of a college environment, determine the functional dependencies that exist in the following table. After these have been determined, convert this table to an equivalent collection of tables that are in 3NF.

STUDENT (STUDENT NUMBER, STUDENT_NAME, NUMBER_CREDITS,
  ADVISOR_NUMBER, ADVISOR_NAME, DEPTNUMB, DEPTNAME,
  (COURSE_NUMBER, COURSE_DESCRIPTION, COURSE_TERM,
  GRADE))

CHAPTER **6**

Database Design 2: Design Methodology

OBJECTIVES

1. Discuss the general process and goals of database design.

2. Define user views and explain their function.

3. Present a methodology for database design at the information level as well as examples illustrating the use of this methodology.

4. Explain how to produce a pictorial representation of a database design.

5. Explain the process of mapping an information-level design to a design that is appropriate for a relational model system.

INTRODUCTION

Now that you have learned how to identify and correct bad designs, you will focus attention on the design process itself; that is, the process of determining the tables and columns that will make up the database and determining the relationships between the various tables.

Database design often is approached as a two-step process. In the first step, a database is designed that satisfies the requirements as cleanly as possible. This step is called **information-level design**, and it is taken *independently* of any particular DBMS that will ultimately be used. In the second step, which is called the **physical-level design**, the information-level design is transformed into a design for the specific DBMS that will be used. Naturally, the characteristics of that DBMS must come into play during this step.

In this text, you will focus on the information-level design process and that portion of the physical-level design process geared towards producing a legitimate design for a typical microcomputer DBMS. This approach represents a subset of the design methodology given by Pratt and Adamski.[*] That methodology, which encompasses both the information and physical levels of design, is intended to be used for the design of complex databases that may be implemented on a variety of DBMSs, on mainframes or microcomputers, and where performance can be a very important concern. For the majority of microcomputer applications, the database design process as presented in this text is more than sufficient.

■　■　■　■　■

INFORMATION-LEVEL DESIGN

No matter which approach is adopted with regards to database design, a complete database design that will satisfy all the requirements only rarely can be a one-step process. Unless the requirements are exceptionally simple, it usually is necessary to subdivide the overall job of database design into smaller tasks. This often is done through the separate consideration of individual pieces of the design problem. In design problems for large organizations, these pieces often are called user views, and you will use the same terminology here. A **user view** is the view of data necessary to support the operations of a particular user. For each user view, a database structure to support the view must be designed and then merged into a cumulative design. Each user view, in general, will be much simpler than the total collection of requirements. Working on these individual tasks will be much more manageable than attempting to turn the design of the entire database into one large task.

The General Database Design Methodology

The database design methodology set forth in this text involves representing individual user views, refining them to eliminate any problems, and then merging them into a cumulative design. A "user" could be a person or a group that will use the system, a report the system must produce, or a type of transaction that the system must support. In the last two instances, you might think of the user as the person who will use the report or enter the transaction. In fact, if the same individual required three separate reports, for example, you probably would be better off to consider each of the reports as a separate user view, even though only one

---

[*] Philip J. Pratt, and Joseph J. Adamski, <u>Database Systems: Management and Design</u>, 3rd edition (Boston: boyd and fraser, 1994).

user was involved, because the smaller the user view, the easier it is to work with.

Now turn to the methodology itself. For each user view, you need to complete the following four steps:

1. Represent the user view as a collection of tables.

2. Normalize these tables.

3. Represent all keys.

4. Merge the result of the previous steps into the design.

THE METHODOLOGY

The following sections give details concerning the steps in the methodology.

Represent the User View as a Collection of Tables

When given a user view or some sort of stated requirement, you must develop a collection of tables that will support it. In some cases, the collection of tables may be obvious. Let's suppose, for example, that a given user view involves departments and employees. Let's assume further that each department can employ many employees but that each employee is assigned to exactly one department—a typical restriction. A design similar to the following may have naturally occurred to you and is an appropriate design.

DEPT (DEPT_NUMBER, NAME, LOCATION)

EMPLOYEE (EMPLOYEE_NUMBER, LAST, FIRST, STREET, CITY, STATE,

ZIP_CODE, WAGE_RATE, SOC_SEC_NUMB, DEPT_NUMBER)

You undoubtedly will find that the more designs you have done, the easier it will be for you to develop such a collection without resorting to any special procedure. The real question is, What procedure should be followed if a correct design is not so obvious? In this case, you can take the following four steps:

Step 1. Determine the entities involved and create a separate table for each type of entity. At this point, you do not need to do anything more than give the table a name. For example, if a user view involves departments and employees, you can create a DEPT table and an EMPLOYEE table. At this point, you will write down something like this:

DEPT (

EMPLOYEE (

That is, you will write down the name of a table and a left parenthesis, and that is all. Later steps will fill in the attributes in these tables.

Step 2. Determine the primary key for each of these tables. This will fill in one or more attributes (depending on how many attributes make up the primary key). Other attributes will not be filled in until a later step. It may seem strange, but even though you have yet to determine the attributes in the table, you usually can determine the primary key. For example, the primary key to an EMPLOYEE table probably will be the Employee Number, and the primary key to a DEPT table probably will be the Department Number.

The **primary key** is the unique identifier, so the essential question here is, What does it take to uniquely identify an employee or a department? Even if you are in the process of trying to automate a system that previously was manual, some unique identifier still usually can be found in the manual system. If not, it is probably time to assign one. Let's say, for example, that in a particular manual system customers did not have numbers. The customer base was small enough that the organization felt they were not needed. Now is a good time to assign them, however, because the company is computerizing. These numbers then would be the unique identifier you are seeking.

Now let's add these primary keys to what you have written down already. At this point, you will have something like the following:

DEPT (<u>DEPT_NUMBER</u>,

EMPLOYEE (<u>EMPLOYEE_NUMBER</u>,

That is, you will have the name of the table and the primary key, but that is all. Later steps will fill in the other attributes.

Step 3. Determine the properties for each of these entities. You can look at the user requirements and then determine the other properties of each entity that are required. These properties, along with the primary key identified in Step 2, will become attributes in the appropriate tables. For example, an EMPLOYEE entity may require Last, First, Street, City, State, Zip Code, Wage Rate, and Soc Sec Numb (social security number). The DEPT entity may require Name (department name) and Location (department location). Adding these to what is already in place would produce the following:

DEPT (<u>DEPT_NUMBER</u>, NAME, LOCATION)

EMPLOYEE (<u>EMPLOYEE_NUMBER</u>, LAST, FIRST, STREET, CITY, STATE,

ZIP_CODE, WAGE_RATE, SOC_SEC_NUMB)

Step 4. Determine relationships among the entities. The basic **relationships** are one-to-many, many-to-many, and one-to-one. You now will see how to handle each of these types of relationships.

One-to-many. A one-to-many relationship is implemented by including the primary key of the "one" table as a foreign key in the "many" table. Let's suppose, for example, that each employee is assigned to a single department but a department can have many employees. Thus *one* department is related to *many* employees. In this case, you would include the primary key of the DEPT table (the "one") as a foreign key in the EMPLOYEE table (the "many"). Thus, the tables now would look like this:

DEPT (<u>DEPT_NUMBER</u>, NAME, LOCATION)

EMPLOYEE (<u>EMPLOYEE_NUMBER</u>, LAST, FIRST, STREET, CITY, STATE,

ZIP_CODE, WAGE_RATE, SOC_SEC_NUMB, DEPT_NUMBER)

Many-to-many. A many-to-many relationship is implemented by creating a new table whose key is the combination of the keys of the original tables. Let's suppose that each employee can be assigned to multiple departments and that each department can have many employees. In this case, you would create a new table whose primary key would be the combination of Employee Number and Dept Number. Because the new table represents the fact that an employee *works in* a department, you might choose to call it WORKS IN, in which case the collection of tables is as follows:

DEPT (<u>DEPT_NUMBER</u>, NAME, LOCATION)

EMPLOYEE (<u>EMPLOYEE_NUMBER</u>, LAST, FIRST, STREET, CITY, STATE,

ZIP_CODE, WAGE_RATE, SOC_SEC_NUMB)

WORKS_IN (<u>EMPLOYEE_NUMBER</u>, <u>DEPT_NUMBER</u>)

In some situations, no other attributes will be required in the new table. The other attributes in the WORKS_IN table would be those attributes that depended on both the employee and the department, if such attributes existed. One possibility, for example, would be the date when the employee was first assigned to the department, because it depends on *both* the employee *and* the department.

One-to-one. If each employee is assigned to a single department and each department consists of only one employee, the relationship between employees and departments is one-to-one. The simplest way to implement a one-to-one relationship is to treat it as a one-to-many relationship. But what is the "one" part of the relationship and what is the "many" part? Sometimes looking to the future helps. For instance, in this example, you might ask, If the relationship changes in the future, is it more likely that one employee will be assigned to many departments or that one department may consist of several employees rather than just one? If you feel, for example, that it is more likely that a department would be allowed to contain more than one employee, you would make EMPLOYEE the "many" part of the relationship. If the answer is that both things very well might happen, you might even treat the relationship as many-to-many. If neither change were likely to occur, you arbitrarily could choose the "many" part of the relationship.

Normalize these Tables

Normalize each table, produced in the previous step, with the target being third normal form.

Represent all Keys

Identify all keys. The types of keys you must identify are primary keys, alternate keys, secondary keys, and foreign keys.

1. Primary. The primary key already has been determined in the earlier steps.

2. Alternate. An **alternate key** is an attribute or collection of attributes that could have been chosen as the primary key but was not. It is not common to have alternate keys; but if they do exist, and if the system is to enforce their uniqueness, they should be so noted.

3. Secondary. If there are any **secondary keys**—attributes that are of interest strictly for the purpose of retrieval—they should be represented at this point. If a user were to indicate, for example, that rapidly retrieving an employee on the basis of his or her last name was important, you would designate Last as a secondary key.

4. Foreign. This is in many ways the most important category because it is through **foreign keys** that relationships are established and that certain types of integrity constraints are enforced in the database. Remember that a foreign key is an attribute, or collection of attributes, in one table that is required either to match the value of the primary key for some row in another table or be null. This is the property called **referential integrity**. Consider, for example, the following tables:

   DEPT (<u>DEPT_NUMBER</u>, NAME, LOCATION)

   EMPLOYEE (<u>EMPLOYEE_NUMBER</u>, LAST, FIRST, STREET, CITY, STATE,
       ZIP_CODE, WAGE_RATE, SOC_SEC_NUMB, DEPT_NUMBER)

   As before, Dept Number in the EMPLOYEE table indicates the department to which the employee is assigned. You say that Dept Number in the EMPLOYEE table is a foreign key that *identifies* DEPT. Thus, the number in this attribute on any row in the EMPLOYEE table either must be the number of a department that is already in the database or be null. Null would indicate that for whatever reason, the employee is not assigned to a department.

Database Design Language (DBDL)

You need a mechanism for representing the tables and keys together with the restrictions discussed above. The standard mechanism for representing tables is fine but it does not go far enough. There is no routine way to represent alternate, secondary, or foreign keys, nor is there a way of representing foreign key restrictions. There is no way of indicating that a given field or attribute can accept null values. Because the methodology is based on the relational model, however, it is desirable to represent tables with the standard method. You will add additional features capable of representing additional information. The end result is **Database Design Language** or **DBDL**.

Figure 6.1a shows sample DBDL documentation for the EMPLOYEE table. In DBDL, tables and their primary keys are represented in the usual manner. Any field that is allowed to be null, such as the Wage Rate field in the EMPLOYEE table, is followed by an asterisk(*).

EMPLOYEE (<u>EMPLOYEE NUMBER</u>, LAST, FIRST, STREET, CITY, STATE, ZIP_CODE,

WAGE_RATE*, SOC_SEC_NUMB, DEPT_NUMBER)

AK   SOC_SEC_NUMB

SK   LAST

FK   DEPT_NUMBER --> DEPT

Figure 6.1a DBDL for EMPLOYEE relation

DBDL (DATABASE DESIGN LANGUAGE)

1.	Relations (tables), attributes (columns), and primary keys are represented in the usual way.
2.	Attributes that are allowed to be null are followed by an asterisk.
3.	Alternate keys are identified by the letters AK followed by the attribute(s) that comprise the alternate key.
4.	Secondary keys are identified by the letters SK followed by the attribute(s) that comprise the secondary key.
5.	Foreign keys are identified by the letters FK followed by the attribute(s) that comprise the foreign key. Foreign keys are followed by an arrow pointing to the relation identified by the foreign key.

Figure 6.1b Summary of DBDL

Underneath the table, the various types of keys are listed. Each is preceded by an abbreviation indicating the type of key (AK — alternate key, SK — secondary key, FK — foreign key). It is sufficient to list the attribute or collection of attributes that forms an alternate or secondary key. In the case of foreign keys, however, you also must represent the table that is identified by the foreign key (i.e., the table whose primary key the foreign key must match). This is accomplished in DBDL by following the foreign key with an arrow pointing to the table that the foreign key identifies.

Figure 6.1b summarizes the details of DBDL. Examples of DBDL will be presented throughout this chapter. The only feature of DBDL not listed actually is more of a tip than a rule. When several tables are listed, a table containing a foreign key should be listed after the table that the foreign key identifies, if possible.

In the example shown in Figure 6.1a, you are saying that there is a table called EMPLOYEE, consisting of fields Employee Number, Last, First, Street, City, State, Zip Code, Wage Rate, Soc Sec Numb (Social Security Number), and Dept Number. The Wage Rate field is the only one that can accept null values. The primary key is Employee Number. Another possible primary key is Soc Sec Numb and so is indicated as an alternate key (AK). You are interested in being able to retrieve information efficiently, based on the employee's name, so you have designated Last as a secondary key. The Dept Number is a foreign key identifying the department to which the employee is assigned (it identifies the appropriate department in the DEPT table).

A Pictorial Representation of the Database

For many people, a pictorial representation, or diagram, of the structure of the database is quite useful. As the old saying goes, "A picture is worth a thousand words." Fortunately, there are many tools for drawing such pictures. In this section, you use the Relationships feature of Microsoft Access to produce the diagram. If you do not have access to such a tool, it also is easy to produce these diagrams by hand.

The procedure for producing the diagram, often called a data structure diagram, by hand is as follows:

1. Draw a rectangle for each table in the DBDL design. Label the rectangle with the name of the corresponding table.

2. For each foreign key, draw an arrow from the rectangle that corresponds to the table being identified to the rectangle that corresponds to the table containing the foreign key.

3. In the rare event that you have two arrows joining the same two rectangles, label the arrows with names that are indicative of the meaning of the relationships represented by the arrows.

4. If the diagram you have drawn is cluttered or messy, redraw the diagram. If possible, avoid crossing arrows, because this makes the diagram more difficult to understand.

Figure 6.2 shows the DBDL from Figure 6.1a together with a corresponding diagram produced by Microsoft Access. Notice there is a DEPT rectangle and an EMPLOYEE rectangle. Each rectangle contains the name of the table and a list of the fields in the table. In fact, these rectangles actually are called field lists in Access. Further, because the EMPLOYEE table contains a foreign key identifying the DEPT table, there is a line from DEPT to EMPLOYEE. This line visually emphasizes the relationship between departments and employees. Such lines represent one-to-many relationships (*one* department to *many* employees) with the "one" end of the relationship indicated by the number 1 and the "many" part of the relationship indicated with the symbol "∞".

DEPT (<u>DEPT NUMBER</u>, NAME, LOCATION)

EMPLOYEE (<u>EMPLOYEE NUMBER</u>, LAST, FIRST, STREET, CITY, STATE, ZIP_CODE,

    WAGE_RATE*, SOC_SEC_NUMB, DEPT_NUMBER)

    AK SOC_SEC_NUMB

    SK LAST

    FK DEPT_NUMBER --> DEPT

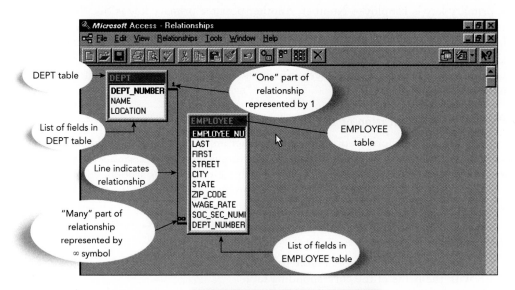

Figure 6.2 DBDL with diagram

Note	If you draw the diagram yourself, you typically will not list all the fields in the rectangle.

Merge the Result into the Design

As soon as you have completed Steps 1 through 3 for a given user view, you can merge these results into the overall design. If the view on which you have been working happens to be the first user view, then the cumulative design will be identical to the design for this first user. Otherwise, you add all the tables for this user to those that are currently in the cumulative design.

    You then combine tables that have the same primary key to form a new table. This table has the same primary key as those tables that have been combined. The new table also contains all the attributes from both tables. In the case of duplicate attributes, you remove all but one copy of the attribute. For example, if the cumulative collection already contained the following:

    EMPLOYEE (<u>EMPLOYEE NUMBER</u>, LAST, FIRST, WAGE_RATE,

        SOC_SEC_NUMB, DEPT_NUMBER)

and the user view just completed contained the following:

    EMPLOYEE (<u>EMPLOYEE NUMBER</u>, LAST, FIRST, STREET, CITY, STATE, ZIP_CODE)

then the two tables would be combined, because they would have the same primary key. All the attributes from both tables would appear in the new table, but without duplicates. Thus, Last and First would appear only once, even though they are in each of the individual tables. The result would be the following:

    EMPLOYEE (<u>EMPLOYEE NUMBER</u>, LAST, FIRST, WAGE_RATE,

        SOC_SEC_NUMB, DEPT_NUMBER, STREET, CITY, STATE, ZIP_CODE)

If you wanted to, you could reorder the attributes at this point. You might feel, for example, that placing Street, City, State, and Zip Code immediately after First would put it in a more natural position. This would give the following:

    EMPLOYEE (<u>EMPLOYEE NUMBER</u>, LAST, FIRST, STREET, CITY, STATE,

        ZIP_CODE, WAGE_RATE, SOC_SEC_NUMB, DEPT_NUMBER)

You then would check the new design to ensure that it was still in third normal form. If it wasn't, you would convert it to 3NF before proceeding.

The process, which is summarized in Figure 6.3, is repeated for each user view until all user views have been examined. At that point, the design is reviewed in order to resolve any problems that may remain and to ensure that the needs of all individual users indeed can be met. Once this has been done, the information-level design is complete.

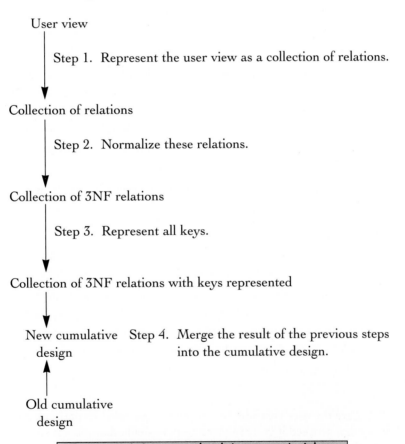

Figure 6.3 Information-level design methodology

DATABASE DESIGN EXAMPLES

Let's now look at some examples of database design.

Example 1:

For an initial example of the design methodology, let's complete an information-level design for a database that must satisfy the following constraints and requirements:

1. For a sales rep, store the sales rep's number, name, address, total commission and commission rate.

2. For a customer, store the customer's number, name, address, balance, and credit limit. In addition, store the number and name of the sales rep who represents this customer. Upon further checking with the user you determine that a sales rep can represent many customers but a customer must have exactly one sales rep (i.e., a customer *must have* a sales rep and cannot have more than *one*).

3. For a part, store the part's number, description, units on hand, item class, the number of the warehouse in which the part is located, and the price.

4. For an order, store the order number, order date, the number, name, and address of the customer who placed the order, and the number of the sales rep who represents that customer. In addition, for each line item within the order, store the part number and description, the number of the part that was ordered, and the quoted price. The following information also has been obtained from the user:

   a. Each order must be placed by a customer who is already in the customer file.

   b. There is only one customer per order.

   c. On a given order, there is at most one line item for a given part. For example, part BT04 cannot appear on several lines within the same order.

   d. The quoted price may be the same as the current price in the part master file, but it need not be. This allows the enterprise the flexibility to sell the same parts to different customers for different prices. It also allows us to change the basic price for a part without necessarily affecting orders that are currently on file.

What are the user views in the preceding example? In particular, how should the design proceed if you are given requirements that are not specifically stated in the form of user views? You actually might be lucky enough to be confronted with a series of well-thought-out user views in a form that can readily be merged into your design. On the other hand, you only might be given a set of requirements like the set you have encountered in this example. Or you might be given a list of reports and updates that a system must support. If you happen to be given the job of interviewing users and documenting their needs as a preliminary to the design process, you can make sure that their views are specified in a form that will be easy to work with when the design process starts. On the other hand, you may just have to take this information as you get it.

If the user views are not spelled out as user views per se, then you should consider each requirement that is specified to be a user view. Thus each report or update transaction that the system must support, as well as any other requirement such as any of those just stated, can be considered an individual user view. In fact, even if the requirements are presented as user views, you may wish to split up a user view that is particularly complex into smaller pieces and consider each piece a user view for the design process.

Let's now proceed with the example.

1. This requirement, or user view, poses no particular difficulty. Only one table is required to support this view:

SALES_REP (<u>SLSREP_NUMBER</u>, LAST, FIRST, STREET, CITY, STATE,
    ZIP_CODE, TOTAL_COMMISSION, COMMISSION_RATE)

This table is in 3NF. Because there are no foreign, alternate, or secondary keys, the DBDL representation of the table is precisely the same as the relational model representation.

Notice you have assumed that the sales rep's number (SlsRep Number) is the primary key to the table. This is a fairly reasonable assumption. But because this information was not given in the first requirement, you would need to verify its accuracy with the user. In each of the following requirements, you shall assume that the obvious attribute (Customer Number, Part Number, and Order Number) is the primary key. Because this is the first user view, the "merge" step of the design methodology will produce a cumulative design consisting of this one table. (See Figure 6.4.)

SALES_REP (<u>SLSREP_NUMBER</u>, LAST, FIRST, STREET, CITY, STATE, ZIP_CODE,
    TOTAL_COMMISSION, COMMISSION_RATE)

Figure 6.4 Cumulative design after first user view

2. Because the first user view was relatively simple, you were able to come up with the necessary table without having to go through the steps mentioned in the design methodology discussion. The second user view is a little more complicated, however, so let's use the steps suggested earlier to determine the tables. (If you've already spotted what the tables should be, you have a natural feel for the process. If so, please be patient while you work through the process here.)

You'll take two different approaches to this requirement so you can see how they can both lead to the same result. The only difference between the two approaches concerns the entities that you initially identify. In the first approach, suppose you identify two entities, SALES REP and CUSTOMER. You then would begin with the two following tables:

SALES_REP (

CUSTOMER (

After determining the unique identifiers, you add the primary keys, which would give:

SALES_REP (<u>SLSREP_NUMBER</u>,

CUSTOMER (<u>CUSTOMER_NUMBER</u>,

Adding attributes for the properties of each of these entities would yield:

SALES_REP (<u>SLSREP_NUMBER</u>, LAST, FIRST

CUSTOMER (<u>CUSTOMER_NUMBER</u>, LAST, FIRST, STREET, CITY, STATE,
    ZIP_CODE, BALANCE, CREDIT_LIMIT

Finally, you would deal with the relationship: *one* sales rep is related to *many* customers. To implement this one-to-many relationship, you would include the key of the "one" table in the "many" table as a foreign key. In this case, you would include Slsrep Number in the CUSTOMER table. Thus, you would have the following:

SALES_REP (<u>SLSREP_NUMBER</u>, LAST, FIRST)

CUSTOMER (<u>CUSTOMER_NUMBER</u>, LAST, FIRST, STREET, CITY, STATE,
    ZIP_CODE, BALANCE, CREDIT_LIMIT, SLSREP_NUMBER)

Both tables are in 3NF, so you can move on to representing the keys. Before doing that, however, let's investigate another approach that could have been used to determine the tables.

Suppose you didn't realize that there really were two entities and thought there was only a single entity, CUSTOMERS. You thus would begin only the single table as follows:

CUSTOMER (

Adding the unique identifier as the primary key would give:

CUSTOMER (<u>CUSTOMER_NUMBER</u>,

Finally, adding the other properties as additional attributes would yield:

CUSTOMER (<u>CUSTOMER_NUMBER</u>, CUST_LAST, CUST_FIRST, STREET, CITY,
    STATE, ZIP_CODE, BALANCE, CREDIT_LIMIT, SLSREP_NUMBER,
    SLSREP_LAST, SLSREP_FIRST)

Note	This table contains first and last names of both customers and sales reps. To distinguish last names, the customer's last name is denoted Cust Last and the sales rep's last name is SlsRep Last. Similarly, the customer's first name is Cust First and the sales rep's first name is Slsrep First.

A problem appears, however, when you examine the functional dependencies that exist in CUSTOMER. Customer Number determines all the other fields, as it should. But Slsrep Number determines Slsrep Last and Slsrep First, yet Slsrep Number is not a candidate key. This table, which is in 2NF because no attribute depends on a portion of the key, is not in 3NF. Thus, converting to 3NF would produce the following two tables:

CUSTOMER (<u>CUSTOMER NUMBER</u>, LAST, FIRST, STREET, CITY, STATE,
    ZIP_CODE, BALANCE, CREDIT_LIMIT, SLSREP_NUMBER)

SALES_REP (<u>SLSREP NUMBER</u>, LAST, FIRST)

Note	The first and last names of customers are now in the CUSTOMER table. The first and last names of sales reps are now in the SALES REP table. Thus, there is no longer any need to have special names to distinguish between the fields. In both cases, they simply can be called First and Last.

Notice these are precisely the same tables that you determined with the other approach. It just took a little longer to get there.

It is these two tables that you merge into the design. Besides the obvious primary keys, Customer Number for CUSTOMER and Slsrep Number for SALES REP, the CUSTOMER table now contains a foreign key, Slsrep Number.

There are no alternate keys, nor did the requirements state anything that would lead to a secondary key. If there were a requirement to retrieve the customer based on his or her last name, for example, you probably would choose to make Last a secondary key. Because last names may not be unique, Last is not an alternate key.

At this point, you could represent the table SALES REP in DBDL in preparation for merging this collection of tables into the collection you already have. Looking ahead, however, you see that because this table has the same primary key as the table SALES REP from the first user view, the two tables will be merged. A single table will be formed that has the common key Slsrep Number as its primary key and that contains all the other attributes from both tables without duplication. For this second user view, the only attributes in SALES REP besides the primary key are Last and First. These attributes were already in the SALES REP table in the cumulative design. Thus, nothing will be added to the SALES REP table that is already in place. The cumulative design now contains the two tables SALES REP and CUSTOMER, as shown in Figure 6.5.

SALES_REP (<u>SLSREP NUMBER</u>, LAST, FIRST, STREET, CITY, STATE, ZIP_CODE,

      TOTAL_COMMISSION, COMMISSION_RATE)

CUSTOMER (<u>CUSTOMER NUMBER</u>, LAST, FIRST, STREET, CITY, STATE, ZIP_CODE,

      BALANCE, CREDIT_LIMIT, SLSREP_NUMBER)

      FK   SLSREP_NUMBER --> SALES_REP

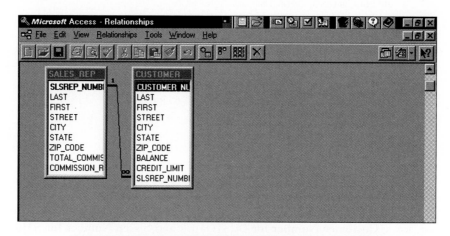

Figure 6.5 Cumulative design after second user view

3. Like the first user view, this one poses no special problems. Only one table is required to support it:

PART (<u>PART NUMBER</u>, PART_DESCRIPTION, UNITS_ON_HAND, ITEM_CLASS,

      WAREHOUSE_NUMBER, UNIT_PRICE)

This table is in 3NF. The DBDL representation is identical to the relational model representation.

Because Part Number is not the primary key of any table you already have encountered, merging this table into the cumulative design produces a design with the three tables SALES REP, CUSTOMER, and PART. (See Figure 6.6.)

SALES_REP (SLSREP_NUMBER, LAST, FIRST, STREET, CITY, STATE, ZIP_CODE,

      TOTAL_COMMISSION, COMMISSION_RATE)

CUSTOMER (CUSTOMER_NUMBER, LAST, FIRST, STREET, CITY, STATE, ZIP_CODE,

      BALANCE, CREDIT_LIMIT, SLSREP_NUMBER)

      FK   SLSREP_NUMBER --> SALES_REP

PART (PART_NUMBER, PART_DESCRIPTION, UNITS_ON_HAND, ITEM_CLASS,

      WAREHOUSE_NUMBER, UNIT_PRICE)

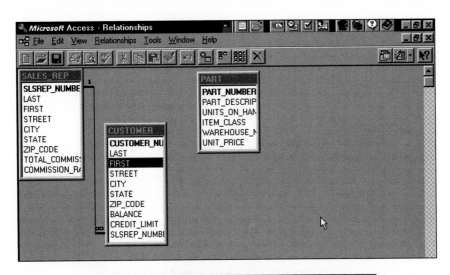

Figure 6.6 Cumulative design after third user view

4. This user view is a bit more complicated, and you could approach it in several ways. Suppose you felt only a single entity was being mentioned, namely ORDERS. In that case, you would create a single table, as follows:

ORDERS (

Because orders are uniquely identified by order numbers, you would add Order Number as the primary key, giving:

ORDERS (ORDER_NUMBER,

Examining the various properties of an order, such as the date, the customer number, and so on, as listed in the requirement, you would add appropriate attributes, giving:

ORDERS (ORDER_NUMBER, ORDER_DATE, CUSTOMER_NUMBER, LAST,

      FIRST, STREET, CITY, STATE, ZIP_CODE, SLSREP_NUMBER,

What about the fact that you are supposed to store the part number, description, number ordered, and quoted price for each order line on this order? One way of doing this would be to include all these attributes within the ORDERS table as a repeating group, because there can be many order lines on an order. This would yield:

ORDERS (<u>ORDER NUMBER</u>, ORDER_DATE, CUSTOMER_NUMBER, LAST,
    FIRST, STREET, CITY, STATE, ZIP_CODE, SLSREP_NUMBER,
    (PART_NUMBER, PART_DESCRIPTION, NUMBER_ORDERED,
    QUOTED_PRICE))

At this point, you have a table that does contain all the necessary attributes. Now you must convert this table to an equivalent collection of tables that are in 3NF. Because this table is not even in 1NF, you would remove the repeating group and expand the key to produce the following:

ORDERS (<u>ORDER NUMBER</u>, ORDER_DATE, CUSTOMER_NUMBER, LAST,
    FIRST, STREET, CITY, STATE, ZIP_CODE, SLSREP_NUMBER,
    <u>PART NUMBER</u>, PART_DESCRIPTION, NUMBER_ORDERED,
    QUOTED_PRICE)

In the new ORDERS table, you have the following functional dependencies:

ORDER_NUMBER --> ORDER_DATE, CUSTOMER_NUMBER, LAST, FIRST,
    STREET, CITY, STATE, ZIP_CODE, SLSREP_NUMBER

CUSTOMER_NUMBER --> LAST, FIRST, STREET, CITY, STATE, ZIP_CODE,
    SLSREP_NUMBER

PART_NUMBER --> PART_DESCRIPTION

ORDER_NUMBER, PART_NUMBER --> NUMBER_ORDERED, QUOTED_PRICE

From the discussion of the quoted price in the statement of the requirement, it should be noted that quoted price indeed does depend on *both* the order number and the part number, not on the part number alone. Because some attributes depend on only a portion of the primary key, the ORDERS table is not in 2NF. Converting to 2NF would yield the following:

ORDERS (<u>ORDER NUMBER</u>, ORDER_DATE, CUSTOMER_NUMBER, LAST,
    FIRST, STREET, CITY, STATE, ZIP_CODE, SLSREP_NUMBER)

PART (<u>PART NUMBER</u>, PART_DESCRIPTION)

ORDER_LINE (<u>ORDER NUMBER</u>, <u>PART NUMBER</u>, NUMBER_ORDERED,
    QUOTED_PRICE)

The tables PART and ORDER_LINE are in 3NF. The ORDERS table is not in 3NF, because Customer Number determines Last, First, Street, City, State, Zip Code, and Slsrep Number, but Customer Number is not a candidate key. Converting the ORDERS table to 3NF and leaving the other tables untouched would produce the following design for this requirement:

ORDERS (<u>ORDER NUMBER</u>, ORDER_DATE, CUSTOMER_NUMBER)

CUSTOMER (<u>CUSTOMER NUMBER</u>, LAST, FIRST, STREET, CITY, STATE,
    ZIP_CODE, SLSREP_NUMBER)

PART (<u>PART NUMBER</u>, PART_DESCRIPTION)

ORDER_LINE (<u>ORDER NUMBER</u>, <u>PART NUMBER</u>, NUMBER_ORDERED,
    QUOTED_PRICE)

This is the collection of tables that will be represented in DBDL and then merged into the cumulative design. Again, however, you can look ahead and see that CUSTOMER will be merged with the existing CUSTOMER table, and PART will be merged with the existing PART table. In neither case will anything new be added to the CUSTOMER and PART tables already in place, so the CUSTOMER and PART tables for this user view will not affect the overall design. The representation for this user view in DBDL is shown in Figure 6.7.

CUSTOMER (<u>CUSTOMER NUMBER</u>, LAST, FIRST, STREET, CITY, STATE, ZIP_CODE,
    SLSREP_NUMBER)

PART (<u>PART NUMBER</u>, PART_DESCRIPTION)

ORDERS (<u>ORDER NUMBER</u>, ORDER_DATE, CUSTOMER_NUMBER)
    FK   CUSTOMER_NUMBER --> CUSTOMER

ORDER_LINE (<u>ORDER NUMBER</u>, PART_NUMBER, NUMBER_ORDERED, QUOTED_PRICE)
    FK ORDER_NUMBER --> ORDERS
    FK PART_NUMBER --> PART

Figure 6.7 DBDL for fourth user view

At this point, you have completed the process for each user. You now should review the design to make sure it cleanly will fulfill all the requirements. If problems are encountered or new information comes to light, the design must be modified accordingly. Based on the assumption that you do not have to further modify the design here, the final information-level design is shown in Figure 6.8.

SALES_REP (<u>SLSREP_NUMBER</u>, LAST, FIRST, STREET, CITY, STATE, ZIP_CODE,

          TOTAL_COMMISSION, COMMISSION_RATE)

CUSTOMER (<u>CUSTOMER_NUMBER</u>, LAST, FIRST, STREET, CITY, STATE, ZIP_CODE,

          BALANCE, CREDIT_LIMIT, SLSREP_NUMBER)

          FK   SLSREP_NUMBER --> SALES_REP

PART (<u>PART_NUMBER</u>, PART_DESCRIPTION, UNITS_ON_HAND, ITEM_CLASS,

          WAREHOUSE_NUMBER, UNIT_PRICE)

ORDERS (<u>ORDER_NUMBER</u>, ORDER_DATE, CUSTOMER_NUMBER)

          FK   CUSTOMER_NUMBER --> CUSTOMER

ORDER_LINE (<u>ORDER_NUMBER</u>, PART_NUMBER, NUMBER_ORDERED, QUOTED_PRICE)

          FK   ORDER_NUMBER --> ORDERS

          FK   PART_NUMBER --> PART

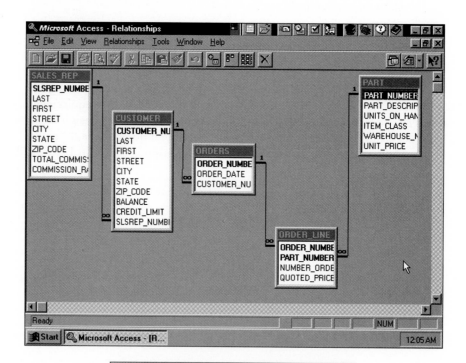

Figure 6.8 Final information-level design

Example 2:   You now will design a database for Henry. Henry wants to keep information on books, authors, publishers, and branches. The only user is Henry, but you don't want to treat the whole project as a single user view. Let's assume you've asked Henry for all the reports the system is to produce, and you will treat each one as a user view. Suppose Henry has given you the following requirements:

1. For each publisher, list the publisher code, the name, and the city in which the publisher is located.

2. For each branch, list the number, the name, the location, and the number of employees.

3. For each book, list its code, title, the code and name of the publisher, the price, and whether or not it is paperback.

4. For each book, list its code, title, and price. In addition, list the number and name of each of the authors of the book. (Note: If there is more than one author, they must be listed in the order in which they are listed on the book. This may or may not be alphabetically.)

5. For each branch, list the number and name. In addition, list the code and title of each book currently in the branch as well as the number of units of the book the branch currently has.

6. For each book, list the code and title. In addition, for each branch currently having the book in stock, list the number and name of each branch along with the number of copies available.

With these six reports as the user views, let's move on to the design of Henry's database.

1. The only entity in this user view is PUBLISHER. The table to support it is as follows:

PUBLISHER (<u>PUBLISHER CODE</u>, NAME, CITY)

This table is in 3NF. The primary key is Publisher Code. There are no alternate or foreign keys. Let's assume Henry wants to be able to access a publisher rapidly on the basis of its name. Then you will make Name a secondary key.

Because this is the first user view, there is no previous cumulative design. So at this point the new cumulative design will consist solely of the design for this user view. It is shown in Figure 6.9.

PUBLISHER (<u>PUBLISHER CODE</u>, NAME, CITY)

    SK   NAME

Figure 6.9 DBDL for BOOK database after first requirement

2. The only entity in this user view is BRANCH. The table to support it is as follows:

BRANCH (<u>BRANCH NUMBER</u>, NAME, LOCATION, NUMBER_EMPLOYEES)

This table is also in 3NF. The primary key is Branch Number, and there are no alternate or foreign keys. Let's assume Henry wants to be able to access a branch rapidly on the basis of its name. Thus you will make Name a secondary key.

Because no table in the cumulative design has Branch Number as its primary key, this table simply will be added to the collection of tables in the cumulative design during the merge step. The result is shown in Figure 6.10.

PUBLISHER (<u>PUBLISHER CODE</u>, NAME, CITY)

    SK NAME

BRANCH (<u>BRANCH NUMBER</u>, NAME, LOCATION, NUMBER_EMPLOYEES)

    SK NAME

Figure 6.10 DBDL for BOOK database after second requirement

3. There are two entities here, PUBLISHER and BOOK, and a one-to-many relationship between them. This leads to the following:

PUBLISHER (<u>PUBLISHER CODE</u>, NAME)

BOOK (<u>BOOK CODE</u>, TITLE, PUBLISHER_CODE, PAPERBACK)

where Publisher Code in BOOK is a foreign key identifying the publisher. Merging these tables with those that are already in place does not add any new attributes to the PUBLISHER table but adds the BOOK table to the cumulative design. The result of the merge is shown in Figure 6.11.

CHAPTER 6

PUBLISHER (<u>PUBLISHER_CODE</u>, NAME, CITY)

       SK   NAME

BRANCH (<u>BRANCH_NUMBER</u>, NAME, LOCATION, NUMBER_EMPLOYEES)

       SK   NAME

BOOK (<u>BOOK_CODE</u>, TITLE, PUBLISHER_CODE, PAPERBACK)

       FK   PUBLISHER_CODE --> PUBLISHER

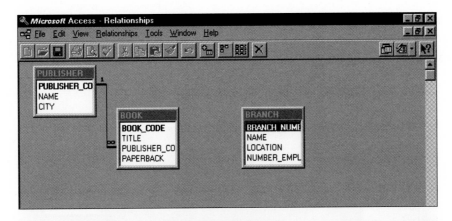

Figure 6.11 Cumulative design for BOOK database after third requirement

■ **4. There are two entities in this user view, BOOK and AUTHOR. The relationship between them is many-to-many (an author can write many books and a book can have many authors). Creating tables for each entity and the relationship gives:**

AUTHOR (<u>AUTHOR_NUMBER</u>, NAME)

BOOK (<u>BOOK_CODE</u>, TITLE, PRICE)

WROTE (<u>BOOK_CODE</u>, <u>AUTHOR_NUMBER</u>)

Because the last table represents the fact that an author *wrote* a particular book, you will call the table WROTE.

In this user view, you need to be able to list the authors for a book in the appropriate order. To accomplish this, you will add a sequence number column to the last table. This completes the tables for this user view, which are:

AUTHOR (<u>AUTHOR_NUMBER</u>, NAME)

BOOK (<u>BOOK_CODE</u>, TITLE, PRICE)

WROTE (<u>BOOK_CODE</u>, <u>AUTHOR_NUMBER</u>, SEQ_NUMBER)

The AUTHOR table is new. Merging the BOOK table adds an additional column: Price. The WROTE table is new. The result of the merge step is shown in Figure 6.12.

PUBLISHER (<u>PUBLISHER CODE</u>, NAME, CITY)

    SK   NAME

BRANCH (<u>BRANCH NUMBER</u>, NAME, LOCATION, NUMBER_EMPLOYEES)

    SK   NAME

BOOK (<u>BOOK CODE</u>, TITLE, PUBLISHER_CODE, PAPERBACK, PRICE)

    FK   PUBLISHER_CODE --> PUBLISHER

AUTHOR (<u>AUTHOR NUMBER</u>, NAME)

WROTE (<u>BOOK CODE</u>, <u>AUTHOR NUMBER</u>, SEQ_NUMBER)

    FK   BOOK_CODE --> BOOK

    FK   AUTHOR_NUMBER --> AUTHOR

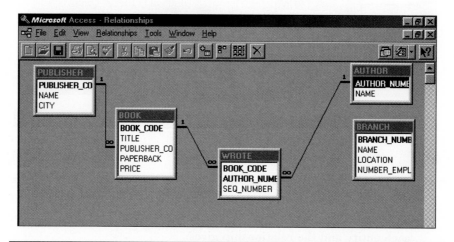

Figure 6.12 Cumulative design for BOOK database after fourth requirement

5. Suppose you were to decide that the only entity mentioned in this requirement was BRANCH. You then would create this table:

BRANCH (

You then would add Branch Number as the primary key, producing the following:

BRANCH (<u>BRANCH_NUMBER</u>,

The other properties include the branch name as well as the book code, book title, and number of units on hand. Because a branch will have several books, the last three columns will form a repeating group. You thus have the following:

BRANCH (<u>BRANCH_NUMBER</u>, NAME, (BOOK_CODE, TITLE, UNITS_ON_HAND))

You convert this table to 1NF by removing the repeating group and expanding the key. This gives:

BRANCH (<u>BRANCH_NUMBER</u>, NAME, <u>BOOK_CODE</u>, TITLE, UNITS_ON_HAND)

In this table, you have the following functional dependencies:

BRANCH_NUMBER --> NAME

BOOK_CODE --> TITLE

BRANCH_NUMBER, BOOK_CODE --> UNITS_ON_HAND

The table is not in 2NF, because some attributes depend on just a portion of the key. Converting to 2NF gives:

BRANCH (<u>BRANCH_NUMBER</u>, NAME)

BOOK (<u>BOOK_CODE</u>, TITLE)

INVENT (<u>BRANCH_NUMBER</u>, <u>BOOK_CODE</u>, UNITS_ON_HAND)

The primary keys are indicated. You call the final table INVENT, because it effectively represents each branch's inventory. In the INVENT table, Branch Number is a foreign key that identifies BRANCH, and Book Code is a foreign key that identifies BOOK. In other words, in order for a row to exist in the INVENT table, *both* the Branch Number *and* the Book Code already must be in the database.

The BRANCH table will merge with the existing BRANCH table without adding anything new. Similarly, the BOOK table will not add anything new to the existing BOOK table. The INVENT table is totally new and will appear as part of the new cumulative design, which is given in Figure 6.13.

PUBLISHER (<u>PUBLISHER_CODE</u>, NAME, CITY)

      SK   NAME

BRANCH (<u>BRANCH_NUMBER</u>, NAME, LOCATION, NUMBER_EMPLOYEES)

      SK   NAME

BOOK (<u>BOOK_CODE</u>, TITLE, PUBLISHER_CODE, PAPERBACK, PRICE)

      FK   PUBLISHER_CODE --> PUBLISHER

AUTHOR (<u>AUTHOR_NUMBER</u>, NAME)

WROTE (<u>BOOK_CODE</u>, <u>AUTHOR_NUMBER</u>, SEQ_NUMBER)

      FK   BOOK_CODE --> BOOK

      FK   AUTHOR_NUMBER --> AUTHOR

INVENT (<u>BRANCH_NUMBER</u>, <u>BOOK_CODE</u>, UNITS_ON_HAND)

      FK   BRANCH_NUMBER --> BRANCH

      FK   BOOK_CODE --> BOOK

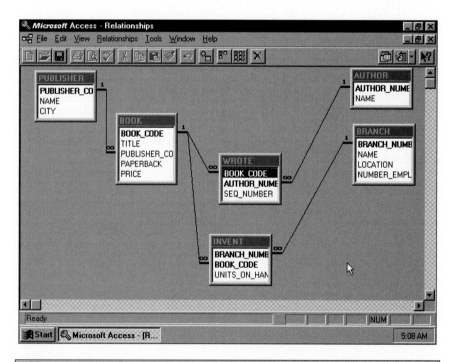

Figure 6.13 Cumulative design for BOOK database after fifth requirement

Question:	How would the design for this user view have turned out if you had started with two entities, BRANCH and BOOK, instead of just the single entity BRANCH?
Answer:	In the first step, you would have these two tables:

    BRANCH (

    BOOK (

Adding the primary keys would give:

BRANCH (<u>BRANCH NUMBER</u>,

BOOK (<u>BOOK CODE</u>,

Filling in the other attributes would give:

BRANCH (<u>BRANCH NUMBER</u>, NAME)

BOOK (BOOK_CODE, TITLE)

Finally, you have to implement the relationship between BRANCH and BOOK. Because a branch can have many books and a book can be in stock at many branches, the relationship is many-to-many. To implement a many-to-many relationship, you add a new table whose primary key is the combination of the primary keys of the other tables. Doing this, you produce the following:

BRANCH (<u>BRANCH NUMBER</u>, NAME)

BOOK (<u>BOOK CODE</u>, TITLE)

INVENT (<u>BRANCH NUMBER</u>, <u>BOOK CODE</u>)

Finally, you add any column that depends on both Branch Number and Book Code to the INVENT table, giving:

BRANCH (<u>BRANCH NUMBER</u>, NAME)

BOOK (<u>BOOK CODE</u>, TITLE)

INVENT (<u>BRANCH NUMBER</u>, <u>BOOK CODE</u>, UNITS_ON_HAND)

Thus you end up with exactly the same collection of tables, which illustrates a point made earlier: there's more than one way of arriving at a correct result.

    ■ **6. This user view leads to precisely the same set of tables that was created for User view 5.**

You now have reached the end of the requirements, and the design shown in Figure 6.13 represents the complete information-level design. You should take a moment to review each of the requirements to make sure they all can be satisfied.

> | | If you compare this design with the BOOK database earlier in the text, you will see a slight difference in the order of some of the columns. In theory it doesn't make any difference. In practice, however, you sometimes rearrange the columns when you are done for convenience. If, for example, you execute an SQL **SELECT** using the asterisk (*), you will see the columns *in the order in which they occur in the table*. Thus, if you have a particular order you prefer, you often will be sure the columns occur in that order.
> | **Note** |

PHYSICAL LEVEL DESIGN

Once the information-level design is complete, you are ready to begin producing the specific design that will be implemented with some typical microcomputer DBMS. This is part of the overall process called physical-level design.

Because most microcomputer DBMSs are relational (at least they claim to be), and because your final information-level design is presented in a relational format, the basic job of producing the design for the chosen DBMS is not difficult. You simply use the same tables and columns. (At this point, you do need to supply format details, of course, like the fact that Customer Number is a character field, three positions in length, but again, this is not difficult.)

Many database management systems support primary, candidate, secondary, and foreign keys. If you are using such systems, you simply use these features to implement the various types of keys that are listed in the final DBDL version of the information-level design.

Unfortunately, there are systems that don't support all these types of keys. If you are using one of these, you need to devise a scheme for handling these keys. Such a scheme must ensure the uniqueness of primary and candidate keys. It must ensure that values in the foreign keys are legitimate; in other words, that they match the value of the primary key on some row in another table. As far as secondary keys are concerned, you merely need to ensure the efficiency of access to rows on the basis of a value of the secondary key.

For instance, suppose you are implementing the EMPLOYEE table shown in Figure 6.1a, in which Employee Number is the primary key, Soc Sec Numb is an alternate key, Last is a secondary key, and Dept Number is a foreign key that matches the DEPT table. You will have to ensure that the following conditions hold true:

1. Employee numbers are unique.

2. Social security numbers are unique.

3. Access to an employee on the basis of his or her last name is rapid. (This restriction differs in that it merely states that a certain type of activity must be efficient, but it is an important restriction nonetheless.)

4. Department numbers are valid; that is, they match the number of a department currently in the database.

The next question is, Who should enforce these restrictions? Two choices are possible, provided the DBMS can't do it. Either the users of the system or programmers could enforce them. In the case of users, they would have to be careful when entering data not to enter two employees with the same Employee Number, not to enter an employee whose department number was invalid, and so on. Clearly, this would put a tremendous burden on the user.

Provided the DBMS can't enforce the restrictions, the appropriate place for the enforcement to take place is in programs. Thus, the burden of responsibility for this enforcement should fall on the programmers who write the programs that users will run to update the database. Incidentally, users *must* update the data through these programs and *not* through the built-in features of the DBMS in such circumstances; otherwise, they would be able to bypass all the controls that you are attempting to program into the system.

Thus, it is the responsibility of programmers to include logic in their programs to enforce all the constraints. With respect to the DBDL shown in Figure 6.1a, this means the following:

1. Before an employee is added, the program should determine three things:

    a. whether an employee with the same Employee Number is already in the database, and if so, the update should be rejected;

    b. whether an employee with the same social security number is already in the database, and if so, the update should be rejected; and

    c. whether the department number that was entered matches the number of a department that is already in the database, and if it doesn't, the update should be rejected.

2. When an employee is changed, if the department number is one of the values that is changed, the program should check to make sure that the new number also matches the number of a department that is already in the database. If it doesn't, the update should be rejected.

3. When a department is deleted, the program should check to make sure that the database contains no employees for this department. If the department does contain employees and it is allowed to be deleted, these employees will have department numbers that no longer are valid. In that case, the update should be rejected.

These actions must be performed efficiently, and in most systems this means creating and using indexes on all key columns. Thus, an index will be created for each column (or combination of columns) that is a primary key, a candidate key, a secondary key, or a foreign key.

SUMMARY

1. Database design is the process of determining an appropriate database structure to satisfy a given set of requirements. It is a two part process:

   a. The information-level design, wherein a clean DBMS-independent design is created to satisfy the requirements.

   b. The physical-level design, wherein the final information-level design is converted into an appropriate design for the particular DBMS that will be used.

2. A user view is the view of data necessary to support the operations of a particular user. In order to simplify the design process, the overall set of requirements is split into user views.

3. The information-level design methodology involves applying the following steps to each user view:

   a. Represent the user view as a collection of tables.

   b. Normalize these tables; that is, convert this collection into an equivalent collection that is in 3NF.

   c. Represent all keys: primary, alternate, secondary, and foreign.

   d. Merge the results of the previous step into the cumulative design.

4. The design is represented in a language called DBDL (Database Design Language).

5. To obtain a pictorial representation of a design, apply the following steps to the DBDL design:

   a. Create a rectangle for each table in the DBDL design.

   b. For each foreign key, create an arrow that (1) begins with the rectangle that corresponds to the table identified by the foreign key and (2) terminates at the rectangle that corresponds to the table containing the foreign key. The foreign key then may be removed, although it is not essential to do so.

6. Assuming that a relational or relational-like microcomputer DBMS is going to be used, the physical-level design process consists of creating a table for each table in the DBDL design. Any constraints (primary key, alternate key, or foreign key) that the DBMS cannot enforce must be enforced by the programs in the system, so this fact must be documented for the programmers.

KEY TERMS

Alternate key

Database design

Database Design Language (DBDL)

Foreign key

Information-level design

Many-to-many

One-to-many

One-to-one

Physical-level design

Primary key

Referential integrity

Relationship

Secondary key

User view

REVIEW QUESTIONS

1. Define the term "user view" as it applies to database design.

2. What is the purpose of breaking down the overall design problem into a consideration of individual user views?

3. Under what circumstances would you not have to break down the overall design into a consideration of individual user views?

4. The information-level design methodology presented contains a number of steps that are to be repeated for each user view. List the steps and briefly describe the kinds of activities that must take place at each step.

5. Describe the function of each of the following types of keys: primary, alternate, secondary, and foreign.

6. Describe the process of mapping an information-level design to a design for a relational model system.

7. Suppose a given user view contains information about employees and projects. Suppose further that each employee has a unique Employee Number and that each project has a unique Project Number. Explain

how you would implement the relationship between employees and projects in each of the following scenarios:

    a.   Many employees can work on a given project, but each employee can work on only a single project.

    b.   An employee can work on many projects but each project has a unique employee assigned to it.

    c.   An employee can work on many projects, and a project can be worked on by many employees.

8.   A database at a college is required to support the following requirements:

    a.   For a department, store its number and name.

    b.   For an advisor, store his or her number and name and the number of the department to which he or she is assigned.

    c.   For a course, store its code and description (i.e., MTH110, ALGEBRA).

    d.   For a student, store his or her number and name. For each course the student has taken, store the course code, the course description, and the grade received. Also, store the number and name of the student's advisor. Assume that an advisor may advise any number of students but that each student has just one advisor.

Complete the information-level design for this set of requirements. Use your own experience to determine any constraints you need that are not stated in the problem. Represent the answer in DBDL.

9.   List the changes that would need to be made in your answer to Review Question 8 if a student could have more than one advisor.

10. Suppose in addition to the requirements specified in Review Question 8, you must store the number of the department in which the student is majoring. Indicate the changes this would cause in the design in these two situations:

    a.   The student must be assigned an advisor who is in the department in which the student is majoring.

    b.   The student's advisor does not necessarily have to be in the department in which the student is majoring.

11. Illustrate mapping to the relational model by means of the design shown in Figure 6.13. List the relations. Identify the keys. List the special restrictions that programs will have to enforce.

12. In Example 2 of the Database Design section, the claim was made that User view 6 led to the same set of tables that had been created for User view 5. Show that this is true.

CHAPTER **7**

Functions of a
Database Management System

OBJECTIVES

1. Discuss the following nine functions, or services, that should be provided by

    a DBMS:

    a. data storage, retrieval, and update

    b. a user-accessible catalog

    c. support for shared update

    d. backup and recovery services

    e. security services

    f. integrity services

    g. services to promote data independence

    h. support for replication

    i. utility services

2. Discuss the manner in which these services typically are provided.

INTRODUCTION

A good DBMS should furnish a number of capabilities. As you might expect, the list of features that a full-scale mainframe DBMS could provide would be more extensive than a comparable list for microcomputer systems. Moreover, mainframe systems often furnish these features in a more sophisticated fashion. In this text, you will learn about these features on microcomputer systems. The list of features that a microcomputer DBMS should furnish includes the following:

1. **Data storage, retrieval, and update**: the capability to store, retrieve, and update the data in the database.

2. A user-accessible **catalog**: where descriptions of data items are stored and are accessible to users.

3. Support for **shared update**: a mechanism to ensure accuracy when several users are updating the database at the same time.

4. **Backup** and **recovery** services: a mechanism for recovering the database in the event the database is damaged in any way.

5. **Security** services: a mechanism to ensure that only authorized users can access the database.

6. **Integrity** services: a mechanism to ensure that certain rules are followed with regard to data in the database and with any changes that are made in the data.

7. Services to promote **data independence**: facilities to support the independence of programs from the structure of the database.

8. **Replication** support: a facility to manage copies of the same data at multiple locations.

9. **Utility services**: DBMS-provided services that assist in the general maintenance of the database.

The preceding list is summarized in Figure 7.1.

■ ■ ■ ■ ■

DATA STORAGE, RETRIEVAL, AND UPDATE

A DBMS must furnish users with the capability to store, retrieve, and update the data that is in the database.

This statement about storage and retrieval almost goes without saying. It defines the fundamental capability of a DBMS. Unless a DBMS provides this facility, further discussion of what a DBMS can do is irrelevant. In storing, updating, and retrieving data, it should not be incumbent upon the user to be aware of the system's internal structures or the procedures used to manipulate these structures. This manipulation is strictly the responsibility of the DBMS.

Functions of a DBMS

1.	Data storage, retrieval, and update
2.	A user-accessible catalog
3.	Shared update support
4.	Backup and recovery services
5.	Security services
6.	Integrity services
7.	Data independence support
8.	Replication support
9.	Utility services

Figure 7.1 Functions of a DBMS

CATALOG

A DBMS must furnish a **catalog** where descriptions of data items are stored and are accessible to users.

This catalog contains crucial information for those who are in charge of a database or who are going to write programs to access a database. Such persons must be able to determine easily what the database "looks like." Specifically, they need to be able to get quick answers to questions like the following:

1. What tables and fields are included in the current structure? What are their names?

2. What are the characteristics of these fields? For example, is the Street field within the Customer table 20 characters long or 30? Is the Customer Number field a numeric field or is it a character field? How many decimal places are in the Unit Price field in the PART table?

3. What are the possible values for the various fields? Are there any restrictions on the possibilities for the Credit Limit field, for example?

4. What is the meaning of the various fields? For example, what exactly is the Item Class field and what does Item Class HW mean?

5. What relationships are present? What is the meaning of each relationship? Must the relationship always exist? For example, must a customer always have a sales rep?

6. Which programs within the system access which data within the database? How do they access it? Do they merely retrieve the data, or do they update it? What kinds of updates do they do? Can a certain program add a new customer, for example, or can it merely make changes regarding information about customers whose names are already in the database? When it makes a change with regards to a customer, can it change all the fields or only the address?

Mainframe DBMSs often are accompanied by a separate entity called a **data dictionary**, which contains answers to all of the above questions and more. The data dictionary forms a sort of super catalog. Microcomputer DBMSs typically are not accompanied by such a comprehensive tool, but they often have built-in capabilities that furnish answers to at least some of these questions. At a minimum, the capabilities they furnish would allow you to obtain the answers to Questions 1 through 5 in the preceding list.

SHARED UPDATE

A DBMS must furnish a mechanism to ensure accuracy when several users are updating the database at the same time.

Microcomputer databases often are used just by one person at one machine. Sometimes several people may be allowed to update a database, but only one person at a time. For example, several people might take turns with one microcomputer to access the database. The advent of microcomputer networks and microcomputer DBMSs that were capable of running on these networks and of allowing several users to access the same database gave rise to a problem that had been a headache to mainframe database management for years: shared update.

Shared update means that two or more users are involved in making updates to the database at the same time. On the surface, it might seem that shared update wouldn't present any problem. Why couldn't two, three, or fifty, for that matter, users update the database simultaneously without incurring a problem?

The Problem

To illustrate the problems involved in shared update, let's assume that there are two users, Ryan and Elena, who both work for Premiere Products. Ryan currently is accessing the database to process orders and, among other things, to increase customers' balances by the amount of the orders. Let's say that Ryan is going to increase the balance of Customer 124 (Sally Adams) by $100.00. Elena, on the other hand, is accessing the database to post payments and, among other things, to decrease customers' balances by the amount of the payments. As it happens, Customer 124 has just made a $100.00 payment, so Elena will decrease her balance by $100.00. The balance of Customer 124 was $418.75 prior to the start of Ryan and Elena's activity and, because the amount of the increase exactly matches the amount of the decrease, the balance still should be $418.75 after the activity has been completed. But will it? That depends.

How exactly does Ryan make the required update? First, the data concerning Customer 124 is read from the database into Ryan's work area in memory (RAM). Second, any changes are made in the data in his work area in memory; in this case, $100.00 is added to the current balance of $418.75, bringing the balance to $518.75. This change has *not* yet taken place in the database, but rather *only* in Ryan's work area in memory. Finally, the information is written to the database and the change now is made in the database itself (Figure 7.2).

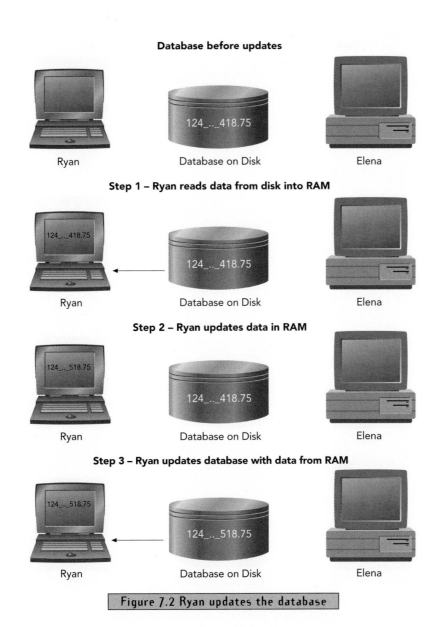

Database before updates

Ryan   Database on Disk   Elena

124_.._418.75

Step 1 – Ryan reads data from disk into RAM

124_.._418.75

Ryan   Database on Disk   Elena

124_.._418.75

Step 2 – Ryan updates data in RAM

124_.._518.75

Ryan   Database on Disk   Elena

124_.._418.75

Step 3 – Ryan updates database with data from RAM

124_.._518.75

Ryan   Database on Disk   Elena

124_.._518.75

Figure 7.2 Ryan updates the database

Suppose Elena begins her update at this point. The data for Customer 124 will be read from the database, including the new balance of $518.75. The amount of the payment, $100.00, then will be subtracted from the balance, thus giving a balance of $418.75 *in Elena's work area in memory*. Finally, this new information is written to the database, and the balance for Customer Number 124 is what it should be (Figure 7.3).

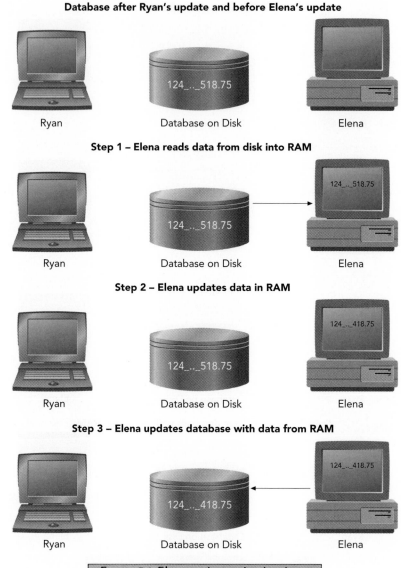

Database after Ryan's update and before Elena's update

Ryan   Database on Disk   Elena

Step 1 – Elena reads data from disk into RAM

Ryan   Database on Disk   Elena

Step 2 – Elena updates data in RAM

Ryan   Database on Disk   Elena

Step 3 – Elena updates database with data from RAM

Ryan   Database on Disk   Elena

Figure 7.3 Elena updates the database

In the preceding scenario, things worked out correctly. But they don't always. Do you see how things could happen in a way that would lead to an incorrect result? What if the scenario shown in Figure 7.4 had occurred instead? Here, Ryan reads the data from the database into his work area in memory, and at about the same time, Elena reads the data from the database into her work area in memory. At this point, both Ryan and Elena have the correct data for Customer 124, including a balance of $418.75. Ryan adds $100.00 to the balance in his work area, and Elena subtracts $100.00 from the balance in her work area. At this point, in Ryan's work area in memory the balance reads $518.75, while in Elena's work area in memory it reads $318.75. Ryan now writes to the database. At this moment, Customer 124 has a balance of $518.75 in the database. Then Elena writes to the database. Now the balance for Customer 124 in the database is **$318.75**! (This is a very good deal for Sally

Adams, but not so for Premiere Products.) Had the updates taken place in the reverse order, the final balance would have been $518.75. In either case, you now have incorrect data in your database (one of the updates has been *lost*). This cannot be permitted to happen.

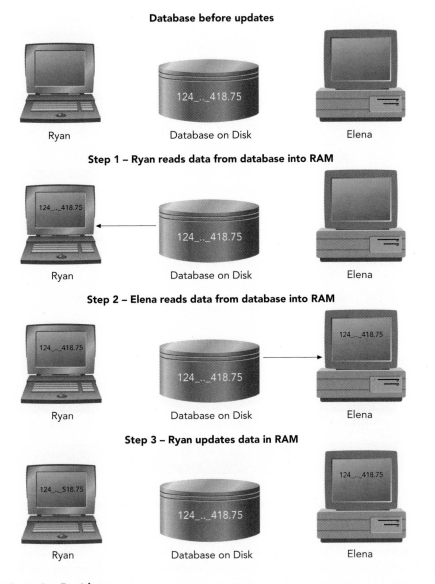

Database before updates

Ryan   Database on Disk   Elena

Step 1 – Ryan reads data from database into RAM

Ryan   Database on Disk   Elena

Step 2 – Elena reads data from database into RAM

Ryan   Database on Disk   Elena

Step 3 – Ryan updates data in RAM

Ryan   Database on Disk   Elena

Avoiding the Problem

One way to prevent this situation from occurring is to prohibit shared update. This may seem drastic, but it is not really so far-fetched. You could permit several users to access the database at the same time, but for *retrieval* only; that is, they would be able to read information *from* the database but they would not be able to write anything *to* the database. When these users entered some kind of transaction to update the database (like posting a payment), the database itself would not be updated. Instead, a record would be placed in a separate file of transactions. A record in this file might indicate, for example, that $100.00 had been received from Customer 124 on a certain date. Periodically, a single update program would read the *batch* of records in this transaction file and perform the appropriate updates to the database; this processing technique is called **batch processing**. Because this program would be the only one to update the database, you would eliminate the problems associated with shared update.

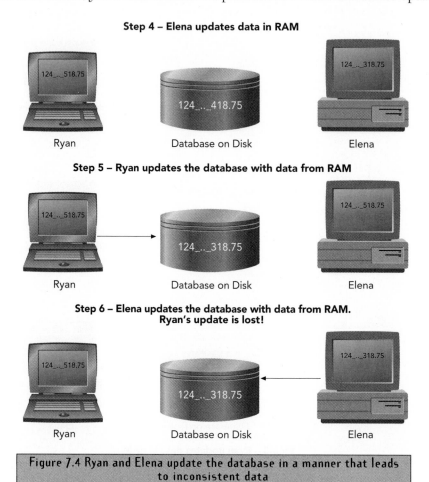

Step 4 – Elena updates data in RAM

Ryan   Database on Disk   Elena

Step 5 – Ryan updates the database with data from RAM

Ryan   Database on Disk   Elena

Step 6 – Elena updates the database with data from RAM. Ryan's update is lost!

Ryan   Database on Disk   Elena

Figure 7.4 Ryan and Elena update the database in a manner that leads to inconsistent data

While this approach would avoid one set of problems, it would create another. From the time users started updating, that is, placing records in the update files, until the time the batch-processing program actually ran, the data in the database would be out of date. Where a customer's balance in the database was $49.50, it actually would be $649.50 if a transaction had been entered that increased it by $600.00. If the customer in question had an $800 credit limit, he or she should be prohibited from charging, say, a $200 item. But according to the data currently in the database, this would not be so. On the contrary — the data in the database would indicate that this customer still had $750.50 of available credit ($800 minus $49.50). In a situation that requires the data in the database to be current, this scheme for avoiding the problems of shared update will not work.

Locking

Assuming you cannot solve the shared update problem by avoiding it, you need a mechanism for dealing with the problem. You need to be able to keep Elena from even beginning the update on Customer 124 until Ryan has completed his update, or vice versa. This can be accomplished by some kind of **locking** scheme. Suppose once Ryan had read the row for Customer 124, it became locked so that no other user could access it, and it remained locked until Ryan had completed the update. For the duration of the lock, any attempt by Elena to read the row would be rejected, and she would be notified that the row was locked. If she chose to do so, she could keep attempting to read the row until it was no longer locked, at which time her update could be completed. This scenario is demonstrated in Figure 7.5. In at least this simple case, the problem of a "lost update" seems to have been solved.

Database before updates

Step 1 – Ryan reads data from database into RAM and locks record

Step 2 – Elena tries to read data from database into RAM and fails

Step 3 – Ryan updates data in RAM; Elena again tries to read data from the database and again fails

Figure 7.5 Ryan and Elena update the database; locking prevents inconsistent data

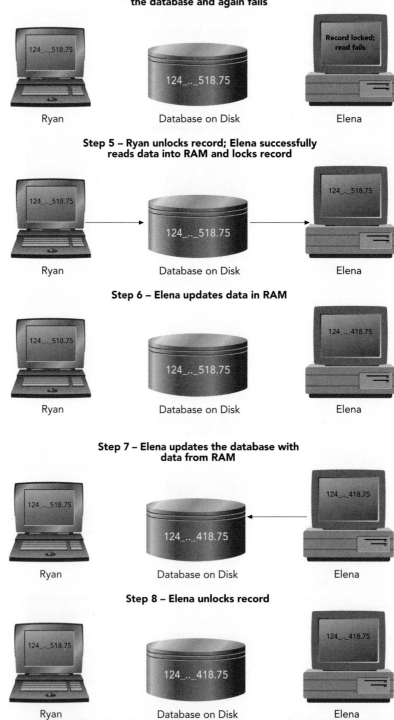

Figure 7.5 Ryan and Elena update the database; locking prevents inconsistent data (cont)

Duration of Locks

How long should a lock be held? If the update involves just changing some values in a single row in a single table (like changing the name of a customer), the lock no longer is necessary once this row has been updated. Sometimes, however, the situation is more involved.

Consider, for example, the process of filling an order. To a user sitting at a workstation, this may seem to involve a single action. A user merely might indicate that an order currently in the database now needs to be filled. Or he or she also may be required to enter certain data on the order. In either case, however, the process still feels like a single action to the user. Behind the scenes, though, lots of activity might be taking place. You might have to update the Units On Hand field in the PART table for each ordered part in order to reflect the number of units of those parts that were shipped and that are consequently no longer on hand. You also might have to update the Balance field in the CUSTOMER table for the customer who placed the order, increasing it by the total amount of the order. Or you might have to update the Total Commission field in the SALES REP table for the sales rep who represents this customer, increasing it by the amount of commission generated by the order.

In circumstances like these, where a single action on the part of a user necessitates several updates in the database, what do you do about locks? How long do you hold each one? For safety's sake, locks should be held until all the required updates have been completed.

Deadlock

Users can hold more than one lock at a time and this may give rise to another potential problem. Let's suppose Elena has locked the row for Customer 124 and is attempting to lock the row for Part BT04. Let's also suppose Ryan already has Part BT04 locked so Elena must wait for him to unlock it. Before Ryan unlocks Part BT04 though, he needs to update, and thus lock, the row for Customer 124, which currently is locked by—you guessed it—Elena. Elena is waiting for Ryan to act (release the lock for Part BT04), while Ryan, on the other hand, is waiting for Elena to act (release the lock for Customer 124). Without the aid of some outside intervention, this dilemma could be prolonged indefinitely. Terms used to describe such situations are **deadlock** and **deadly embrace**. Obviously, some strategy is necessary either to prevent or handle deadlock.

Locking on Microcomputer DBMSs

Mainframe DBMSs typically offer sophisticated schemes for locking as well as for detecting and handling deadlocks. Microcomputer DBMSs provide facilities for the same purposes, but they usually are much more limited than the facilities provided by mainframe DBMSs. These limitations, in turn, put an additional burden on the programmers who write the programs that allow several users to update the same database simultaneously.

Although the exact features for handling these problems vary from one microcomputer DBMS to another, the following list is fairly typical of the types of facilities provided:

1. Programs can lock a whole table or an individual row within a table, but only one or the other. As long as one program has a row or table locked, no other program may access that row or table.

2. Programs can release any or all of the locks they currently hold.

3. Programs can inquire whether a given row or table is locked.

This list, although it is short, comprises the complete set of facilities provided by many systems. Consequently, the following guidelines have been devised for writing programs for a shared-update environment:

1. If more than one row in the same table must be locked during an update, the whole table must be locked.

2. When a program attempts to read a row that is locked, it may wait a short period of time and then try to read the row again. This process could continue until the row becomes unlocked. It usually is preferable, however, to impose a limit on the number of times a program may attempt to read the row. In this case, reading is done in a loop, which proceeds until either (a) the read is successful, or (b) the maximum number of times that the program can repeat the operation is reached. Programs vary in terms of what action is taken should the loop be terminated without the read being successful. One possibility is to notify the user of the problem and let him or her decide whether to try the same update again or move on to something else.

3. Because there is no facility to *detect and handle* deadlocks, you must try to *prevent* them. A common approach to this problem is for every program in the system to attempt to lock all the rows and/or tables it needs before beginning an update. Assuming it is successful in this attempt, each program then can perform the required updates. If any row or table that the program needs already is locked, it immediately should release *all* the locks that it currently holds, wait some specified period of time, and then try the entire process again. In some cases, it may be better to notify the user of the problem and see whether the user wants to try again. In effect, this means that any program that encounters a problem immediately will get out of the way of all the other programs, rather than be involved in a deadlock situation.

4. Because locks prevent other users from accessing a portion of the database, it is important that no user keeps rows or tables locked any longer than necessary. This is especially significant for online update programs. Suppose, for example, a user is employing some online update program to update customers. Suppose further that once the user enters the number of the customer to be updated, the customer row is locked and remains locked until the user has entered all new data and the update has taken place. What if the user is interrupted by a phone call before he or she has completed filling in the new data? What if the user goes to lunch? The row might remain locked for an extended period of time. If the update involves several rows, all of which must be locked, the problem becomes that much worse. In fact, in many microcomputer DBMSs, if more than one row from the same table must be locked, the whole table must be locked, which means that whole tables may be locked for extended periods of time. Clearly, this cannot be permitted to occur.

The trick here is for programs to read the information they need at the beginning of the update and then immediately *release all locks*. After the user has entered all the new data, the update takes place as described earlier; that is, attempt to lock all required rows, proceed with the update if successful, and release all locks if not successful. This does pose a problem, however. Suppose your program read the data for Customer Number 124 and then released its lock on this customer while the user of your program was filling in new data on the screen. What if a user of another program updated Customer 124 in the meantime and the update was completed before your user finished filling in the new data? If your user then were to finish filling in the new data and your program blindly went ahead to update the row for Customer 124 with this new data, the other user's update would be lost, that is, overwritten with your user's data. So, your program should take a further precautionary step. Before blindly updating the database with your user's data, your program should make sure that nobody else has updated the data in the meantime. If someone has, your program cannot update the database with your user's data; instead, your user must be informed of the situation and permitted to decide whether he or she wants to redo the update or move on to something else.

How will your program know whether or not some other user has updated the row for Customer 124? Several methods can be used to provide the answer. One is to include an additional field in each record, perhaps a three-digit number called Update Counter. Every time any program updates a row in any way, it also should update the value in this field by adding 1 to it. (If the previous value was 999, the new value produced by adding one to the old value would be too big for the field. In such a case, the program updating the row would have to set the update count back to zero.) Assuming that every program in the system were to adhere to this approach, you could utilize the following logic:

1. Read all the data from the row for Customer Number 124, including the value of Update Counter. (Let's assume for the purposes of this example that the value is 478.) Store this value in some variable for future reference. Unlock the row.

2. Get all the new data from the user.

3. When it is time to do the update, lock the row for Customer Number 124, read the current data, and examine the value of Update Counter. If it is still the same (in this case, 478), the row has not been updated and you can finish your update. If it is different (479 or 480, for example), you know that at least one other program has updated the data in the meantime and you cannot complete your update.

4. If you have to lock multiple rows, the same procedure is followed for each one; that is, for each of the rows involved, store its update count in some variable. When it is time to do the update, lock all the rows, read each row's update count, and compare it with the count you have stored. If the counts *all* agree, you can perform the update. If one or more counts don't agree, the update cannot take place.

Two crucial points arise from the preceding discussion. First, the logic to support shared update certainly adds a fair amount of complexity to each of the programs in the system. Second, cooperation among programs is essential. Every program must do its job. If one program doesn't update the Update Counter field, for example, another program may assume that a row has not been updated when, in fact, it has been. If a program doesn't release all its locks when it encounters a row or table it needs that is locked by some other program, the possibility of deadlock arises. If a program does not release its locks while its user is entering data on the screen, the performance of the whole system may suffer.

One naturally might ask at this point, Is it worth it? Is the ability to have several users updating the database simultaneously worth the complexity that it adds to every program in the system? In some cases, the answer will be no.

Shared update may be far from a necessity. In other cases, however, shared update will be necessary to the productivity of the users of the system. In these cases, implementation either of the ideas discussed or of some similar scheme is essential to the proper performance of the system.

BACKUP AND RECOVERY

A DBMS must furnish a mechanism for recovering the database in the event the database is damaged in any way.

A database can be damaged or destroyed in a number of ways. Users can enter data that is incorrect; programs that are updating the database can end abnormally during an update; a hardware problem can occur; and so on. After any such event has occurred, the database may contain invalid data. It even may have been totally destroyed.

Obviously, a situation in which data has been damaged or destroyed cannot be allowed to go uncorrected. The database must be returned to a correct state. This process is called **recovery**; that is, you say that you **recover** the database. In situations where indexes or other physical structures in the database have been damaged but the data has not, many DBMSs provide a feature you can use to repair the database automatically to recover it.

If the data in a database has been damaged, the simplest approach to recovery involves periodically making a copy of the database (called a **backup** or a **save**). If a problem occurs, the database is recovered by copying this backup copy over it. In effect, the damage is undone by returning the database to the state it was in when the last backup was made.

Unfortunately, other activity besides that which caused the destruction also is undone. Suppose the database is backed up at 10:00 P.M. and users begin updating it at 8:00 A.M. the next morning. Suppose further that at 11:30 A.M. something happens that destroys the database. If the previous night's backup is used to recover the database, the *entire* database is returned to the state it was in at 10:00 P.M. the previous night. *All* updates made in the morning are lost, not just the update or updates that were in progress at the time the problem occurred. This would mean that during the final part of the recovery process, users would have to redo all the work they had done since 8:00 A.M.

As you might expect, mainframe DBMSs provide sophisticated facilities to avoid the costly and time-consuming process of having users redo their work. These facilities maintain a record, which is called a **journal** or **log**, of all updates to the database.

Such features generally are not available at this time on microcomputer DBMSs. Most of them furnish users with a simple way to make backup copies and to recover the database later by copying the backup over the database; but this is all they furnish in this regard.

Given this state of affairs, how should you handle backup and recovery in any application system you develop with a microcomputer DBMS? You simply could use the features of the DBMS to periodically make backup copies, and use the most recent backup if a recovery were necessary. The more crucial it is to avoid redoing work, the more often you would make backup copies. For example, if a backup were made every eight hours, you might have to redo up to eight hours of work. If one were made every two hours, on the other hand, at most two hours of work would have to be redone.

In many situations, this approach, although not particularly desirable, is acceptable. For some systems, however, it is not. In such cases, the necessary recovery features that are not supplied by the DBMS must be included in the application programs. Each of the programs that update the database, for example, also could write a record to a separate file, the journal, indicating the update that had taken place. A separate program could be written that would look at this file and recreate all of the updates indicated by the records in the file. The recovery process would then consist of (a) copying the backup over the actual database, and (b) running this special program.

While this approach does simplify the recovery process for the users of the system, it also causes some problems. First, each of the programs in the system becomes more complicated because of the extra logic involved in adding records to the special file. Second, a separate program to update the database with the information in this file must be written. Finally, every time a user completes an update, the system now has extra work to do, and this additional processing may slow down the system to an unacceptable pace. Thus, in any application, you must determine whether the ease of recovery furnished by this approach is worth the price you may have to pay for it. The answer will vary from one system to another.

SECURITY

A DBMS must furnish a mechanism that restricts access to the database to authorized users.

The term **security** refers to the protection of the database against unauthorized (or even illegal) access, either intentional or accidental. The more common features used by microcomputer DBMSs to provide for security are passwords and encryption.

Passwords

Many microcomputer DBMSs furnish sophisticated schemes whereby system administrators can assign **passwords**. Each password may be associated with a list of actions that the user who furnishes it is permitted to take. A user who furnished the password XY1JE, for example, might be allowed to view and alter any customer data, whereas another user who furnished the password GS36Y might be permitted to view and alter a customer's name or address, view but not alter a customer's credit limit, and not even view a customer's balance.

Encryption

Encryption refers to the storing of the data in the database in an encrypted format. Any time a user stores or modifies data in the database, the DBMS will encrypt the data before actually updating the database. Before a legitimate user retrieves the data via the DBMS, the data will be decrypted. The whole encryption process is transparent to a legitimate user; that is, he or she is not even aware it is happening. If an unauthorized user attempts to bypass all the controls of the DBMS and get to the database directly, however, he or she will be able to see only the encrypted version of the data.

Views

If a DBMS provides a facility that allows various users to have their own **views** of a database, this can be used for security purposes. Tables or fields to which the user does not have access in his or her view effectively do not exist for that user.

INTEGRITY

A DBMS must furnish a mechanism to ensure that both the data in the database and changes in the data follow certain rules.

In any database, there will be conditions, called **integrity constraints**, that must be satisfied by the data within the database. The types of constraints that may be present fall into the following four categories:

1. Data type. The data entered for any field should be consistent with the data type for that field. For a numeric field, only numbers should be allowed to be entered. If the field is a date, only a legitimate date should be permitted. For instance, February 30, 1999 would be an illegitimate date that should be rejected by the DBMS.

2. Legal values. It may be that for certain fields, not every possible value that is of the right type is legitimate. For example, even though Credit Limit is a numeric field, only the values 750, 1,000, 1,500, and 2,000 may be valid. It may be that only numbers between 2.00 and 800.00 are legal values for the Unit Price field.

3. Format. It may be that certain fields have a very special format that must be followed. Even though the Part Number field is a character field, for example, only specially formatted strings of characters may be acceptable. Legitimate part numbers may have to consist of two letters followed by a hyphen, followed by a three-digit number. This is an example of a format constraint.

4. Key constraints. There are two types of key constraints: primary key constraints and foreign key constraints. **Primary key constraints** enforce the uniqueness of the primary key. For example, forbidding the addition of a sales rep whose number matched the number of a sales rep already in the database would be a primary key constraint. **Foreign key constraints** enforce the fact that a value for a foreign key must match the value of the primary key for some row in another table. Forbidding the addition of a customer whose sales rep was not already in the database would be an example of a foreign key constraint.

An integrity constraint can be treated in one of four ways:

1. The constraint can be ignored, in which case, no attempt is made to enforce the constraint.

2. The burden of enforcing the constraint can be placed on the users of the system. This means that users must be careful that any changes they make in the database do not violate the constraint.

3. The burden can be placed on programmers. Logic to enforce the constraint then is built into programs. Users must update the database only by means of these programs and not through any of the built-in entry facilities provided by the DBMS, because these would allow violation of the constraint. The programs are designed to reject any attempt on the part of the user to update the database in such a way that the constraint is violated.

4. The burden can be placed on the DBMS. The constraint is specified to the DBMS, which then rejects any attempt to update the database in such a way that the constraint is violated.

Question	Which of these approaches is best?

Answer

The fourth approach. Here is why.

The first approach is undesirable, because it can lead to invalid data in the database (two customers with the same number, part numbers with an invalid format, illegal credit limits, and so on).

The second approach is a little better, because at least an attempt is made to enforce the constraints. It puts the burden of enforcement, however, on the user. Not only does this mean extra work for the user, but any mistake on the part of a single user, no matter how innocent, can lead to invalid data in the database.

The third approach removes the burden of enforcement from the user and places it on the programmers. This is better still, because it means that users will be unable to violate the constraints. The disadvantage is that all of the update programs in the system are made more complex. This complexity makes the programmers less productive and makes the programs more difficult to create and modify. It also makes changing an integrity constraint more difficult, because this may mean changing all the programs that update the database. Further, any program in which the logic that is used to enforce the constraints is faulty could permit some constraint to be violated *without your even being aware that this had happened* until some problem that occurred at a later date brought it to your attention. Finally, you would have to guard carefully against a user bypassing the programs in the system in order to enter data directly into the database (for example, by using some built-in facility of the DBMS). If this should happen, all controls you had so diligently placed into your programs would be helpless to prevent a violation of the constraints.

The best approach is the one in which you put the burden on the DBMS. You would specify any constraints to the DBMS and the DBMS would ensure that they are never violated.

Most popular microcomputer DBMSs today have most of the necessary capabilities to enforce the various types of integrity constraints (as do almost all mainframe DBMSs). Consequently, you let the DBMS enforce all the constraints that it is capable of enforcing; then any other constraints are enforced by application programs. You also might create a special program whose sole purpose would be to examine the data in the database to determine whether any constraints had been violated. This program would be run periodically. Corrective action could be taken to remedy any violations that were discovered by means of this program.

Current Microcomputer DBMSs and Integrity

This section concludes with a discussion of the constraints that current microcomputer DBMSs are able to enforce.

- Virtually all microcomputer DBMSs do an excellent job of enforcing data type constraints. At a minimum, they typically allow data types of numeric, character, and date. Users are prevented from entering nonnumeric data into numeric fields or invalid dates into date fields.
- Most microcomputer DBMSs provide direct support for enforcing constraints that involve legal values. For example, most microcomputer DBMSs enforce constraints for a range of numbers (unit price must be between 2.00 and 800.00) and for selected numbers (credit limit must be 750, 1,000, 1,500, or 2,000) as shown in Figure 7.6. Of the few systems that don't provide direct support, some will supply support if users update the data through custom-generated forms; in other words, the constraints can be specified during the description of a form and the constraints will be enforced for any user who employs that form to update the data in the database. If the database is updated in some other way, however, these constraints will not be enforced.

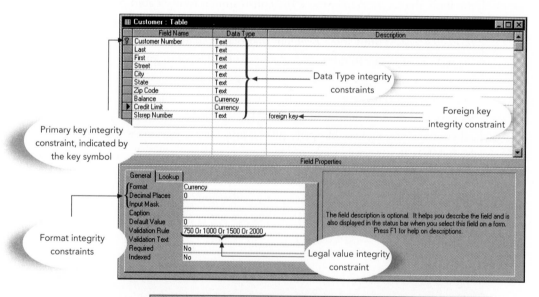

Figure 7.6 Integrity constraints in a microcomputer DBMS

- Most microcomputer DBMSs provide direct support for enforcing a substantial number of format constraints, and these constraints are enforced no matter how the data is entered into the database.
- Most microcomputer DBMSs support key constraints. They allow a primary key to be specified and build a unique index automatically for the designated primary key. Most systems also support foreign key constraints.

DATA INDEPENDENCE

A DBMS must include facilities that provide programs with independence in terms of their relationship to the database structure.

Some of you may have written or worked with application systems that accessed a collection of files. Were any changes ever required in the types of data stored in the files? Did users ever propose any further requirements that necessitated the addition of fields? What about changing the characteristics of a field; for example, expanding the number of characters in the Part Description field from 25 to 30 or the number of digits in a Zip Code field from 5 to 9? What about additional processing requirements; for example, a new requirement to access rapidly a customer on the basis of his or her name?

If any of these things have happened to you, you know that even the simplest of them can be very painful. Adding a new field or changing the characteristics of an existing field, for example, usually entails writing a program that will read each record from the existing file and will write a corresponding record with the new layout to a new file. In addition, each of the programs in the existing system must be changed to reflect the new layout, and these changes must be tested.

One of the advantages of working with a DBMS is **data independence**, that is, the property that changes can be made in the structure of a database without application programs necessarily being affected. Let's examine how the various types of changes that can be made in the structure of the database would affect programs that access the database.

1. Addition of a field. No program should need to be changed except, of course, those programs that will utilize the new field. Some programs may need to be changed, however. If, for example, a program used something like the SQL "SELECT * FROM ..." to select all the fields from a given table, the user suddenly would be presented with an extra field. To prevent this from happening, the output of the program would have to be restricted to only the desired fields. To avoid the imposition of this extra work, it's a good idea to list specific fields in an SQL SELECT command instead of using the asterisk (*).

2. Changing the length of a field. In general, programs should not have to change because the length of a field has been changed. For the most part, the DBMS will handle all the details concerning this change in length. If, however, a program is designed to set aside a certain portion of the screen or a report for the field and the length of the field has increased to the point where the previously allocated space is inadequate, clearly the program will need to be changed.

3. Creating a new index. Typically, a simple command is all that is required to create a new index. Most DBMSs will use the new index automatically for all updates and queries. For some DBMSs, you might need to make minor changes in already existing programs to use the new index.

4. Adding or changing a relationship. This change is the trickiest of all and is best illustrated with an example. Let's suppose that at Premiere Products you now have the following requirements:

   a. Customers are assigned to territories.

   b. Each territory is assigned to a single sales rep.

   c. A sales rep can have more than one territory.

   d. A customer is represented by the sales rep who covers the territory to which the customer is assigned.

To implement these changes, you might choose to restructure the database as follows:

SALES_REP (SLSREP_NUMBER, LAST, FIRST, STREET, CITY, STATE, ZIP_CODE, TOTAL_COMMISSION, COMMISSION_RATE)

TERRITORY (TERRITORY NUMBER, TERRITORY_DESCRIPTION, SLSREP_NUMBER)

CUSTOMER (CUSTOMER NUMBER, LAST, FIRST, STREET, CITY, STATE, ZIP_CODE, BALANCE, CREDT_LIMIT, TERRITORY_NUMBER)

Now let's suppose that a user is accessing the database via the following view, called SLSCUST:

CREATE VIEW SLSCUST (SNUMB, SLAST, SFIRST, CNUMB, CLAST, CFIRST) AS

    SELECT SALES_REP.SLSREP_NUMBER, SALES_REP.LAST, SALES_REP.FIRST,

    CUSTOMER.CUSTOMER_NUMBER, CUSTOMER.LAST, CUSTOMER.FIRST

    FROM SALES_REP, CUSTOMER

    WHERE SALES_REP.SLSREP_NUMBER = CUSTOMER.SLSREP_NUMBER

The defining query no longer is legitimate, because there is no SlS Rep_Number field in the CUSTOMER table. A relationship still exists between sales reps and customers, however. The difference is that you now must go through the TERRITORY table to relate the two. If users have been accessing the tables directly to form the relationship, their programs will have to change. If they are using the SLSCUST view, then only the definition of the view will have to change. The new definition will be as follows:

CREATE VIEW SLSCUST (SNUMB, SLAST, SFIRST, CNUMB, CLAST, CFIRST) AS

    SELECT SALES_REP.SLSREP_NUMBER, SALES_REP.LAST, SALES_REP.FIRST,

    CUSTOMER.CUSTOMER_NUMBER, CUSTOMER.LAST, CUSTOMER.FIRST

    FROM SALES_REP, TERRITORY, CUSTOMER

    WHERE SALES_REP.SLSREP_NUMBER = TERRITORY.SLSREP_NUMBER

    AND TERRITORY.TERRITORY_NUMBER = CUSTOMER.TERRITORY_NUMBER

The defining query now is more complicated than it was before, but this will not affect users of the view. They will continue to access the database in exactly the same way they did before, and their programs will not need to change.

You've now seen how the use of views can allow changes to be made in the logical structure of the database without application programs being affected. As helpful as this is, however, all is not quite as positive as it might seem. For one thing, this entire discussion would not even be relevant to the many DBMSs that do not permit the use of views. Second, even those DBMSs that support views often limit the types of updates that can be accomplished through a view. In particular, if the view involves a join, often little or no updating is allowed to take place. So the benefits that can be derived from the use of views very well may be unavailable to the user who needs to update the database. This problem is the focus of a great deal of current research and should be resolved in the near future.

REPLICATION

A DBMS must furnish a facility to manage copies of the same data at multiple locations.

Sometimes data should be duplicated (technically, called **replicated**) at more than one site, for performance or other reasons. For example, accessing data at a local site is much more efficient than accessing data at remote sites, because it does not involve data communication and network time delays, it avoids contending for data with other users, and it keeps data available to local users at times when the data might not be available at other sites. If certain information needs to be accessed frequently from all sites, a company might choose to store the information at all its locations. At other times, laptop computer users on the road, for example sales reps meeting at their customers' sites or executives waiting at an airport, might need access to data but don't have this access unless it's stored on their laptops.

Replication lets users at different sites use and modify copies of a database and then share their changes with other users. Replication is a two-step process. First, the DBMS creates copies, called **replicas**, of the database at one or more sites (Figure 7.7a). The master database and all replicas form a replica set. Users then update their individual replicas, just as if they were updating the master database. Periodically, the DBMS exchanges all updated data between two databases in the replica set in a process called **synchronization** (Figure 7.7b).

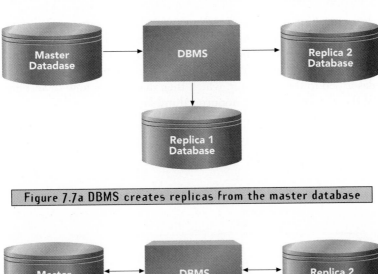

Figure 7.7a DBMS creates replicas from the master database

Figure 7.7b DBMS synchronizes two databases in the replica set

Ideally, the DBMS should handle all issues associated with replication for you. Any work to keep the various copies of data consistent should be done behind the scenes; users should be unaware of it. You'll learn more about replication in Chapter 9.

UTILITIES

A DBMS should provide a set of utility services.

In addition to the services already discussed, a DBMS can provide a number of utility-type services that assist in the general maintenance of the database. Following is a list of such services that might be provided by a microcomputer DBMS:

1. Services that permit changes to be made in the database structure (adding new tables or fields, deleting existing tables or fields, changing the name or characteristics of a field, and so on).

2. Services that permit the addition of new indexes and the deletion of indexes that are no longer needed.

3. Access to DOS, Windows, and other operating system services from within the DBMS.

4. Services that provide export to and import from other microcomputer software products. For example, these services allow data to be transferred in a relatively easy fashion between the DBMS and a spreadsheet, word processing, or graphics program, or even another DBMS.

5. Support for easy-to-use edit and query capabilities, screen generators, report generators, and so on.

6. Access to both procedural and nonprocedural languages. With a procedural language, the computer must be told precisely how a given task is to be accomplished; BASIC, Pascal, and COBOL are examples of procedural languages. With a nonprocedural language, the task merely is described to the computer, which then determines how to accomplish it. SQL is an example of a nonprocedural language.

7. An easy-to-use menu-driven or switchboard-driven interface that allows users to tap the power of the DBMS without having to resort to a complicated set of commands.

SUMMARY

1. A DBMS must furnish users with the capability to store, retrieve, and update the data that is in the database.

2. A DBMS must furnish a catalog in which descriptions of the structure of a database are stored and which can be queried by users.

3. A DBMS must provide support for shared update, allowing more than one user to update the database at the same time.

   a. If care is not taken, incorrect results can be produced in the database.

   b. Locking is one approach that ensures correct results. As long as a portion of the database is locked by one user, other users cannot gain access to it.

   c. Deadlock or deadly embrace are terms used to describe the situation wherein two or more users each are waiting for the other to give up a lock before they can proceed. Mainframe DBMSs have sophisticated facilities for detecting and handling deadlock. Most microcomputer DBMSs do not have such facilities, which means that programs that access the database must be written in such a way that deadlocks are avoided.

4. A DBMS must provide facilities for recovering the database in the event that it is damaged or destroyed. Most microcomputer DBMS provide facilities for periodically making a backup copy of the database. To recover the database when it is damaged or destroyed, the backup is copied over the database.

5. A DBMS must provide security facilities; that is, features that prevent unauthorized access to the database. Such facilities typically include passwords, encryption (the storing of data in an encoded form), and views (which limit users to accessing only the tables and fields included in the view).

6. An integrity constraint is a rule that data in the database must follow. A DBMS should include features that prevent integrity constraints from being violated.

7. A DBMS must include facilities that promote data independence—the property that the database structure can change without application programs necessarily being affected.

8. A DBMS must furnish a facility to handle replication by managing copies of a database at multiple locations.

9. The DBMS must provide a set of utility services.

KEY TERMS

Backup

Batch processing

Catalog

Data dictionary

Data independence

Data storage, retrieval, and update

Deadlock

Deadly embrace

Encryption

Foreign key constraints

Integrity

Integrity constraint

Journal

Locking

Log

Password

Primary key constraints

Recovery

Replicas

Replication

Save

Security

Shared update

Synchronization

Utility services

View

REVIEW QUESTIONS

1. What do you mean when you say that a DBMS should provide facilities for storage, retrieval, and update?

2. What is the purpose of the catalog? What types of information usually are found in the catalogs that accompany microcomputer DBMSs? What additional types of information often are found in the catalogs that accompany mainframe DBMSs?

3. What is meant by shared update?

4. Describe a situation, other than the one used in the text, in which uncontrolled shared update would produce incorrect results.

5. What is meant by locking?

6. How long should locks be held?

7. What is deadlock? How does it occur?

8. Are most microcomputer systems capable of detecting and breaking deadlocks?

9. Assuming that you are using a microcomputer DBMS that provides the locking facilities described in the text, how should programs be written to (a) avoid deadlock, (b) guarantee correct results, and (c) keep any individual user from tying up portions of the database for extended periods of time?

10. What is meant by recovery? What facilities typically are provided by microcomputer DBMSs to handle backup and recovery? What main feature is lacking in such facilities? What problems can this cause for users?

11. What is meant by security?

12. How are passwords used by microcomputer DBMSs to promote security?

13. What is encryption? How does it relate to security?

14. How do views relate to security?

15. What is meant by integrity? What is an integrity constraint? Describe four different ways of handling integrity constraints. Which approach is the most desirable?

16. What is meant by data independence? What benefit does it provide?

17. Describe a situation, other than the ones given in the text, when replication would be useful to an organization.

18. Name some utility services that a DBMS should provide.

19. How well does your school's DBMS fulfill the functions of a DBMS described in this chapter? Which functions are supported fully, which are supported partially, and which are not supported at all?

20. Many computer magazines and a number of Web sites present comparisons of several DBMSs. Find one such DBMS comparison and compare the functions in this chapter to the listed features and functions in the comparison. Which functions from this chapter are included in the comparison, which functions are missing from the comparison, and what additional functions are included in the comparison?

CHAPTER 8

Database Administration

OBJECTIVES

- Discuss the need for database administration (DBA).

- Explain the role of DBA in formulating and implementing database policies.

- Discuss the role of DBA with regards to the data dictionary, user training, and the selection and support of a DBMS.

- Discuss the role of DBA in the database design process.

INTRODUCTION

You already have seen that the database approach confers many benefits. On the other hand, it involves potential hazards, especially when the database serves more than one user. Problems are associated with shared update and with security: Who is allowed to access various parts of the database, and in what way? How do we prevent unauthorized accesses? Just managing the database involves fundamental difficulties. Each user must be made aware of the database structure, or at least, that portion of the database that he or she is allowed to access. Any changes that are made in the structure must be communicated to all users, along with information about how the changes will affect them. Backup and recovery must be coordinated carefully, much more so than in a single-user environment, which presents another complication.

In order to surmount these problems, the services of a person or group commonly referred to as **database administration (DBA)** are essential. DBA, usually a group rather than an individual, is responsible for supervising both the database and the use of the DBMS. Sometimes the term "DBA" is used to refer to the database administrator, the individual in charge of this group. Usually, the context makes clear which meaning is intended.

In this chapter, you will investigate the role of DBA, which is summarized in Figure 8.1. You'll be focusing on the role of DBA in a microcomputer environment. In the next section, DBA's role in formulating and implementing important policies with respect to the database and its use will be discussed. Then you will examine DBA's role in the use of the data dictionary and its crucial role in training various users. Next, you'll learn about the data dictionary and its crucial role in training various users. Finally, the role plays in the database design process will be discussed.

■ ■ ■ ■ ■

RESPONSIBILITIES OF DBA

- Policy Formulation and Implementation

  a. Access privileges

  b. Security

  c. Planning for disaster

  d. Archives

- Data Dictionary Management

- Training

- DBMS Support

  a. DBMS evaluation and selection

  b. Responsibility for DBMS

- Database Design

Figure 8.1 Responsibilities of DBA

POLICY FORMULATION AND IMPLEMENTATION

DBA formulates database policies and communicates these policies to users. DBA also is charged with the implementation of these policies.

Access Privileges

Access to every table and column in the database is not a necessity for every user. Sam, for example, is an employee at Premiere Products whose main responsibility is the inventory. While he very well may need access to the entire PART table, does he also need access to the SALES_REP table? He probably should be able to print inventory reports, but should he be able to change the layout of these reports? Betty, whose responsibility is customer mailings, clearly requires access to customers' names and addresses, but what about their balances or credit limits? Should she be able to change an address? While sales rep 03 (Mary Jones) should be able to obtain information about her own customers, should she be able to obtain the same information about other customers? Figures 8.2a through 8.2c illustrate permitted and denied access for these employees.

You don't have enough information about the policies of Premiere Products to answer the foregoing questions. The DBA, however, must answer questions like these and take steps to ensure that users access the database only in ways to which they are entitled. Policies concerning such access should be clearly documented, and communicated to all concerned parties.

SALES REP

SLSREP NUMBER	LAST	FIRST	STREET	CITY	STATE	ZIP CODE	TOTAL COMMISSION	COMMISSION RATE
03	Jones	Mary	123 Main	Grant	MI	49219	2150.00	.05
06	Smith	William	102 Raymond	Ada	MI	49441	4912.50	.07
12	Diaz	Miguel	419 Harper	Lansing	MI	49224	2150.00	.05

Sam

PART

PART NUMBER	PART DESCRIPTION	UNITS ON HAND	ITEM CLASS	WAREHOUSE NUMBER	UNIT PRICE
AX12	Iron	104	HW	3	$24.95
AZ52	Dartboard	20	SG	2	$12.95
BA74	Basketball	40	SG	1	$29.95
BH22	Cornpopper	95	HW	3	$24.95
BT04	Gas Grill	11	AP	2	$149.99
BZ66	Washer	52	AP	3	$399.99
CA14	Griddle	78	HW	3	$39.99
CB03	Bike	44	SG	1	$299.99
CX11	Blender	112	HW	3	$22.95
CZ81	Treadmill	68	SG	2	$349.95

Access denied

Access permitted

Figure 8.2a Permitted and denied access for Sam

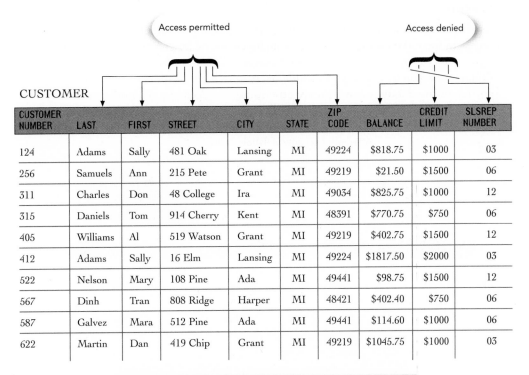

Figure 8.2b Permitted and denied access for Betty

CUSTOMER

CUSTOMER NUMBER	LAST	FIRST	BALANCE	CREDIT LIMIT	SLSREP NUMBER
124	Adams	Sally	$818.75	$1000	03
256	Samuels	Ann	$21.50	$1500	06
311	Charles	Don	$825.75	$1000	12
315	Daniels	Tom	$770.75	$750	06
405	Williams	Al	$402.75	$1500	12
412	Adams	Sally	$1817.50	$2000	03
522	Nelson	Mary	$98.75	$1500	12
567	Dinh	Tran	$402.40	$750	06
587	Galvez	Mara	$114.60	$1000	06
622	Martin	Dan	$1045.75	$1000	03

Access permitted

Access denied

Access denied

Figure 8.2c Permitted and denied access for Mary Jones

Security

As you learned earlier, the term security refers to the prevention of unauthorized access to the database. Of course, this includes access by someone who has no right to access the database at all, for example, someone who is not connected with Premiere Products. It also can include users who have legitimate access to some portion of the database but who are attempting to access a portion to which they are not entitled. Figures 8.3a and 8.3b illustrate both types of security violation.

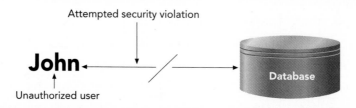

Figure 8.3a Attempted security violation; John is not an authorized user

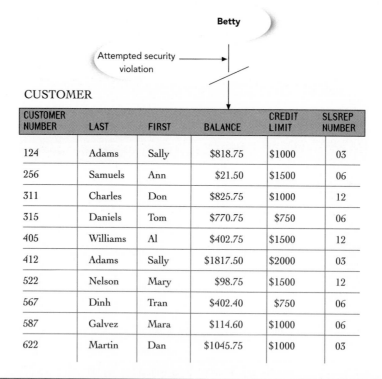

CUSTOMER

CUSTOMER NUMBER	LAST	FIRST	BALANCE	CREDIT LIMIT	SLSREP NUMBER
124	Adams	Sally	$818.75	$1000	03
256	Samuels	Ann	$21.50	$1500	06
311	Charles	Don	$825.75	$1000	12
315	Daniels	Tom	$770.75	$750	06
405	Williams	Al	$402.75	$1500	12
412	Adams	Sally	$1817.50	$2000	03
522	Nelson	Mary	$98.75	$1500	12
567	Dinh	Tran	$402.40	$750	06
587	Galvez	Mara	$114.60	$1000	06
622	Martin	Dan	$1045.75	$1000	03

Figure 8.3b Attempted security violation; although Betty is an authorized user, she is not authorized to access customers' balances

DBA must take steps to ensure the database is secure. Once access privileges have been specified, DBA should draw up policies to explain them and then should distribute these policies to authorized users. Whenever security is violated, DBA must research and track down who breached security and how.

Whatever facilities are present in the DBMS (such as passwords, encryption, and views), should be utilized by DBA to implement these policies. Any necessary features that the DBMS lacks should be supplemented by DBA through the use of special programs. Figures 8.4a and 8.4b show security features of the DBMS both with and without DBA.

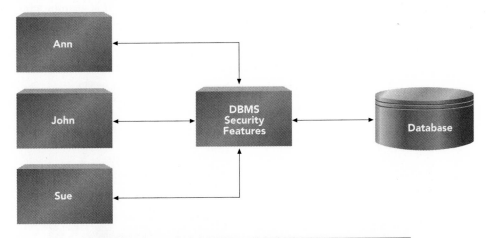

Figure 8.4a Security features of DBMS as sole security

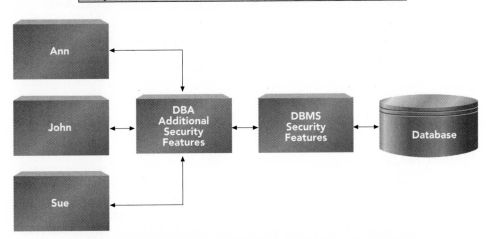

Figure 8.4b Security features of DBMS supplemented by DBA

One security feature, passwords, deserves further attention. Sometimes people think that simply establishing a password scheme will ensure security. After all, Tim can't get access to Pam's data if he doesn't know her password, assuming, of course, that Tim doesn't have a password of his own that allows access to the same data.

But what if Tim observes Pam entering her password? What if he guesses her password? You might think this sort of occurrence is so unlikely that there is nothing to worry about. In fact, it is not so unlikely. Many people often choose passwords that they can remember easily. A very common choice, for example, is the name of a family member. So if Pam is a typical user, Tim might very well be able to obtain her password just by trying names of family members. Other users choose unusual passwords or have such passwords assigned to them but, in order to remember them, they often write them down. Without giving it much thought, such users might be careless about the paper on which a password is written, giving people like Tim still another vehicle for obtaining one. Figure 8.5 illustrates the careless use of passwords.

Figure 8.5 Careless use of passwords: Tim is trying to look over Pam's shoulder to see the paper on which her password is written

It is up to DBA to educate users on the use of passwords. The pitfalls just discussed should be stressed, as should precautionary measures, including the need for frequent changes of passwords.

Planning for Disaster

The type of security discussed so far, concerns harm done by unauthorized users. A database can be harmed in another way as well, and that is through some physical occurrence such as an aborted program, a disk problem, a power outage, or a computer malfunction. This issue was discussed in Chapter 7 in the material on recovery, but it is listed here as well because it is DBA's responsibility to establish and implement backup and recovery procedures. As in other cases, DBA will use the built-in features of the DBMS where possible and will supplement them where they are lacking.

For example, many microcomputer DBMSs lack facilities to maintain a journal of changes in the database. Thus, recovery usually is limited to copying the most recent backup over the live database. This means, as you already have seen, that any changes made since this backup have to be redone by the users. If this presents a major problem, DBA may decide to supplement the DBMS facilities. A typical solution would be to have each program that updates the database also make appropriate entries in a journal (Figure 8.6a) and then make use of this journal in the recovery process (Figure 8.6b). The database first is recovered by copying the backup version over the live database. Then, it is brought up-to-date through a special DBA-created program that updates the database with changes recorded in the journal.

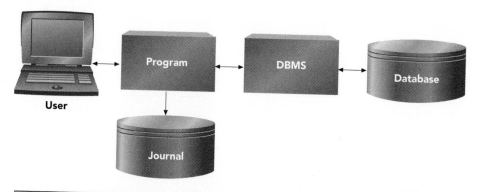

Figure 8.6a Programs involved in database processing also maintain a journal

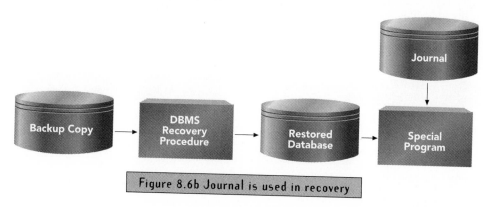

Figure 8.6b Journal is used in recovery

Archives

Often, data needs to be kept in the database for only a limited time. An order that has been filled, has appeared on some statement, and has been paid, is in one sense no longer important. Should the order be left in the database? If data always is left in the database as a matter of policy, the database continually will grow. Along with this, the disk space that is occupied by the database expands, and the performance of programs that access the database may deteriorate. Both of these events ultimately can lead to difficulties. This is a reason for removing an already filled order and all of its associated order lines from the database.

On the other hand, it may be necessary to retain such data for future reference. Possible reasons could include customer inquiries, government regulations, auditing requirements, and so on. Apparently, you may have a conflict on your hands: you may need to remove something, and yet may not be able to afford to remove it.

The solution is to use what is known as a **data archive**. In ordinary usage an **archive** (technically, archives) is a place where public records and documents are kept. A data archive is similar. It is a place where a record of certain corporate data is kept. In fact, a data archive simply is referred to as an archive. In the case of the aforementioned order, you would remove it from the database and place it in the archive, thus storing it for future reference (Figure 8.7).

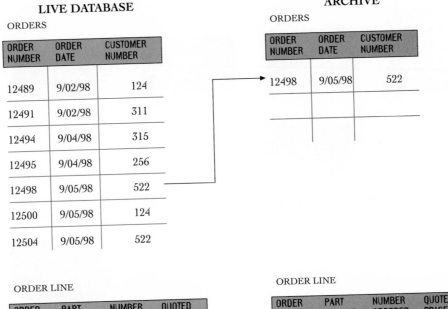

Figure 8.7 Movement of order 12498 from live database to archive

Typically, the archive will be kept on some magnetic form — for example, a disk, diskette, or tape. On mainframes, the most common medium for an archive is tape. On micros, tape also might be used, but another common choice is a collection of diskettes. Still another option would be to keep the data in printed form only. Whichever medium is used, it's important that copies of both archives and backups be kept off-site, so recovery can take place even if a company's buildings and contents are destroyed. Once again, it is up to DBA to establish and implement procedures for the use, maintenance, and storage of the archive.

DATA DICTIONARY MANAGEMENT

In addition to administering the database, DBA also manages the **data dictionary**. The data dictionary is essentially the catalog mentioned in Chapter 7, but it often contains a wider range of information, including at least, information on tables, columns, indexes, and programs.

DBA establishes naming conventions for tables, columns, indexes, and so on. It creates the data definitions for all tables as well as any data integrity rules. It also is charged with the update of the contents of the data dictionary. The creation and distribution of appropriate reports from the data dictionary is another of its responsibilities.

TRAINING

DBA provides training in the use of the DBMS and in how to access the database. It also coordinates the training of users. In cases where training is provided by the vendor of software the organization has purchased, DBA handles the scheduling in order to make sure the right users receive the training they require.

DBMS SUPPORT

DBMS Evaluation and Selection

DBA is responsible for the evaluation and selection of the DBMS. In order to oversee this responsibility, DBA sets up a checklist like the one shown below. (This checklist applies specifically to a relational system, because this text deals with microcomputer DBMSs and more of these are, at least in part, relational. If you already had not selected a model for your focus, a category called "Choice of Data Model" would have to be added to the list. A corresponding checklist for mainframe systems would be slightly larger than the following checklist. This example, however, is representative of a checklist for a relational DBMS.) DBA must evaluate each prospective purchase of a DBMS in terms of all categories shown in the figure. An explanation of the various categories follows.

DBMS EVALUATION CHECKLIST

1. Data Definition
   a. Data types
      (1) Numeric
      (2) Character
      (3) Date
      (4) Logical (T/F)
      (5) Memo
      (6) Currency
      (7) Binary object (pictures, drawings, sounds, and so on)
      (8) Link to an Internet, Web, or other address
      (9) User-defined data types
      (10) Other
   b. Support for nulls
   c. Support for primary keys
   d. Support for foreign keys
   e. Unique indexes
   f. Views
2. Data Restructuring
   a. Possible restructuring
      (1) Add new tables
      (2) Delete old tables
      (3) Add new columns
      (4) Change layout of existing columns
      (5) Delete columns
      (6) Add new indexes
      (7) Delete old indexes
   b. Ease of restructuring
3. Nonprocedural Languages
   a. Nonprocedural languages supported
      (1) SQL
      (2) QBE
      (3) Natural language
      (4) Own language. Award points on the basis of ease of use as well as the types of operations (joining, sorting, grouping, calculating various statistics, and so on) that are available in the language. SQL can be used as a standard against which such a language can be judged.
   b. Optimization done by one of the following:
      (1) User, in formulating the query
      (2) DBMS (through built-in optimizer)
      (3) No optimization possible. System will do only sequential searches.
4. Procedural Languages
   a. Procedural languages supported
      (1) Own language. Award points on the basis of the quality of this language both in terms of the types of statements and control structures available and the database manipulation statements included in the language.
      (2) C or C++
      (3) GUI language, such as PowerBuilder or Visual Basic
      (4) COBOL
      (5) Other
   b. Can nonprocedural language be used in conjunction with the procedural language (e.g., could SQL be embedded in COBOL programs)?

DBMS EVALUATION CHECKLIST (CONT)

5. Data Dictionary
    a. Type of entities
        (1) Tables
        (2) Columns
        (3) Indexes
        (4) Relationships
        (5) Programs
        (6) Other
    b. Integration of data dictionary with other components of the system
6. Shared Update
    a. Level of locking
        (1) Column
        (2) Row
        (3) Page
        (4) Table
    b. Type of locking
        (1) Shared
        (2) Exclusive
        (3) Both
    c. Responsibility for handling deadlock
        (1) Programs
        (2) DBMS (automatic rollback of transaction causing deadlock)
7. Backup and Recovery Services
    a. Backup facilities
    b. Journaling facilities
    c. Recovery facilities
        (1) Recover from backup copy only
        (2) Recover using backup copy and journal
    d. Rollback of individual transactions
    e. Incremental backup
8. Security
    a. Passwords
        (1) Access to database only
        (2) Read or write access to any column or combination of columns
    b. Encryption
    c. View
    d. Difficulty in bypassing security controls
9. Integrity
    a. Support for entity integrity
    b. Support for referential integrity
    c. Support for data type integrity
    d. Support for other types of integrity constraints
10. Replication and Distributed Databases
    a. Partial replicas
    b. Handling of duplicate updates in replicas
    c. Procedure support
        (1) Language used
        (2) Procedures stored in database
        (3) Support for remote stored procedures
        (4) Trigger support
11. Limitations
    a. Number of tables
    b. Number of columns
    c. Length of individual column
    d. Total length of all columns in a table
    e. Number of rows per table
    f. Number of files that can be open at the same time
    g. Sizes of database, tables, and other objects
    h. Types of hardware supported
    i. Types of LANs supported
    j. Other

DBMS EVALUATION CHECKLIST (CONT)

12. Documentation and Training
    a. Clearly written manuals
    b. Tutorial
        (1) Written
        (2) Online
    c. Online help available
        (1) General help
        (2) Context-sensitive help
    d. Training
        (1) Vendor or other company
        (2) Location
        (3) Types (DBA, programmers, users, others)
        (4) Cost
13. Vendor Support
    a. Type of support available
    b. Quality of support available
    c. Cost of support
    d. Reputation of support
14. Performance
    a. Tests comparing the performance of various DBMSs in such areas as sorting, indexing, reading all rows, changing data values in all rows, and so on, are available from a variety of periodicals.
    b. If you have special requirements, you might want to design your own benchmark tests that could be performed on each DBMS under consideration.
    c. Includes a performance monitor
15. Portability
    a. Operating systems
        (1) Unix
        (2) Microsoft Windows
        (3) Microsoft Windows NT
        (4) NetWare
        (5) OS/2
        (6) Other
    b. Import/export/linking file support
        (1) Other databases
        (2) Other applications (e.g., spreadsheets and graphics)
    c. Internet and intranet support
16. Cost
    a. Cost of basic DBMS
    b. Cost of any additional components
    c. Cost of any additional hardware that is required
    d. Cost of network version (if required)
    e. Cost and types of support
17. Future Plans
    a. What does the vendor plan for future of system?
    b. What is the history of the vendor in terms of keeping the system up-to-date?
    c. When changes are made in the system, what is involved in converting to the new version?
        (1) How easy is the conversion?
        (2) What will it cost?
18. Other Considerations (Fill in your own special requirements.)
    a. Special Purpose Reports
    b. ?
    c. ?
    d. ?

1. Data definition. What types of data are supported? Is support for nulls provided? What about primary and foreign keys? The DBMS undoubtedly will provide indexes, but is it possible to specify that an index is unique and then have the system enforce the uniqueness? Is support for views provided?

2. Data restructuring. What type of database restructuring is possible? How easy is it to do this restructuring? Will the system do most of the work or will the DBA have to create special programs for this purpose?

3. Nonprocedural languages. What type of nonprocedural language is supported? The possibilities are SQL, QBE, natural language, or a DBMS built-in language. If one of the standard languages is supported, how good a version is provided by the DBMS? If the DBMS furnishes its own language, how good is it? How does its functionality compare to that of SQL?

   How does the DBMS achieve optimization of queries? Either the DBMS itself optimizes each query, the user must do so by the manner in which he or she states the query, or no optimization occurs. Most desirable, of course, is the first alternative.

4. Procedural languages. What types of procedural languages are supported? Are they common languages, such as C or C++, COBOL, or a GUI language, or does the DBMS come with its own language? In the latter case, how complete is the language? Does it contain all the required types of statements and control structures? What facilities are provided for accessing the database? Is it possible to make use of the nonprocedural language while using the procedural language?

5. Data dictionary. What kind of data dictionary support is available? Is it a simple catalog, or can it contain more, such as information about programs and the various data items these programs access? How well is the data dictionary integrated with other components of the system — for example, the nonprocedural language?

6. Shared update. Is support provided for shared update? What is the unit that may be locked (field, row, page, or table)? Are exclusive locks the only ones permitted or are shared locks also allowed? (A shared lock permits other users to read the data; with an exclusive lock, no other user may access the data in any way.) How is deadlock handled? Will the DBMS take care of it, or is it the responsibility of programs to ensure that it is handled correctly?

7. Backup and recovery services. What type of backup and recovery facilities are provided? Can the DBMS maintain a journal of changes in the database and use the journal during the recovery process? If a transaction has aborted, is the DBMS capable of rolling it back (that is, undoing the updates of the transaction)? Can the DBMS perform an incremental backup of just the data that has changed?

8. Security. What type of security features does the system make available? Are passwords supported? Do passwords simply regulate whether a user may access the database, or is it possible to associate read or write access to a combination of fields with a password? Is encryption supported? Does the system have some type of view mechanism that can be used for security? How difficult is it to bypass the security controls?

9. Integrity. What type of integrity constraints are supported? Is there support for entity integrity (the fact that the primary key cannot be null)? What about referential integrity (the property that values in foreign keys must match values already in the database)? Does the DBMS support data type integrity (the property where values that do not match the data type for the field into which they are being entered are not allowed to occur in the database)? Is there support for any other types of constraints?

10. Replication and distributed databases. Does the DBMS support replication? If so, does it allow partial replicas (copies of selected rows and fields from tables in a database)? How does it handle updates to the same data from two or more replicas? Can a database be distributed, that is, stored on more than one computer? If so, what types of distribution are allowed and what types of procedure support exists?

11. Limitations. What limitations exist with respect to the number of tables, fields, and rows per table? How many files can be open at the same time? (For many databases, each table and each index is in a separate file. Thus, a single table with three indexes, all in use at the same time, would account for four files. Problems may arise if the number of files that can be open is relatively small and many indexes are in use.) On what types of hardware is the DBMS supported? What types of local area networks (LANs) can be used?

   (A **local area network (LAN)** is a configuration of several computers all hooked together, thereby allowing users to share a variety of resources. One of these resources is the database. In a local area network, support for shared update is very important, because many users may be updating the database at the same time. The relevant question here, however, is not how well the DBMS supports shared update, but which of the LANs can be used in conjunction with this DBMS?)

12. Documentation and Training. How good are the manuals? Are they easy to use? Is there a good index? Is a tutorial, in either printed or online form, available to assist users in getting started with the system? Is online help available? If so, is it general help or context-sensitive? (Context-sensitive help means that if a user is having trouble and asks for help, the DBMS will provide assistance for that particular problem at the time the user asks for it.) Does the vendor provide training classes; do other companies offer training? Are the classes on-site or off-site? Are there classes for DBA and separate classes for programmers, for users, and for others? What is the cost for each type of training?

13. Vendor support. What type of support is provided by the vendor, and how good is it? What is the cost? What is the vendor's reputation for support among current users?

14. Performance. How well does the system perform? This is a tough one to answer. One way to determine relative performance is to look into benchmark tests that have been performed on several DBMSs by various periodicals. Beyond this, if an organization has some specialized needs, it may have to set up its own benchmark tests. Does the DBMS provide a performance monitor that measures different types of performance while the DBMS is operational?

15. Portability. On what types of operating systems is the DBMS supported? What types of files can be imported or exported? Can the DBMS link to other data sources such as other types of DBMSs? Does the DBMS provide Internet and intranet support? (An intranet is a company internal network using software tools typically used on the Internet and the World Wide Web.)

16. Cost. What is the cost of the DBMS and of any components the organization is planning to purchase? Is additional hardware required and, if so, what is the associated cost? If the organization requires a special version of the DBMS for a network, what is the additional cost? What is the cost of vendor support, and what types of support plans are available?

17. Future plans. What plans has the vendor made for the future of the system? This information often is difficult to obtain, but you can get an idea by looking at the performance of the vendor with respect to keeping the existing system up-to-date. How easy has it been for users to convert to new versions of the system?

18. Other considerations. This is a final, catch-all category that contains any special requirements not covered in the other categories.

Once each DBMS has been examined with respect to all the preceding categories, the results can be compared. Unfortunately, this process can be difficult, owing to the number of categories and their generally subjective nature. To make the process more objective, a numerical ranking can be assigned to each DBMS for its performance in each category (for example, a number between zero and ten, where zero is poor and ten is excellent). Further, the categories can be assigned weights. This allows an organization to signify which categories are more critical than others. Then, each of the numbers being used in the numerical ranking can be multiplied by the appropriate weight. The results are added up, producing a weighted total. The weighted totals for each DBMS then can be compared, producing the final evaluation.

How does DBA arrive at the numbers to assign each DBMS in the various categories? Several methods are used. It can request feedback from other organizations that are currently using the DBMS in question. It can read journal reviews of the various DBMSs. Sometimes a trial version of the DBMS can be obtained, in which case members of the staff can perform a hands-on test. In practice, all three methods sometimes are combined. Whichever method is used, however, it is crucial that the checklist and weights be carefully thought out; otherwise, the findings may be inadvertently slanted in a particular direction.

Responsibility for DBMS

Once the DBMS has been selected, DBA continues to be primarily responsible for it. DBA installs the DBMS in a way that is suitable for the organization. If the DBMS configuration needs to be changed, it is DBA that will make the changes.

When a new version of the DBMS is released, DBA will review it and determine whether the organization should convert to it. If the decision is made to convert to the new version or perhaps to a new DBMS, DBA coordinates the conversion. Any fixes to problems in the DBMS that are sent by the vendor also are handled by DBA.

DATABASE DESIGN

DBA is responsible for carrying out the process of database design. It must ensure that a sound methodology for database design, such as the one discussed in Chapter 6, is established and followed by all personnel involved in the process. It also must ensure that all pertinent information is obtained from the appropriate users.

DBA is responsible for the implementation of the final information-level design; in other words, it is responsible for the physical-level design process. If performance problems surface, it is up to DBA to make the changes that will improve the system's performance. This is called **tuning** the design.

DBA also is responsible for establishing documentation standards of all the steps in the database design process. It also has to ensure these standards are followed, the documentation is kept up-to-date, and the appropriate personnel have access to the documentation they need.

Requirements don't remain stable over time; they constantly are changing. DBA must review such changes and determine whether a change in the database design is warranted. If so, it must make such changes in the design and in the data in the database. It then also must make sure that all programs affected by the change are modified in any way necessary and that the corresponding documentation also is modified.

SUMMARY

1. Database administration (DBA) is the person or group assigned responsibility for supervising the database and the use of the DBMS.

2. DBA formulates and implements policies concerning the following:

    a. those who can access the database, which portions of the database these persons may access, and in what manner;

    b. security, that is, the prevention of unauthorized access to the database;

    c. recovery of the database in the event that it is damaged; and

    d. management of an archive for data that is no longer needed in the database but must be retained for reference purposes.

3. DBA is in charge of maintaining the data dictionary.

4. DBA is in charge of training with respect to the use of the database and the DBMS. Training that is provided by an outside vendor is scheduled by DBA, which ensures that users receive the vendor training they need.

5. DBA is in charge of supporting the DBMS. This has two facets:

    a. The evaluation and selection of a new DBMS; DBA develops a checklist of desirable features for a DBMS and evaluates each prospective purchase of a DBMS against this list.

    b. DBA is responsible for installing and maintaining the DBMS after it has been selected and procured.

6. DBA is in charge of database design, both the information level and the physical level. It is also in charge of evaluating changes in requirements to determine whether a change in the database design is warranted. If so, DBA makes the change and reports it to affected users.

KEY TERMS

Archive

Data archive

Data dictionary

Database administration (DBA)

Local area network (LAN)

Security

Tuning

REVIEW QUESTIONS

1. What is DBA? Why is it necessary?

2. What is DBA's role in regards to access privileges?

3. What is DBA's role in regards to security? What problems can arise in the use of passwords? How should these problems be handled?

4. Suppose a typical microcomputer DBMS is being used by company X. Suppose further that in the event the database is damaged in some way, it is essential that it be recovered without the users having to redo any work. What action should DBA take?

5. What are data archives? What purpose do they serve? What is the relationship between databases and data archives?

6. What is DBA's responsibility in regards to the data dictionary?

7. Who trains computer users within an organization? What is DBA's role in this training?

8. Describe the method that should be used to select a new DBMS.

9. Describe the meaning of the following categories on a DBMS checklist:

    a. Data definition

    b. Data restructuring

    c. Nonprocedural languages

    d. Procedural languages

    e. Data dictionary

    f. Shared update

    g. Backup and recovery services

    h. Security

    I. Integrity

    j. Replication and distributed databases

    k. Limitations

    l. Documentation and training

    m. Vendor support

    n. Performance

    o. Portability

    p. Cost

    q. Future plans

    r. Other considerations

10. How does DBA obtain the necessary information to award points for the various categories on the checklist?

11. What is DBA's role regarding the DBMS once it has been selected?

12. What is DBA's role in database design?

13. Many computer magazines and a number of Web sites present comparisons of several DBMSs using an evaluation checklist. Find one such DBMS evaluation checklist for microcomputer DBMSs and compare it with the checklist in this chapter. What items appear on one checklist but not the other? If a DBMS is recommended in your selected comparison, why was it recommended?

CHAPTER **9**

Advanced Topics

OBJECTIVES

- Describe distributed database management systems.

- Discuss client/server systems.

- Define data warehouses and explain their uses.

- Discuss the general concepts of object-oriented database management systems.

- Summarize the impact of the Internet and intranets on database management systems.

INTRODUCTION

Previous chapters of this text have focused on relational database management systems, which dominate the database market today. In this chapter, it's time to examine several advanced database topics, most of which are applicable to relational systems.

The centralized approach to processing data, by which users access a central computer through terminals and workstations, was cost effective through the 1970s. The advent of reasonably priced minicomputers and microcomputers, however, facilitated the placement of computers at various locations within an organization, which meant that users could be served directly at those various locations. These computers were linked in some kind of network that allowed users to access data not only in their local computer but anywhere along the entire network. Thus, distributed processing was born. In the next section, you will examine the issues involved in distributed databases—the database component of distributed processing.

It has been common practice for some time to use special front-end computers to off-load communications functions from a central computer. Recently, client/server systems have appeared to off-load database access functions from workstations and a central computer. These systems are the subject of the second section.

The next section covers special database systems that focus on the rapid, timely, and accurate retrieval of data; these systems are called data warehouses. Next you examine object-oriented systems, which treat data as objects, complete with the actions that can occur on the objects. The final section briefly reviews the impact of the Internet and intranets on database systems.

■ ■ ■ ■ ■

DISTRIBUTED SYSTEMS

Suppose Premiere Products has many locations, or sites, around the country. For the most part, each location has its own sales reps and customer base, and maintains its own inventory. Instead of using a single, centralized mainframe computer accessed by all the separate locations, Premiere Products is considering installing a computer at each site. If it did so, each site would maintain its own data concerning its sales reps, customers, parts, and orders. Occasionally an order at one site, however, might involve parts from another site. Also, customers from one site might place orders occasionally at another site. Thus, the computer at each site would have to be able to communicate with the computers at all other sites. The computers would have to be connected in some kind of **communications network**, as illustrated in Figure 9.1.

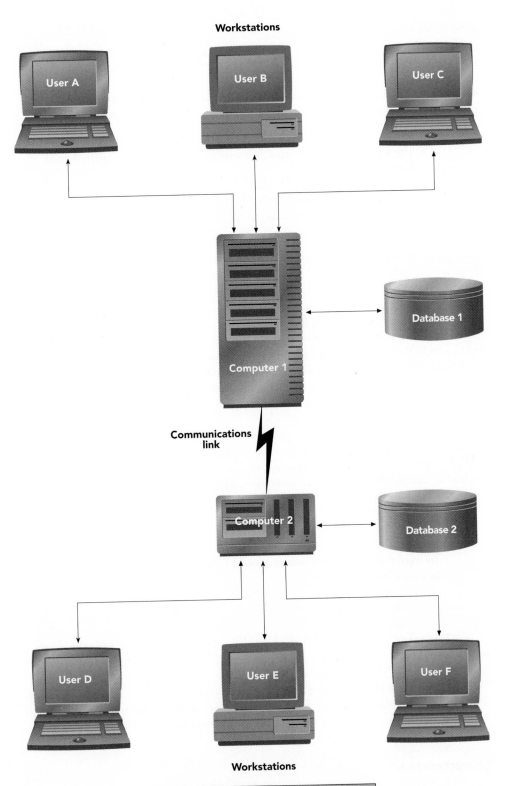

Figure 9.1 Communications network

Description

Distributed databases fall within the realm of database management and are involved in the networks just described.

Definition: A **distributed database** is a database stored on computers at several sites of a computer network and in which users can access data at any site in the network.

On the basis of this definition, we can go on to describe a distributed database management system.

Definition: A **distributed database management system (DDBMS)** is a DBMS capable of supporting and manipulating distributed databases.

Communication between computers in the network is achieved through **messages**; that is, one computer sends a message to another. The word "message" is used in a fairly broad way here. It could mean a request for data. It could be used to indicate a problem. For example, one computer could send a message to another computer indicating that the requested data was not available. Finally, a message could be the data itself. Although the mechanics of sending a message are not going to be discussed, it is important to be aware that the length of time required to send one message depends on the length of the message together with the characteristics of the network. There will be a fixed amount of time, sometimes called the access delay, required for every message. In addition, the time for each message must include the time it takes to transmit all the characters. The formula is as follows:

Communication time =

access delay + (data volume / transmission rate)

As an example, suppose you have an access delay of two seconds and a transmission rate of 30,000 bits per second. Assuming that a message consists of 1,000 records, each of which is 800 bits long, the communication time would be as follows:

Communication time = 2 + (1,000 * 800) / 30,000

= 2 + 800,000 / 30,000

= 2 + 26.67

= 28.67 seconds

To transmit a 10-byte message would take:

Communication time = 2 + 100 / 30,000

= 2 + .003

= 2.003 seconds or, for practical purposes

= 2 seconds

As you can see, in short messages the access delay can become the dominant feature. Thus, in general, a small number of lengthy messages is preferable to a large number of short messages.

This form of communication is substantially slower than accessing data on a disk. In a centralized system, design decisions are made to minimize disk accesses, but in general, in a distributed system, it is more important to minimize messages.

Characteristics

Because a distributed database management system (DDBMS) effectively contains a local DBMS at each site, an important property of such systems is that they either are homogeneous or heterogeneous. A **homogeneous DDBMS** is one that has the same local DBMS at each site. A **heterogeneous DDBMS** is one that does not; there are at least two sites at which the local DBMSs are different. Heterogeneous systems are more complex than homogeneous systems and, consequently, have more problems and are more difficult to manage.

All DDBMSs share several important characteristics. Among them are location transparency, replication transparency, and fragmentation transparency.

1. Location transparency. The definition of a distributed database says nothing about the *ease* with which users access data stored at another site. Still, systems that support distributed databases should enable a user to access data at a **remote site**—a site other than the one at which the user is currently operating—just as easily as he or she accesses data at the **local site**—the site at which the user is working. Response times for accessing data stored at a remote site might be much greater, but except for this difference, the user should feel as though the entire database is stored at his or her location. This property is called **location transparency** and is one of the major objectives of distributed systems.

2. Replication transparency. As described in Chapter 7, **replication** lets users at different sites use and modify copies of a database and then share their changes with other users. While this replication of data can improve the efficiency of certain types of processing, it creates update problems and causes associated problems with data consistency. If you update the record of a single part at Premiere Products, the update must be made at each of the locations at which data concerning this part is stored. Not only does this make the update process more cumbersome, but should one of the copies of data for this part be overlooked, there would be inconsistent data in the database.

   Ideally, the DDBMS should handle this problem for us. Any work to keep the various copies of data consistent should be done behind the scenes; the user should be unaware of it. This property is called **replication transparency**.

3. Fragmentation transparency. When customers at each Premiere Products site are stored at that site, you have what is termed **data fragmentation**. A system supports data fragmentation if a logical object, such as the collection of all records of a given type, can be divided among the various locations. The main purpose of data fragmentation is to place data at the site where it most often is accessed.

   Fragmentation can occur in a variety of ways. Assume, for example, Premiere Products has three sites called SITE1, SITE2, and SITE3. Also assume that an additional column in the CUSTOMER table, called Site Number, identifies the primary site with which a customer is associated.

   Using an SQL-like language, you could define the following fragments:

```
DEFINE FRAGMENT F1 AS
        SELECT CUSTOMER_NUMBER, LAST, FIRST, STREET, CITY, STATE,
                ZIP_CODE, BALANCE, CREDIT_LIMIT, SLSREP_NUMBER,
                SITE_NUMBER
        FROM CUSTOMER
        WHERE SITE_NUMBER = 'SITE1'
DEFINE FRAGMENT F2 AS
        SELECT CUSTOMER_NUMBER, LAST, FIRST, STREET, CITY, STATE,
                ZIP_CODE, BALANCE, CREDIT_LIMIT, SLSREP_NUMBER,
                SITE_NUMBER
        FROM CUSTOMER
        WHERE SITE_NUMBER = 'SITE2'
DEFINE FRAGMENT F3 AS
        SELECT CUSTOMER_NUMBER, LAST, FIRST, STREET, CITY, STATE,
                ZIP_CODE, BALANCE, CREDIT_LIMIT, SLSREP_NUMBER,
                SITE_NUMBER
        FROM CUSTOMER
        WHERE SITE_NUMBER = 'SITE3'
```

Each of these fragment definitions indicates what is to be selected from the global CUSTOMER relation that will be included in the fragment. Note the global CUSTOMER relation will not actually exist in any one place. Rather, parts of it will exist in three pieces. These pieces, or fragments, will be assigned to locations. Here, fragment F1 is assigned to SITE1, fragment F2 is assigned to SITE2, and fragment F3 is assigned to SITE3. The effect of this assignment is that each customer is stored at the site at which he or she is a customer.

The Premiere Products data shown in Figure 9.2 is used as the basis for the fragmentation illustrated in Figure 9.3. Creation of the complete CUSTOMER relation entails taking the union of these three fragments.

CUSTOMER

CUSTOMER NUMBER	LAST	FIRST	STREET	CITY	STATE	ZIP CODE	BALANCE	CREDIT LIMIT	SLSREP NUMBER	SITE NUMBER
124	Adams	Sally	481 Oak	Lansing	MI	49224	$ 818.75	$1000	03	SITE1
256	Samuels	Ann	215 Pete	Grant	MI	49219	$ 21.50	$1500	06	SITE1
311	Charles	Don	48 College	Ira	MI	49034	$ 825.75	$1000	12	SITE3
315	Daniels	Tom	914 Cherry	Kent	MI	48391	$ 770.75	$ 750	06	SITE2
405	Williams	Al	519 Watson	Grant	MI	49219	$ 402.75	$1500	12	SITE3
412	Adams	Sally	16 Elm	Lansing	MI	49224	$1817.50	$2000	03	SITE1
522	Nelson	Mary	108 Pine	Ada	MI	49441	$ 98.75	$1500	12	SITE3
567	Dinh	Tran	808 Ridge	Harper	MI	48421	$ 402.40	$ 750	06	SITE2
587	Galvez	Mara	512 Pine	Ada	MI	49441	$ 114.60	$1000	06	SITE2
622	Martin	Dan	419 Chip	Grant	MI	49219	$1045.75	$1000	03	SITE3

Figure 9.2 Customer data for Premiere Products including Site Number

Fragment F1

CUSTOMER

CUSTOMER NUMBER	LAST	FIRST	STREET	CITY	STATE	ZIP CODE	BALANCE	CREDIT LIMIT	SLSREP NUMBER	SITE NUMBER
124	Adams	Sally	481 Oak	Lansing	MI	49224	$ 818.75	$1000	03	SITE1
256	Samuels	Ann	215 Pete	Grant	MI	49219	$ 21.50	$1500	06	SITE1
412	Adams	Sally	16 Elm	Lansing	MI	49224	$1817.50	$2000	03	SITE1

Fragment F2

CUSTOMER

CUSTOMER NUMBER	LAST	FIRST	STREET	CITY	STATE	ZIP CODE	BALANCE	CREDIT LIMIT	SLSREP NUMBER	SITE NUMBER
315	Daniels	Tom	914 Cherry	Kent	MI	48391	$770.75	$ 750	06	SITE2
567	Dinh	Tran	808 Ridge	Harper	MI	48421	$402.40	$ 750	06	SITE2
587	Galvez	Mara	512 Pine	Ada	MI	49441	$114.60	$1000	06	SITE2

Fragment F3

CUSTOMER

CUSTOMER NUMBER	LAST	FIRST	STREET	CITY	STATE	ZIP CODE	BALANCE	CREDIT LIMIT	SLSREP NUMBER	SITE NUMBER
311	Charles	Don	48 College	Ira	MI	49034	$ 825.75	$1000	12	SITE3
405	Williams	Al	519 Watson	Grant	MI	49219	$ 402.75	$1500	12	SITE3
522	Nelson	Mary	108 Pine	Ada	MI	49441	$ 98.75	$1500	12	SITE3
622	Martin	Dan	419 Chip	Grant	MI	49219	$1045.75	$1000	03	SITE3

Figure 9.3 Fragmentation of CUSTOMER data by site

Again, users should not be aware of the underlying activity, in this case the fragmentation. They should feel as if they are using a single central database. If users are unaware of fragmentation, you say the system has **fragmentation transparency**.

Advantages

As compared with a single centralized database, distributed databases offer some advantages. They are listed in Figure 9.4 and are discussed below.

Advantages to Distributed Databases

1.	Local control of data
2.	Increasing capacity
3.	System availability
4.	Added efficiency

Figure 9.4 Advantages to distributed databases

1. Local control of data. Because each location can retain its own data, it can exercise greater control over that data. With a single centralized database, on the other hand, the central data processing center that maintains the database usually will not be aware of all the local issues at the various sites served by the database.

2. Increasing capacity. In a properly designed and installed distributed database, the process of increasing system capacity often is simpler than in a centralized system. If the size of the database at a single site becomes inadequate, potentially only the local database at that site needs to be changed. Further, the capacity of the database as a whole can be increased by merely adding a new site.

3. System availability. When a centralized database becomes unavailable for any reason, *no* users are able to continue processing. In contrast, if one of the local databases in a distributed database becomes unavailable, only users who need data in that particular database are affected; other users can continue processing in a normal fashion. In addition, if the data has been replicated (another copy of it exists in other local databases) potentially all users can continue processing. Processing for users at the site of the unavailable database, however, will be much less efficient, because data formerly obtained locally now must be obtained through communication with a remote site.

4. Added efficiency. As you saw earlier, the fact that data is available locally means the efficiency with which that data can be retrieved is much greater than with a remote centralized system.

Disadvantages

Distributed databases also offer some disadvantages. They are listed in Figure 9.5 and are discussed below.

Disadvantages to Distributed Databases

1.	Update of replicated data
2.	More complex query processing
3.	More complex treatment of shared update
4.	More complex recovery measures
5.	More difficult management of data dictionary
6.	Database design is more complex

Figure 9.5 Disadvantages to distributed databases

1. Update of replicated data. It often is desirable to replicate data both for the sake of performance and to ensure that the overall system will remain available even when the database at one site is not. Replication can cause severe update problems, most obviously in terms of overhead. Instead of one copy being updated, several must be, and because most of these copies are at sites other than the site initiating the update, communication overhead must be added to the update overhead.

There is another, slightly more serious problem, however. Let's assume that data at five sites must be updated, and that the fifth site currently is unavailable. If all updates must be made or none at all, the whole update fails. Thus, data is unavailable for update if even one of the sites that is the target of the update is not available. This certainly contradicts earlier remarks about *additional* availability. On the other hand, if you do not require all updates to be made, the data will be inconsistent.

Often, a compromise strategy is used. One copy of the data is designated the **primary copy**. As long as the primary copy is updated, the update is deemed complete. It is the responsibility of the primary copy to ensure that all other copies are in sync. The site holding the primary copy sends update transactions to all other sites to accomplish the update and notes whether any sites currently are unavailable. If it discovers an unavailable site, the primary site must try to send the update again at some later time and continue trying until successful. This strategy overcomes the basic problem, but it obviously incurs more overhead. Further, if the primary site itself is unavailable, the problem remains unresolved.

2. More complex query processing. The issues involved in processing queries can be much more complex in a distributed environment. The problem stems from the difference between the time it takes to send messages between sites and the time it takes to access a disk. As you saw earlier, minimizing message traffic is extremely important.

To illustrate the problems involved, consider the following query: List all parts in Item Class SG and whose unit price is more than $100.00.

For this query, you will assume that (1) the PART table contains 1,000 rows and is stored at a remote site; (2) there is no special structure, such as an index, which would be useful in processing this query; and (3) only 10 of the 1,000 rows in the PART table satisfy the conditions. How would you process this query?

One solution would involve retrieving each row from the remote site and examining the item class and unit price to determine whether the row should be included in the result. For each row, this solution would require two messages: a message from the local site to the remote site requesting a row, followed by a message from the remote site to the local site containing either the data or, ultimately, an indication that there is no more data. Thus, in addition to the database accesses themselves, this strategy would require 2,000 messages.

A second solution would involve sending a single message from the local site to the remote site requesting the complete answer, followed by a single message from the remote site back to the local site containing all the rows in the answer. The second message might be quite lengthy, especially where many rows satisfied the conditions, but this solution still would be a vast improvement over the first one. A small number of lengthy messages is preferable to a large number of short messages.

The net result is that systems that are only record-at-a-time oriented can create severe performance problems in distributed systems. If the only choice is to transmit every record from one site to another as a message, then examine it at the other site, the communication time can become intolerable. Systems that permit a request for a set of records, as opposed to an individual record, will inherently outperform record-at-a-time systems.

3. More complex treatment of shared update. **Shared update** in a distributed system is treated in basically the same way as it is treated in nondistributed systems: **locks** are acquired; locking is **two-phase** (locks are acquired in a **growing phase**, during which no locks are released, and then all locks are released in the **shrinking phase**); **deadlocks** must be detected and broken; and offending updates must be **rolled back**. The primary distinction lies not in the kinds of activities that take place but in the additional level of complexity created by the very nature of a distributed database.

If all the records to be updated by a particular transaction occur at one site, the problem is essentially the same as in a nondistributed database. The records might be stored at a number of different sites, however, and if the data is replicated, each occurrence might be stored at several sites, each requiring the same update to be performed. Assuming each record occurrence has replicas at three different sites, an update that would affect five record occurrences in a nondistributed system might affect twenty different occurrences in a distributed system (each occurrence together with its three replicas). Further, these 20 different occurrences conceivably could be stored at 20 different sites.

Having more occurrences to update is only part of the problem. Assuming each site keeps its own locks, several messages must be sent for each record to be updated: a request for a lock; a message indicating that either the record already is locked by another user or that the lock has been granted; a message indicating the update to be performed; an acknowledgment of the update; and finally, a message indicating that the record is to be unlocked. Because all these messages must be sent for each record and the number of records can be much larger than in a nondistributed system, the total time for an update can be substantially longer in a distributed environment.

There is a partial solution to this problem. It involves the use of the primary copy mentioned earlier. You will recall that one of the replicas of a given record occurrence was designated as the primary copy. If this is done, then merely locking the primary copy rather than all copies will suffice. This will cut down on the number of messages concerned with the process of locking and unlocking records. The number of messages still might be large, however, and the unavailability of the primary copy can cause an entire transaction to fail. Thus, even this partial solution presents problems.

As in a nondistributed system, deadlock is a possibility. Here there are two types, **local deadlock** and **global deadlock**. Local deadlock can be detected at one site. If two transactions are each waiting for a record held by the other at the same site, this fact can be detected from information internal to the site (the waiting-for information is only at that site). Another possibility is that one transaction might require a record held by another transaction at one site, while the second transaction required a record held by the first at a different site. In this case, neither site would contain information individually to allow this deadlock to be detected; this is a global deadlock, and it can be detected only through global waiting-for information. Maintaining such global waiting-for information, however, necessitates many more messages.

As you can see, the various factors involved in supporting shared update greatly add to the communications overhead in a distributed system.

4. More complex recovery measures. While the basic **recovery** process is the same as the one described in Chapter 7, there is a potential problem. Each database update either should be made permanent or aborted and rolled back, in which case *none* of its changes will be made. In a distributed environment, with several local databases being updated by an individual transaction, the updates might be committed at some sites and rolled back at others, thereby creating an inconsistent state in the global database. This *cannot* be allowed to happen.

This possibility usually is prevented through the use of the principle of **two-phase commit**. The basic idea of the two-phase commit is that one site, often the site initiating the update, will act as **coordinator**. In the first phase, the coordinator sends messages to all other sites requesting they prepare to update the database; in other words, they acquire all necessary locks. They do not update at this point, however, but send a message to the coordinator that they are ready to update. If for any reason they cannot secure the necessary locks, or if the update must be aborted at their site, they send a message to the coordinator that they must abort.

The coordinator waits for replies from all sites involved before determining whether to commit the update. If all replies are positive, the coordinator sends a message to each site to commit the update. At this point, each site *must* proceed with the commit process. If any reply is negative, the coordinator sends a message to each site to abort the update and each site *must* follow this instruction. In this way, consistency is guaranteed.

While a process similar to the two-phase commit is essential to database consistency, there are two problems associated with it. For one thing, as you may have noticed, many messages are sent in the process. For another, during the second phase, each site must follow the instructions from the coordinator; otherwise, the process will not accomplish its intended result. This means the sites are not as independent as you might like them to be.

5. More difficult management of data dictionary. The distributed environment introduces further complexity to the management of the **data dictionary** or **catalog**. Where should the data dictionary entries be stored? There are several possibilities:

a. Choose one site and store the complete data dictionary only at this site.

b. Store a complete copy of the data dictionary at each site.

c. Distribute (possibly with replication) the dictionary entries among the various sites.

While storing the complete dictionary at a single site is a relatively simple approach to administer, retrieval of information in the dictionary from any other site will suffer because of the communication involved. Storing a complete copy at every site solves the retrieval problem, because any retrieval completely can be satisfied locally. Because this approach involves total replication (every occurrence is replicated at every site), it suffers from severe update problems. If the dictionary is updated with any frequency, the update overhead probably will be intolerable. Thus, some intermediate strategy usually is implemented.

One fairly obvious partitioning of the dictionary involves storing dictionary entries at the site at which the data they describe is located. Interestingly, this approach also suffers from a problem. If a user is querying the dictionary in an attempt to access an entry not stored at the site, the system has no way of knowing where the data is. Satisfying this user's query may well involve sending a message to every other site, which involves a considerable amount of overhead.

6. Database design is more complex. The distributed environment adds another level of complexity to database design. The information level of design is unaffected by the fact that the system is distributed, but, during the physical level phase of design, an additional factor must be considered, and that is communication. In a nondistributed environment, one of the principal concerns during the physical design is disk activity, both numbers of disk accesses and volumes of data to be transported. While this also is a factor in the distributed environment, there is another important factor to consider: communication activity. Because transmitting data from one site to another is *much* slower than transferring data to and from the disk, in many situations this will be the most important factor of all.

In addition to the standard issues encountered for nondistributed systems, possible fragmentation and/or replication must be considered during the physical level of database design. The process of analyzing and choosing among alternative designs must include any message traffic necessitated by each alternative. While much has been done concerning database design for distributed systems, much work remains.

Rules for Distributed Systems

C. J. Date[*] formulated 12 rules that distributed systems should follow. The basic goal of these systems is that a distributed system should feel like a nondistributed system to the user; that is, the user need not be aware that the system is distributed. The 12 rules are as follows:

1. Sites should be autonomous. No site should depend on another site to function.

2. No master site. There should not be reliance on a single site, often called a master site, to control specific types of operations. A system, for example, in which one site was in charge of update management would violate this rule.

3. No need for planned shutdowns. Performing functions, such as adding sites, changing versions of DBMSs, and modifying hardware, should not require planned shutdowns of the entire distributed system.

---

[*]C.J. Date, "Twelve Rules for a Distributed Database," <u>Computer World</u> 21.23 June, 1987.

4. Location transparency. Users should not need to be concerned with the location of any specific data in the network. It should feel to users as though the entire database is stored at their location.

5. Fragmentation transparency. Users should not be aware of any fragmentation that has taken place. They should feel as if they are using a single central database.

6. Replication transparency. Users should not be aware of any replication that has taken place. Any work to keep the various copies of data consistent should be done behind the scenes; the user should be unaware of it.

7. Query processing. You already have learned about the complexities of query processing in a distributed environment. It is critical that the DDBMS be able to process these queries efficiently.

8. Update management. You already have learned about the complexities of update management and the need for the two-phase commit protocol. It is essential that the DDBMS effectively manage this activity.

9. Not dependent on specific hardware. Because installations typically have a number of different types of hardware, it is desirable that the distributed system is able to integrate these various types. Without this, users would be restricted to only the data stored on similar machines.

10. Not dependent on a specific operating system. Even though the hardware in use may be the same, there may be different operating systems in use. For the same reasons that it is desirable for a distributed system to support various types of hardware, it also is advantageous for it to support various operating systems.

11. Not dependent on a specific network. Because different sites within an organization may employ different communications networks, it is desirable for a distributed system to support the various types of networks within the organization and not to be restricted to a single type.

12. Not dependent on a specific DBMS. Another way of stating this requirement is that the DDBMS should be heterogeneous; that is, capable of supporting local DBMSs that are different. This is a difficult task. In practice, the way it will be accomplished is for each of the local DBMSs to be capable of *speaking* a common language. As you might guess, this common language most likely will be SQL.

CLIENT/SERVER SYSTEMS

Until recently, it was common for a local area network (LAN) to contain a **file server** as shown in Figure 9.6. The server contained the files required by the individual workstations on the network. When a workstation required a particular file, it sent a request to the server. The server then sent the requested file or files to the workstation. While this approach worked, it generated a large amount of traffic on the network. As users' networks grew in the number of workstations and the amount of data processed, this approach caused severe performance problems.

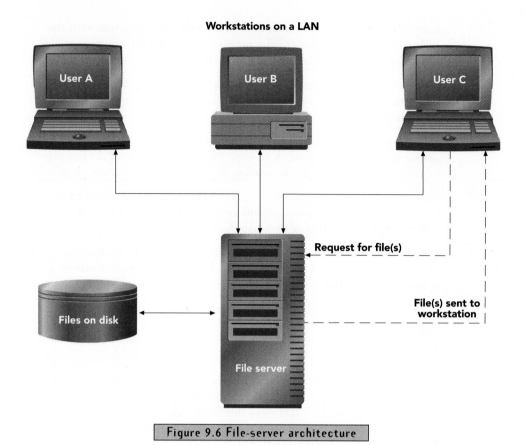

Workstations on a LAN

Request for file(s)

File(s) sent to
workstation

Files on disk

File server

Figure 9.6 File-server architecture

The alternative, which is called **client/server**, is illustrated in Figure 9.7. In "client/server" terminology, the "server" is the computer providing data to the "clients," who are the users accessing the data through their workstations. With this alternative, a DBMS runs on the server. Users send requests, not for entire *files*, but only for specific *data*. The DBMS on the server processes the request and then extracts the requested data, which then is sent back to the workstation.

Clients: workstations on a LAN

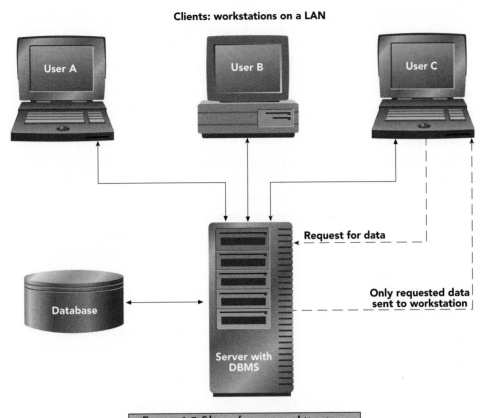

Figure 9.7 Client/server architecture

In order for a workstation to take advantage of this approach, the software running on the workstation has to be capable of communicating with the DBMS running on the server. Currently, there are several DBMSs that can be used on servers. The common language that they use is, as you might expect, SQL. There also are many software products that have been modified to be able to communicate with one or more of these DBMSs.

It should be emphasized that the changes to these software products do not affect the way the users interact with them. The screens still look the same. The options still work in the same fashion they always did. The users don't even need to be aware that the data they are accessing resides on the server rather than on their own PCs. Note that a client/server system stores the database on a single server, and the DBMS resides and processes on that server. Only in a distributed database management system is the database itself distributed.

Advantages to Client/Server

There are several advantages to the client/server approach.

1. It is more efficient. Only the necessary data, rather than the entire file, is transmitted across the network.

2. It provides for the possibility of distributing work among several processors.

3. The workstations do not necessarily need to be as powerful as they would in a file-server environment, because the server will handle more of the work.

4. As far as a user is concerned, the software runs on the workstations just as it does on a stand-alone system. The user does not need to learn any special commands or techniques to work in the client/server environment.

5. Because client/servers use SQL as a common language, it is easier for users to access data from a variety of sources. A single operation potentially could access data from multiple networks and multiple platforms. Without a common language, this would be a very difficult process.

6. Client/servers provide a greater level of security than file servers.

7. Client/servers have proven to be powerful enough that users have replaced mainframe applications and mainframe databases with microcomputer applications and databases managed by client/servers at a considerable savings.

Features of Client/Servers

Client/servers typically offer several useful features:

1. They support SQL.

2. They have a central data dictionary.

3. They are heavily optimized to provide maximum performance.

4. They provide support for data integrity. This includes support for all the various types of integrity constraints discussed in Chapter 7.

5. They support shared update as discussed in Chapter 7. This includes support for locking, deadlock detection, and deadlock correction.

6. They provide support for security as discussed in Chapter 7.

7. They provide support for backup and recovery as discussed in Chapter 7.

Triggers and Stored Procedures

One special aspect of the support client/servers provide for integrity is the use of triggers. A **trigger** is an action that will take place automatically when an associated database operation takes place. Triggers are created with special SQL statements similar to the following:

```
CREATE ADDORDER TRIGGER ON ORDERS
        FOR INSERT, UPDATE AS
        IF NOT EXISTS
                (SELECT CUSTOMER_NUMBER
                        FROM INSERTED
                        WHERE CUSTOMER_NUMBER IN
                                (SELECT CUSTOMER_NUMBER
                                        FROM CUSTOMER))
        BEGIN
                Print ("Invalid Customer Number.")
        END
```

This trigger, which is called ADDCUST ensures that the customer number entered for an order matches a customer in the CUSTOMER table. It will be applied on both INSERT and UPDATE of a row in the ORDERS table. The row to be changed is in the special temporary table called INSERTED. If the customer number in the new row is not in the collection of customer numbers in the CUSTOMER table, then the update will not take place. Instead the system would display the message "Invalid Customer Number."

Another important aspect of client/server systems relates to performance. If the same collection of SQL statements will be executed repeatedly, the statements can be placed in a special file, called a **stored procedure**. The statements in a stored procedure are compiled and optimized. From that point on, whenever users execute the collection of statements, they will execute the compiled, optimized code in the stored procedure.

DATA WAREHOUSES

Among the objectives that organizations have when they use relational database management systems (RDBMSs) are data integrity, high performance, and ample availability. The leading RDBMSs are able to satisfy these requirements. Typically, when users interact with an RDBMS, they use transactions, such as add a new order and change a customer's sales rep. These types of systems thus are called **online transaction processing (OLTP)** systems. For each transaction, OLTP typically deals with a small number of rows from the tables in a database in a highly structured, repetitive, and predetermined way. If you need to know the status of specific customers, parts, and orders, or if you need to update data for specific customers, parts, and orders, for example, an RDBMS and OLTP are the ideal tools to use.

When you need to analyze data from a database, however, an RDBMS and OLTP often suffer from severe performance problems. For example, finding total sales by region and by month requires the joining of all the rows in many tables; such processing takes a considerable number of database accesses and considerable time to accomplish. Consequently, many organizations continue to use RDBMSs and OLTP for their normal, day-to-day processing, or for *operational purposes*, but have turned to data warehouses for the analysis of their data. The following definition for a data warehouse is credited to W. H. Inmon[*] who originally coined the phrase.

Definition: A **data warehouse** is a subject-oriented, integrated, time-variant, nonvolatile collection of data in support of management's decision-making process.

Subject-oriented means data is organized by entity rather than by the application that uses it. For example, Figure 9.8 shows the databases for typical operational applications such as inventory, order entry, production, and accounts payable. When the data from these operational databases is loaded into a data warehouse, it's transformed into subjects such as product, customer, vendor, and financial. Data about products appears once in the warehouse, even though it might appear in many files and databases in the operational environment.

Note	The operational applications in this example use a variety of DBMSs and file-processing systems, because they've been developed over the past 30 years, a typical situation for many organizations.

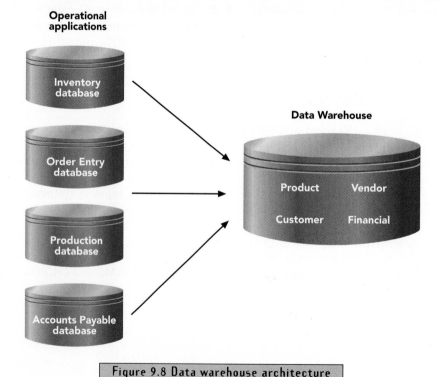

Figure 9.8 Data warehouse architecture

[*]W. H. Inmon, "Building the Data Warehouse," <u>QED</u> (1990).

Integrated means data is stored in one place in the data warehouse, even though it originates from everywhere in the organization and from a variety of external sources. The data can come from recently developed applications or from legacy systems developed many years ago.

Time-variant means data in a data warehouse represents a snapshot of data at one point in time in the past, unlike an operational application whose data is accurate as of the moment. Data warehouses also retain historical data for long periods of time, summarized to specific time periods such as daily, weekly, monthly, and annual.

Nonvolatile means data is read-only. Data is loaded into it periodically but users cannot update a data warehouse directly.

In summary, a data warehouse contains read-only snapshots of highly consolidated and summarized data from multiple internal and external sources that are refreshed periodically, usually on a daily or weekly basis. Companies use data warehouses in support of their decision-making processing, which typically consists of unstructured and nonrepetitive requests for exactly the type of information contained in a data warehouse.

Data Warehouse Structure

A typical data warehouse structure is shown in Figure 9.9. The central *Sales Fact* table is called a fact table. A **fact table** consists of many rows that contain consolidated and summarized data. The fact table contains a multipart primary key, each part of which is a foreign key to the surrounding dimension tables. Each **dimension table** contains a single-part primary key that serves as an index into the fact table and also contains other fields associated with the primary key value. The overall structure shown in Figure 9.9 generically is called a **multidimensional database** because of its structure, and the specific type of multidimensional database shown is called a **star-join schema** because of its conceptual shape.

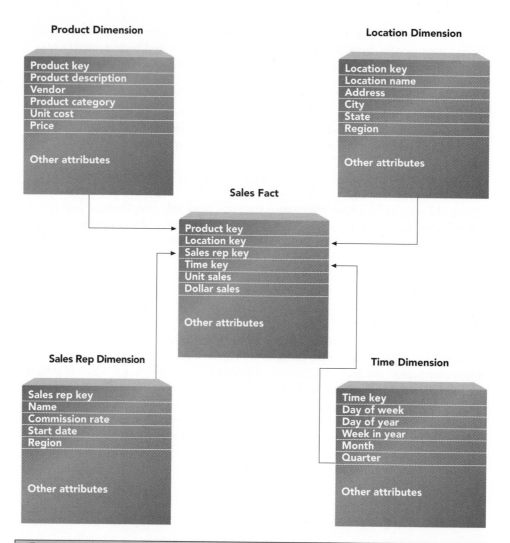

Figure 9.9 A star-join schema with four dimension tables and a central fact table

Access to a multidimensional database is accomplished through the use of **online analytical processing (OLAP)** software. OLAP software is optimized to work efficiently with multidimensional databases in a data warehouse environment.

Rules for OLAP Systems

E. F. Codd* formulated 12 rules that OLAP systems should follow. The 12 rules are as follows:

1. Multidimensional conceptual view. Users must be able to view data in a multidimensional way, matching the way data appears naturally in an organization.
2. Transparency. Users should not have to know the physical location of the OLAP software.
3. Accessibility. Users should perceive data as a single user view, even though it may be located physically in several heterogeneous locations.

---

*E. F. Codd, S. B. Codd, and C. T. Salley, "Providing OLAP (On-line Analytical Processing) to User Analysts: An IT Mandate," <u>Arbor Software</u> August, 1993.

4. Consistent reporting performance. Retrieval performance should not degrade as the number of dimensions and size of the warehouse grows.
5. Client/server architecture. The server component of OLAP software must be intelligent enough so that a variety of clients can be connected with minimal effort.
6. Generic dimensionality. Every data dimension must be equivalent in both its structural and operational capabilities. For example, you should be able to obtain information about products as easily as you obtain information about sales reps.
7. Dynamic sparse matrix handling. Missing data should be handled correctly and efficiently.
8. Multi-user support. OLAP software must provide secure, concurrent access. Because you don't update a data warehouse when you're using it, shared update is not an issue, so problems of security and access are less difficult than in an OLTP environment.
9. Unrestricted, cross-dimensional operations. Users must be able to perform the same operations across any number of dimensions. For example, you should be able to ask for statistics based on the dimensions of time, location, and product just as easily as you ask for statistics based on the single dimension of location.
10. Intuitive data manipulation. Users should be able to act directly on individual data values without needing to use menus or other interfaces. Of course, these other interfaces can be used, but they should not be the required method of processing.
11. Flexible reporting. Users should be able to report data results any way they want.
12. Unlimited dimensions and aggregation levels. OLAP software should allow at least 15 data dimensions and an unlimited number of aggregation (summary) levels.

OBJECT-ORIENTED DATABASE MANAGEMENT SYSTEMS

In the past, people used databases to store data consisting only of text and numbers. Today, people additionally store graphics, drawings, photographs, video, sound, voice mail, spreadsheets, and other complex objects in their databases. Relational database management systems store complex objects using special data types, generically called **binary large objects (BLOBs)**. Some applications, such as computer-aided design and manufacturing (CAD/CAM) and geographic information systems (GIS), have as their primary focus the storage and management of complex objects. For these systems, many companies use object-oriented database management systems.

What Is an Object-Oriented Database Management System?

The relational model, which has a strong theoretical foundation, is the basic standard for relational database management systems. Although object-oriented database management systems do not have a corresponding standard, they all exhibit several common characteristics. The concept of an object is at the core of all such systems. An **object** is some unit of data along with the actions that can take place on that object. A customer object, for example, would consist of the data relevant to customers (number, name, balance, and so on) together with the actions that can take place on customer data (add-customer, change-credit-limit, delete-customer, and so on).

The primary emphasis in the object-oriented systems is on the *data* rather than the actions. The actions are defined as part of the data definition. They then can be used whenever required. In contrast, in the more traditional, non-object-oriented systems, the actions are created as part of data manipulation (in the programs that update the database), rather than data definition. The data and actions actually are **encapsulated**, which means that they are hidden from the end user. In other words, you don't need to know the details of how the actions act on the data in order to use the actions or access the data. These ideas lead to the following definition:

Definition: An **object-oriented database management system (OODBMS)** is one in which data and the methods that operate on data are encapsulated into objects.

To become familiar with OODBMSs, you should have a general understanding of the following five key concepts:

1. Objects
2. Classes
3. Methods
4. Messages
5. Inheritance

Objects and Classes

Let's illustrate these terms by examining an object-oriented representation of the Premiere Products database (Figure 9.10). Actually, there is a slight variation of the Premiere Products database. There is an extra field, Allocated, in the PART table that represents the number of units of a given part currently on order (allocated).

SALES REP

SLSREP NUMBER	LAST	FIRST	STREET	CITY	STATE	ZIP CODE	TOTAL COMMISSION	COMMISSION RATE
03	Jones	Mary	123 Main	Grant	MI	49219	$2150.00	.05
06	Smith	William	102 Raymond	Ada	MI	49441	$4912.50	.07
12	Diaz	Miguel	419 Harper	Lansing	MI	49224	$2150.00	.05

CUSTOMER

CUSTOMER NUMBER	LAST	FIRST	STREET	CITY	STATE	ZIP CODE	BALANCE	CREDIT LIMIT	SLSREP NUMBER
124	Adams	Sally	481 Oak	Lansing	MI	49224	$ 818.75	$1000	03
256	Samuels	Ann	215 Pete	Grant	MI	49219	$ 21.50	$1500	06
311	Charles	Don	48 College	Ira	MI	49034	$ 825.75	$1000	12
315	Daniels	Tom	914 Cherry	Kent	MI	48391	$ 770.75	$ 750	06
405	Williams	Al	519 Watson	Grant	MI	49219	$ 402.75	$1500	12
412	Adams	Sally	16 Elm	Lansing	MI	49224	$1817.50	$2000	03
522	Nelson	Mary	108 Pine	Ada	MI	49441	$ 98.75	$1500	12
567	Dinh	Tran	808 Ridge	Harper	MI	48421	$ 402.40	$ 750	06
587	Galvez	Mara	512 Pine	Ada	MI	49441	$ 114.60	$1000	06
622	Martin	Dan	419 Chip	Grant	MI	49219	$1045.75	$1000	03

ORDERS

ORDER NUMBER	ORDER DATE	CUSTOMER NUMBER
12489	9/02/98	124
12491	9/02/98	311
12494	9/04/98	315
12495	9/04/98	256
12498	9/05/98	522
12500	9/05/98	124
12504	9/05/98	522

ORDER LINE

ORDER NUMBER	PART NUMBER	NUMBER ORDERED	QUOTED PRICE
12489	AX12	11	$ 21.95
12491	BT04	1	$149.99
12491	BZ66	1	$399.99
12494	CB03	4	$279.99
12495	CX11	2	$ 22.95
12498	AZ52	2	$ 12.95
12498	BA74	4	$ 24.95
12500	BT04	1	$149.99
12504	CZ81	2	$325.99

PART

PART NUMBER	PART DESCRIPTION	UNITS ON HAND	ITEM CLASS	WAREHOUSE NUMBER	UNIT PRICE	ALLOCATED
AX12	Iron	104	HW	3	$ 24.95	11
AZ52	Dartboard	20	SG	2	$ 12.95	2
BA74	Basketball	40	SG	1	$ 29.95	4
BH22	Cornpopper	95	HW	3	$ 24.95	0
BT04	Gas Grill	11	AP	2	$149.99	2
BZ66	Washer	52	AP	3	$399.99	1
CA14	Griddle	78	HW	3	$ 39.99	0
CB03	Bike	44	SG	1	$299.99	4
CX11	Blender	112	HW	3	$ 22.95	2
CZ81	Treadmill	68	SG	2	$349.95	2

Figure 9.10 Premiere Products sample data

Figure 9.11 shows a representation of this database as a collection of objects.

> **Note** This is just one approach to representing objects. There are many different ways of doing so. They all represent the same general features, however.

At first glance, it doesn't look much different from the relational model representation you are used to working with (Figure 9.12). If you look closer, however, you'll see some differences:

1. For each entity SLSREP, CUSTOMER, and so on) there is an object rather than a relation.

2. The properties (attributes) are listed vertically under the object names. In addition, each property is followed by the set of values with which the property is associated.

3. Objects can contain other objects. The SLSREP object, for example, contains as one of its properties, the CUSTOMER object. The letters "*MV*" following the CUSTOMER object indicate it is multivalued. In other words, a single occurrence of the SLSREP object can contain multiple occurrences of the CUSTOMER object. Roughly speaking, this is analogous to a relation containing a repeating group.

4. An object can contain just a portion of another object. The CUSTOMER object, for example, contains the SLSREP object. The word "SUBSET" indicates, however, that it only contains a subset of the object. In this case, it only contains three of the properties: Slsrnumber, Slsrlast, and Slsrfirst.

Notice that two objects each can appear to contain the other. The SLSREP object, for example, contains the CUSTOMER object, and the CUSTOMER object contains the SLSREP object (or at least a subset of it). The important thing to keep in mind here is that users deal with *objects*. If the users of the CUSTOMER object require the sales rep's number and name, they will be part of this object. If the users of the SLSREP object require data about all the customers of the sales rep, the CUSTOMER object will be viewed as part of the SLSREP object. This is not to imply, of course, that the data will be stored physically in this fashion. Rather this is the way it appears as far as users are concerned.

Objects can contain more than one other object. Consider the ORDERS object, for example. It contains the CUSTOMER object and the ORDERLINE object, with the ORDERLINE object being multivalued. Nevertheless, to users of this object, it is a single unit.

SLSREP OBJECT

Slsrnumber:	Slsrep-numbers
Slsrlast:	Names
Slsrfirst:	Names
Slsrstreet:	Addresses
Slsrcity:	Cities
Slsrstate:	States
Slsrzip:	Zip-codes
Totcomm:	Commissions
Commrate:	Commission-rates
CUSTOMER:	CUSTOMER OBJECT; MV

PART OBJECT

Partnumber:	Part-numbers
Partdesc:	Part-descriptions
Unonhand:	Units
Itemclass:	Item-classes
Warehouse:	Warehouse-numbers
Unitprice:	Prices
Allocated:	Units
ORDERLINE:	ORDERLINE OBJECT; MV

ORDERLINE OBJECT

Ordnumber:	Order-numbers
Partnumber:	Part-numbers
Numordered:	Units
Quoteprice:	Prices

CUSTOMER OBJECT

Custnumber:	Customer-numbers
Custlast:	Names
Custfirst:	Names
Custstreet:	Addresses
Custcity:	Cities
Custstate:	States
Custzip:	Zip-codes
Currbal:	Balances
Credlimit:	Credit-limits
SLSREP:	SLSREP OBJECT; SUBSET [Slsrnumber, Slsrlast, Slsrfirst]

ORDERS OBJECT

Ordnumber:	Order-numbers
Orddate:	Dates
CUSTOMER:	CUSTOMER OBJECT; SUBSET[Custnumber, Custlast, Custfirst, Slsrnumber]
ORDERLINE:	ORDERLINE OBJECT; MV

Figure 9.11 Object-oriented representation of Premiere Products database

SALES_REP (<u>SLSREP_NUMBER</u>, LAST, FIRST, STREET,
CITY, STATE, ZIP_CODE, TOTAL_COMMISSION,
COMMISSION_RATE)

CUSTOMER (<u>CUSTOMER_NUMBER</u>, LAST, FIRST, STREET,
CITY, STATE, ZIP_CODE, SLSREP_NUMBER)

PART (<u>PART_NUMBER</u>, PART_DESCRIPTION, UNITS_ON_HAND, ITEM_CLASS,
WAREHOUSE_NUMBER, UNIT_PRICE, ALLOCATED)

ORDERS (<u>ORDER_NUMBER</u>, ORDER_DATE, CUSTOMER_NUMBER)

ORDER_LINE (<u>ORDER_NUMBER</u>, <u>PART_NUMBER</u>, NUMBER_ORDERED,
QUOTED_PRICE)

Figure 9.12 Underlying relations for Premiere Products database

Technically, what you have defined are not objects, but classes. The term **class** refers to the general structure. The term object really refers to a specific occurrence of a class. Thus, SLSREP is a class, whereas the data for sales rep 12 would be an object. Often, however, you don't need to bother with this distinction and you use the words almost interchangeably.

Methods and Messages

The actions defined for an object (class) are called **methods**. Figure 9.13 shows two methods associated with the ORDERS object. The first, ADD-ORDER, is used to add an order. The data for the order is to be found in W-ORDERS.

Question	Describe the steps in the ADD-ORDER method.
Answer	The steps accomplish the following: 1. Add an appropriate row to the ORDERS table. 2. For each order line record associated with the order, add an appropriate row to the ORDERLINE table. 3. Also for each order line record, update the *Allocated* value for the appropriate part.

The other method, DELETE-ORDER, is used to delete an order. The only data required as input to this method is the number of the order to be deleted.

METHODS

ADD-ORDER (W-ORDERS)

    Add row to ORDERS table

        Ordnumber   := W-Ordnumber

        Orddate   := W-Orddate

        Custnumber   := W-Custnumber

    For each order line record in W-ORDERS DO

        Add row to ORDERLINE table

            Ordnumber   := W-Ordnumber

            Partnumber   := W-Partnumber

            Numordered   := W-Numordered

            Quoteprice   := W-Quoteprice

        Update Part table (WHERE Partnumber = W-Partnumber)

            Allocated   := Allocated + W-Numordered

DELETE-ORDER (W-ORDNUMBER)

    Delete row from ORDERS table (WHERE Ordnumber = W-Ordnumber)

    For each order line record (WHERE Ordnumber = W-Ordnumber) DO

        Delete row from ORDERLINE table

        Update part table (WHERE PART.Partnumber = ORDERLINE.Partnumber)

            Allocated   := Allocated - Numordered

Figure 9.13 Two methods for Premiere Products database

Question	Describe the steps in the DELETE-ORDER method.
Answer	The steps accomplish the following: 1. Delete the order with the indicated number from the ORDERS table. 2. For each ORDERLINE record on which the order number matches the indicated number, delete the record. 3. Also for each such ORDERLINE record, subtract the Numordered value from the Allocated value for the corresponding part. (With this record deleted, the parts no longer are allocated.)

| Note | The methods just illustrated are fairly complicated, each involving many separate updates. Many methods are much simpler. |

These methods are defined during the data definition process. To actually execute the steps indicated in a method, you send what is termed a message to the object. A **message** is a request to execute the method. As part of sending the message, you must send the required data (for example, full order data for ADD-ORDER; only the order number for DELETE-ORDER). The whole process is similar to the process of calling a subroutine in a standard programming language.

Inheritance

One of the key features of object-oriented systems is **inheritance**. For any class, you can define a subclass. Every occurrence of the subclass also is considered to be an occurrence of the class. The subclass *inherits* the structure of the class as well as the methods. In addition, you can define additional properties and methods for the subclass.

As an example, suppose Premiere Products has a special type of order. It has all the characteristics of other orders. In addition, it contains a freight amount and a discount that are calculated in a special way. Rather than create a new class for this type of order, it will be a subclass of ORDERS. In that way, it automatically has all the properties of ORDERS. It has all the same methods, including the appropriate updating of Allocated whenever orders are added or deleted. The only thing you would have to add would be those properties and methods that are specific to this new type of order, thus greatly simplifying the entire process.

Object-Oriented Database Design

There are some database designers who use an "object-oriented" approach to database design. Usually, this means the design process is oriented toward objects. Each user view is designed and documented using some object-oriented representation. These objects still need to be normalized, however, and converted to a representation appropriate for the selected DBMS.

Rules for Object-Oriented Systems

Just as there are rules indicating desired characteristics for DDBMSs and OLAP, there is a similar set of rules for object-oriented systems. They are as follows:

1. Complex objects. The DBMS supports the creation of complex objects from simple objects such as integers, characters, and so on.

2. Object identity. The DBMS must furnish a way to identify objects; that is, there must be a way to distinguish between one object and another.

3. Encapsulation. The data and the procedures that act on data should be stored as part of the database. Details concerning the way the data is stored and the actual implementation of the procedures are hidden from the users of the database.

4. Types or classes. You already are familiar with the idea of a class. Types are very similar to classes and correspond to abstract data types in programming languages. The differences between the two are subtle and we will not explore them here. It is important that an object-oriented DBMS supports either types or classes (it doesn't matter which).

5. Inheritance. You already learned about the important concept of inheritance and the benefits that can come from it. An object-oriented DBMS should support inheritance.

6. Late Binding. **Binding**, in this case, refers to the association of operations to actual program code. With late binding this association does not happen until runtime; that is, until some user actually invokes the operation. This allows the use of the same name for what are, in fact, different operations. For example, an operation to display an object on the screen will require a different program code if the object is a picture than if the object is text. With late binding, you could use the same name for both operations. At the time a user invokes this "display" operation, the system will determine the object being displayed and then bind the operation to the appropriate program code.

7. Computational completeness. Functions for performing various computations can be expressed in the language of the DBMS.

8. Extensibility. Any DBMS, object-oriented or not, comes with a set of predefined types, such as Numeric and Character. An OODBMS should be **extensible**, meaning that it is possible to define new types. Further, there should be no distinction between the types furnished by the system and these new types.

9. Persistence. In object-oriented programming, **persistence** refers to the ability to have a program *remember* its data from one execution to the next. Although this is unusual in programming languages, it is common in all database systems. After all, one of the fundamental capabilities of any DBMS is the capability to store data for later use.

10. Performance. An OODBMS should have sufficient performance capabilities to effectively manage very large databases.

11. Shared update support. An OODBMS should support shared update. (This concept was discussed in Chapter 7.)

12. Recovery support. An OODBMS should provide recovery services. (This concept was discussed in Chapter 7.)

13. Query facility. An OODBMS should provide some type of query facility. (Query facilities like SQL and QBE were discussed in Chapter 2 and Chapter 3, respectively.)

THE INTERNET AND INTRANETS

Over the past few years, the Internet and the closely related World Wide Web (Web) have shown phenomenal growth, both in numbers of users and the availability of software tools. In particular, many database vendors now allow their products to connect to the Web; this is clearing the way for **electronic commerce (e-commerce)** based on an organization's databases. Internally, organizations are constructing **intranets** (internal Internets) to do their internal processing, using a combination of Web browsers, RDBMSs, DDBMSs, OODBMSs, client/server systems, and data warehouses. Figure 9.14 shows a typical use of Web browsers through the Internet and on an intranet to access and update a company's database.

Externally, companies benefit in two ways from their use of the Web for database processing. First, they can export and link data from their databases to suppliers, customers, and others outside the company; this provides current information in a timely way to those needing the information. Second, companies can allow customers, for example, to place orders that directly update the organization's database and trigger the processing required to fulfill the order.

Over the next few years, more and more database processing will be Internet and Web enabled. This will allow organizations to be more efficient and effective in the way they carry out their business functions.

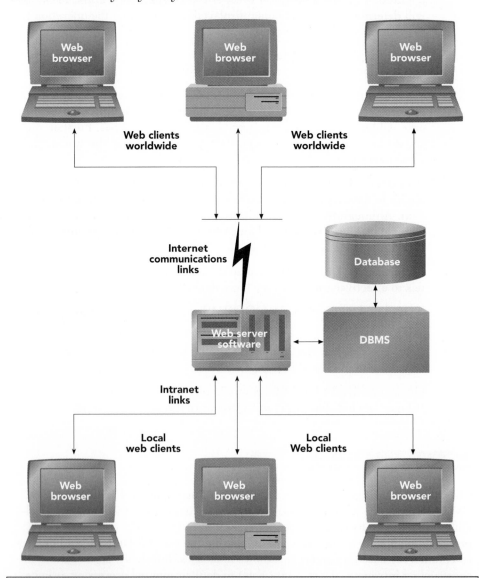

Figure 9.14 Using Web browsers on the Internet and on an intranet to access and update a company's database

SUMMARY

1. A distributed database is a database stored on several computers linked in some kind of network. A user at any site can access data at any other site. A distributed database management system (DDBMS) is a DBMS capable of supporting and manipulating distributed databases.

2. A homogenous DDBMS is one that has the same local DBMS at each site, whereas a heterogeneous DDBMS is one that does not.

3. Location transparency, replication transparency, and fragmentation transparency are characteristics of DDBMSs.

4. DDBMSs permit local control of data, increased capacity, improved system availability, and increased efficiency.

5. DDBMSs are more complicated in the areas of the update of replicated data, the processing of queries, the treatment of shared updates, the measures for recovery, the management of the data dictionary, and the design of databases.

6. C. J. Date presented 12 rules that a DDBMS should follow.

7. In a client/server system, a DBMS runs on a server, handling requests for data from the individual workstations, or clients.

8. A trigger is an action that will take place automatically when an associated database operation takes place in a client/server system.

9. Online transaction processing (OLAP) is used with relational database management systems, and online analytical processing (OLAP) is used with data warehouses.

10. A data warehouse is a subject-oriented, integrated, time-variant, nonvolatile collection of data in support of management's decision-making process.

11. The typical data warehouse data structure is a multidimensional database, consisting of a central fact table, surrounded by dimension tables.

12. E. F. Codd presented 12 rules that an OLAP system should follow.

13. Object-oriented systems deal with data as objects. Each of the properties of an object is associated with a class (domain). The key concept is that the actions that manipulate an object are defined as part of the definition of the object. These actions are called methods. To cause a particular method to be executed, you send a message to the object. You can define subclasses that inherit both the structure and methods of another class.

14. Thirteen rules describe the desired characteristics for object-oriented systems.

15. The Internet and the Web are playing an increasingly important role in an organization's database processing in an electronic commerce (e-commerce) environment. Web browsers can be used to access and update databases both through the Internet and through internal networks (intranets).

KEY TERMS

Binary large object (BLOB)

Binding

Catalog

Class

Client/server system

Communications network

Coordinator

Data dictionary

Data fragmentation

Data warehouse

Deadlock

Dimension table

Distributed database

Distributed database management system (DDBMS)

Electronic commerce (e-commerce)

Encapsulated

Extensible

Fact table

File server

Fragmentation transparency

Global deadlock

Growing phase

Heterogeneous DDBMS

Homogeneous DDBMS

Inheritance

Integrated

Intranet

Local deadlock

Local site

Location transparency

Lock

Message

Method

Multidimensional database

Nonvolatile

Object

Object-oriented database management system (OODBMS)

Online analytical processing (OLAP)

Online transaction processing (OLTP)

Persistence

Primary copy

Recovery

Remote site

Replication

Replication transparency

Roll back

Shared update

Shrinking phase

Star-join schema

Stored procedure

Subject-oriented

Time-variant

Trigger

Two-phase commit

Two-phase locking

REVIEW QUESTIONS

1. What is a distributed database? What is a distributed database management system (DDBMS)?

2. How does a homogeneous DDBMS differ from a heterogeneous DDBMS? Which is more complex?

3. What is meant by a local site? By a remote site?

4. What is location transparency?

5. What is replication? Why is it used? What benefit is derived from using it? What are the biggest potential problems?

6. What is replication transparency?

7. What is data fragmentation? What purpose does it serve?

8. What is fragmentation transparency?

9. Explain why each of the following features of distributed systems is advantageous:

    a. Local control of data

    b. Capability to increase system capacity

    c. System availability

    d. Increased efficiency

10. Why is query processing more complex in a distributed environment?

11. What is meant by local deadlock? By global deadlock?

12. Describe the principle of two-phase commit. How does it work? Why is it necessary?

13. Describe the various possible approaches to storing data dictionary entries in a distributed system.

14. What additional factors must be considered during the information-level design process if the design is for a distributed database?

15. What additional factors must be considered during the physical-level design process if the design is for a distributed database?

16. List and briefly describe the 12 rules that a distributed system should follow.

17. What is the difference between a file-server and a client/server system?

18. List the advantages to the client/server approach.

19. List the features client/server systems should possess.

20. What are triggers? What purpose do they serve?

21. What are stored procedures? What purpose do they serve?

22. What are the characteristics of online transaction processing (OLTP) systems?

23. What is a data warehouse?

24. What does it mean that a data warehouse is nonvolatile?

25. What are the names of the different tables in a multidimensional database?

26. When is online analytical processing (OLAP) used?

27. List and briefly describe the 12 rules that an OLAP system should follow.

28. What is an object? What is a class? How do classes relate to objects?

29. What is the meaning of encapsulation in an object-oriented system?

30. What is a method? What is a message? How do messages relate to methods?

31. What is inheritance? What are the benefits to inheritance?

32. List and briefly describe the 13 rules that an object-oriented system should follow.

33. How are organizations employing their databases on the Internet and the Web?

34. If your school is using the Internet and/or an intranet to manipulate data stored in a database, investigate how this is being accomplished (which software and database entities are used). If not, what are your school's future plans in this arena?

ANSWERS TO ODD-NUMBERED QUESTIONS

CHAPTER 1 — INTRODUCTION TO DATABASE MANAGEMENT

1. A file is a structure that is used to store data about a single entity; it can be viewed as a table. A record is a row in the table. A field is a column.

3. A relationship is an association between entities.

5. A database is a structure that can house information about several types of entities, the attributes of these entities, and the relationships among them.

7. The purchase price of microcomputer DBMSs is relatively low, ranging from $100 to $800. In contrast, the cost of a good mainframe DBMS can run as high as $400,000.

9. Sharing of data means that many users will have access to the same data.

11. Redundancy is the duplication of data. It wastes space, makes updating more difficult, and may lead to inconsistencies in the data.

13. Integrity means that the data in the database follows certain rules (called integrity constraints) that users have established.

15. Data independence is the property by which the structure of a database can be altered without changes having to be made in the programs that access the database. With data independence, it is easy to change the structure of the database when the need arises.

17. The more complex a product is in general (and a DBMS, in particular, is complex), the more difficult it is to understand and correctly apply its features. As a result of this complexity, serious problems may result from mistakes made by the user of the DBMS.

19. Recovery can be more difficult in a database environment, partly because of the greater complexity of the structure. It is also likely that in the database environment several users will be making updates at the same time, which means that recovering the database involves not only restoring it to the last state in which it was known to be correct, but also performing the complex task of redoing all the updates made since that time.

CHAPTER 2 — THE RELATIONAL MODEL 1: INTRODUCTION, QBE, AND THE RELATIONAL ALGEBRA

3. A relation is a two-dimensional table in which (1) the entries in the table are single-valued; (2) each column has a distinct name; (3) all of the values in a column are values of the same attribute; (4) the order of the columns is immaterial; (5) each row is distinct; and (6) the order of the rows is immaterial.

5. An unnormalized relation is a structure that satisfies all the properties of a relation except the restriction that entries must be single-valued. It is not a relation.

7. In the shorthand representation, each table is listed, and after each table, all the columns of the table are listed in parentheses. Primary keys are underlined.
   BRANCH (<u>BRANCH_NUMBER</u>, BRANCH_NAME, BRANCH_LOCATION, NUMBER_OF_EMPLOYEES)

PUBLISHER (<u>PUBLISHER_CODE</u>, PUBLISHER_NAME,
PUBLISHER_CITY)
AUTHOR (<u>AUTHOR_NUMBER</u>, AUTHOR_NAME)
BOOK (<u>BOOK_CODE</u>, BOOK_TITLE, PUBLISHER_CODE,
　　　BOOK_TYPE, BOOK_PRICE, PAPERBACK)
WROTE (<u>BOOK_CODE</u>, <u>AUTHOR_NUMBER</u>,
　　　SEQUENCE_NUMBER)
INVENT (<u>BOOK_CODE</u>, <u>BRANCH_NUMBER</u>,
　　　UNITS_ON_HAND)

9.　The primary key is the column or collection of columns that uniquely identifies a given row. The primary key of the BRANCH table is BRANCH_NUMBER. The primary key of the PUBLISHER table is PUBLISHER_CODE. The primary key of the AUTHOR table is AUTHOR_NUMBER. The primary key of the BOOK table is BOOK_CODE. The primary key of the WROTE table is the concatenation (combination) of BOOK_CODE and AUTHOR_NUMBER. The primary key of the INVENT table is the concatenation of BOOK_CODE and BRANCH_NUMBER.

11.　Place a check mark under the name of the table. Do not enter any conditions.

13.　Place check marks in the CUSTOMER_NUMBER, LAST, and FIRST columns. Type 03 in the SLSREP_NUMBER column and 1000 in the CREDIT_LIMIT column.

15.　Both the ORDERS table and the CUSTOMER table must be on the screen. Place check marks in the ORDER_NUMBER, ORDER_DATE, CUSTOMER_NUMBER, and LAST fields. Place the same example in the CUSTOMER_NUMBER field of the CUSTOMER table and the CUSTOMER_NUMBER field of the ORDERS table.

17.　Place CALC COUNT in the CUSTOMER_NUMBER field and type 1000 in the CREDIT LIMIT field.

19.　Place check marks in the PART_NUMBER and PART_DESCRIPTION columns. Type AP in the ITEM_CLASS column. Place examples in the UNITS_ON_HAND and UNIT_PRICE columns and then use these examples to indicate the calculation for on-hand value.

21.　SELECT PART WHERE PART_NUMBER = 'BT04' GIVING ANSWER

CHAPTER 3 — THE RELATIONAL MODEL 2: SQL

1.　To create a table in SQL, use a CREATE TABLE command that gives the name of the table followed by the names and data types of the columns that comprise the table. INTEGER allows the field to contain integers. SMALLINT allows the field to contain "small" integers (integers less than 32767). DECIMAL allows the field to contain numbers that have a decimal part. CHAR allows the field to contain character strings. DATE allows the field to contain dates.

3.　Compound conditions are formed by connecting simple conditions using AND, OR, or NOT. A compound condition using AND is true only if all the simple conditions contained in it are true. A compound condition using OR is true if one (or more) of the simple conditions contained in it are true. Preceding a condition, simple or compound, by NOT reverses the truth or falsity of the original condition. You enter compound conditions in SQL in the WHERE clause just as you enter simple conditions.

5. Use a SQL built-in function (COUNT, SUM, AVG, MAX, and MIN) by including it in the SELECT clause followed by the name of the field to which it applies.

7. To join tables in SQL, use a SELECT command that lists two or more tables to be joined in the FROM clause, and then specifies the columns to be matched in the WHERE clause.

9. The update command in SQL are INSERT, which allows you to insert new rows in a table, UPDATE, which allows you to make changes to all the rows that satisfy some condition, and DELETE, which allows you to delete all the rows that satisfy a condition.

11. SELECT *
    FROM SALES_REP

13. SELECT ORDER_NUMBER
    FROM ORDERS
    WHERE CUSTOMER_NUMBER = 124
    AND ORDER_DATE = '9/05/98'

15. SELECT CUSTOMER_NUMBER, LAST, FIRST
    FROM CUSTOMER
    WHERE LAST = 'Nelson'

17. SELECT COUNT(CUSTOMER_NUMBER)
    FROM CUSTOMER
    WHERE CREDIT_LIMIT = 1000

19. SELECT ORDER_NUMBER, ORDER_DATE,
    CUSTOMER,CUSTOMER_NUMBER, LAST, FIRST
    FROM ORDERS, CUSTOMER
    WHERE ORDERS.CUSTOMER_NUMBER =
        CUSTOMER.CUSTOMER_NUMBER

21. SELECT SALES_REP.SLSREP_NUMBER, SALES_REP.LAST,
    SALES_REP.FIRST
    FROM SALES_REP, CUSTOMER
    WHERE SALES_REP.SLSREP_NUMBER =
        CUSTOMER.SLSREP_NUMBER
    AND CREDIT_LIMIT = 1000

23. UPDATE PART
    SET PART_DESCRIPTION = 'Gas Stove'
    WHERE PART_NUMBER = 'BT04'

25. DELETE FROM CUSTOMER
    WHERE BALANCE < 100.00
    AND SLSREP_NUMBER = '12'

CHAPTER 4 — THE RELATIONAL MODEL 3: ADVANCED TOPICS

1. A view is an individual user's picture of the database. It is defined through a defining query. The data in the view never actually exists in the form described in the view. Rather, when a user accesses the view, his or her query is merged with the defining query of the view to form a query that pertains to the whole database.

3. a.

CREATE VIEW CUSTORD AS
        SELECT CUSTOMER.CUSTOMER_NUMBER,
        LAST, FIRST, BALANCE, ORDER_NUMBER, DATE
        FROM CUSTOMER, ORDERS
        WHERE CUSTOMER.CUSTOMER_NUMBER=
        ORDERS.CUSTOMER_NUMBER

   b.

SELECT CUSTOMER_NUMBER, LAST, FIRST,
        ORDER_ NUMBER, DATE
        FROM CUSTORD WHERE BALANCE > 100

   c.

SELECT CUSTOMER.CUSTOMER_NUMBER, LAST, FIRST,
        ORDER_NUMBER, DATE
        FROM CUSTOMER, ORDERS
        WHERE CUSTOMER.CUSTOMER_NUMBER =
        ORDERS.CUSTNUMB AND BALANCE > 100

5. On relational mainframe DBMSs, the optimizer (a part of the DBMS) makes the decision to use a particular index. On microcomputer DBMSs, the user or programmer makes this decision.

7. The catalog is the place where information about the database structure is maintained. Tables, columns, and indexes are three components of a database structure about which information is maintained in the catalog.

9. Nulls are special values used for missing information. The primary key should never be allowed to be null.

11. Adding an order for which the customer number does not match a row in the customer table would violate referential integrity as would changing the customer number for an order to one that does not match. If delete does not cascade, deleting a customer who has orders would violate referential integrity. If delete cascades, all the orders for a customer would be deleted when the customer is deleted.

13. Users must perceive data as tables. The SELECT, PROJECT, and JOIN operations of the relational algebra must be supported and the support must be independent of any pre-defined access paths.

15. A relational DBMS must be able to manage data entirely through its relational capabilities. All data should be represented by values in tables. Users should be able to access any value in a database by giving the name of the table, the name of the column, and a value for the primary key of the table. A relational DBMS should support null data values. A relational DBMS should furnish a user-accessible catalog. A relational DBMS must furnish at least one language capable of supporting all the following: data definition, view definition, data manipulation, integrity constraints, authorizations, and logical transactions. Any view updatable in theory must be updatable by a relational DBMS. A relational DBMS should furnish facilities for retrieving, adding, updating, or deleting a set of rows with a single command. In a relational DBMS, changes to the physical storage and/or access methods used in a database should not impact users or programs. In a relational DBMS, changes to the logical structure of a database should not impact users or

programs. The data sublanguage must support the definition of integrity constraints. A relational DBMS that manipulates a distributed database should allow users and programs to access data at a remote site in exactly the same fashion they do at the local site. Any low-level (record-at-a-time) language in a relational DBMS should not be able to be used to bypass the integrity constraints that have been specified by the high-level language.

CHAPTER 5 — DATABASE DESIGN 1: NORMALIZATION

1. Column B is functionally dependent on column A if a value for A determines a unique value for B at any time.

3. The primary key of a table is the column or collection of columns that determines all other columns in the table and for which there is no subcollection that also determines all other columns.

5. A table is in first normal form if it does not contain a repeating group.

7. A table is in third normal form if it is in second normal form and if the only determinants it contains are candidate keys. If a table is not in 3NF, redundant data will cause wasted space and update problems. Inconsistent data may also be a problem.

9. Many answers are possible. See the guidelines in Chapter 5.

11. INVOICE_NUMBER —> CUSTOMER_NUMBER, LAST, FIRST, STREET, CITY, STATE, ZIP_CODE, INVOICE_DATE CUSTOMER_NUMBER —> LAST, FIRST, STREET, CITY, STATE, ZIP_CODE
    PART_NUMBER —> PART_DESCRIPTION, UNIT_PRICE
    INVOICE_NUMBER, PART_NUMBER —> NUMBER_SHIPPED

    INVOICE (<u>INVOICE_NUMBER</u>, CUSTOMER_NUMBER, INVOICE_DATE)
    CUSTOMER (<u>CUSTOMER_NUMBER</u>, LAST, FIRST, STREET, CITY, STATE, ZIP_CODE)
    PART (<u>PART_NUMBER</u>, PART_DESCRIPTION, UNIT_PRICE)
    INVOICE_LINE (<u>INVOICE_NUMBER</u>, <u>PART_NUMBER</u>, NUMBER_SHIPPED)

CHAPTER 6 — DATABASE DESIGN 2: DESIGN METHODOLOGY

1. A user view is the view of data that is necessary to support the operations of a particular user. By considering individual user views rather than the complete design problem, we greatly simplify the database design process.

3. If the design problem were extremely simple, the overall design might not have to be broken down into a consideration of individual user views.

5. The primary key is the column or columns that uniquely identify a given row and that furnish the main mechanism for directly accessing a row in the table. An alternate key is a column or combination of columns that could have functioned as the primary key but was not chosen to do so. A secondary key is a column or combination of columns that is not any other type of key but is of interest for purposes of retrieval. A foreign key is a column or combination of columns in one table whose values that are required to match the primary key in another table. Foreign keys furnish the mechanism through which relationships are made explicit.

7. a. Include the project number as a foreign key in the employee table.

   b. Include the employee number as a foreign key in the project table.

   c. Create a new table whose primary key is the concatenation of employee number and project number.

9. Instead of the advisor number being included as a foreign key in the student table, there would be an additional table whose primary key was the concatenation of student number and advisor number.

11. BRANCH (<u>BRANCH_NUMBER</u>, BRANCH_NAME, BRANCH_LOCATION, NUMBER_OF_EMPLOYEES)
    Secondary key BRANCH_NAME
    BRANCH_NUMBER must be unique
    PUBLISHER (<u>PUBLISHER_CODE</u>, PUBLISHER_NAME, PUBLISHER_CITY)
    PUBLISHER_CODE must be unique
    AUTHOR (<u>AUTHOR_NUMBER</u>, AUTHOR_NAME)
    AUTHOR_NUMBER must be unique
    BOOK (<u>BOOK_CODE</u>, BOOK_TITLE, PUBLISHER_CODE, BOOK_TYPE, BOOK_PRICE, PAPERBACK)
    Foreign key PUBLISHER_CODE matches PUBLISHER
    BOOK_CODE must be unique
    WROTE (<u>BOOK_CODE</u>, <u>AUTHOR_NUMBER</u>, SEQUENCE_NUMBER)
    Foreign key BOOK_CODE matches BOOK
    Foreign key AUTHOR_NUMBER matches AUTHOR
    The combination of BOOK_CODE and AUTHOR_NUMBER must be unique
    BOOK_CODE must match the code of a book in the BOOK table
    AUTHOR_NUMBER must match the number of an author in the AUTHOR table
    INVENT (<u>BOOK_CODE</u>, <u>BRANCH_NUMBER</u>, UNITS_ON_HAND)
    Foreign key BOOK_CODE matches BOOK
    Foreign key BRANCH_NUMBER matches BRANCH
    The combination of BOOK_CODE and BRANCH_NUMBER must be unique
    BOOK_CODE must match the code of a book in the BOOK table
    BRANCH_NUMBER must match the number of a branch in the BRANCH table

CHAPTER 7 — FUNCTIONS OF A DATABASE MANAGEMENT SYSTEM

1. The DBMS must furnish a mechanism for storing data and for enabling users to retrieve data from the database and to update data in the database. This mechanism should not require the users to be aware of the details with respect to how the data is actually stored.

3. Shared update refers to two or more users updating data in a database at the same time.

5. Locking is the process whereby only one user is allowed to access a specific portion of a database at a time. When a user is accessing a portion of the database, it is locked, meaning that it is unavailable to any other user.

7. Deadlock is the circumstance in which user A is waiting for resources that have been locked by user B, and user B is waiting for resources that have been locked by user A; unless action to the contrary is taken, the two will wait for each other forever. It occurs when each of the two users is attempting to access data that is held by the other.

9. a. Each user must attempt to lock all the resources he or she needs before beginning any updates. If any of the resources are already locked by another user, all locks must be released and the process must begin all over again.

    b. Before updating a record, user 1 should make sure that the record has not been updated by user 2 since the time user 1 first read it. To understand why this is necessary, read part c of this answer.

    c. After reading a record, a user should immediately release the lock on it.

11. Security is the prevention of unauthorized access to the database.

13. Encryption is the process whereby data is transformed into another form before it is stored in the database. The data is returned to its original form when it is retrieved by a legitimate user. This process prevents a person who bypasses the DBMS and accesses the database directly from seeing the relevant data.

15. A database has integrity when the data in it follows certain established rules, called integrity constraints. Integrity constraints can be handled in four ways: (1) They can be ignored. (2) The responsibility for enforcing them can be assigned to the user (that is, it would be up to the user not to enter invalid data). (3) They can be enforced by programs. (4) They can be enforced by the DBMS. Of these four, the most desirable is the last. When the DBMS enforces the integrity constraints, users don't have to constantly guard against entering incorrect data, and programmers are spared having to build the logic to enforce these constraints into the programs they write.

17. Many examples are possible; if you need help in remembering some, see the list in this chapter.

19. The answer depends on the particular DBMS being used at your school.

CHAPTER 8 — DATABASE ADMINISTRATION

1. DBA is database administration, the person or group that is responsible for the database. The responsibilities of DBA are crucial to success in the database environment, especially if the database is to be shared among several users; these responsibilities include determining access privileges; establishing and enforcing security procedures; determining and enforcing policies with respect to the use of a data dictionary; and so on.

3. DBA determines access privileges, uses the DBMS security facilities such as passwords, encryption, and views, and supplements these features, where necessary, with special programs.
    Users often choose passwords that are easy for others to guess, such as the names of family members. Users can also be careless with the paper on which passwords are written. To prevent others from guessing their passwords, users should guard against doing either of these things and should also change their passwords frequently.

5. Certain corporate data, though no longer required in the active database, must be kept for future reference. A data archive is a place for storing this type of data. The use of data archives allows an. organization to keep records indefinitely, without causing the database to become unnecessarily large. Data can be removed from the database and placed in the data archive, instead of just being deleted.

7. DBA does some of the training of computer users. Other training, such as that which is provided by a software vendor, is coordinated by DBA.

9. a. What facilities are provided by the system for defining a new database? What data types are supported?

   b. What facilities are present to assist in the restructuring of a database?

   c. What nonprocedural language (a language in which we tell the computer what the task is rather than how to do it) is furnished by the system? How does its functionality compare with that of SQL?

   d. What procedural language (a language in which we tell the computer how to do the task) is provided by the system? How complete is it? How is the integration between the procedural language and the nonprocedural language accomplished?

   e. What data dictionary is included? What types of information can be held in the dictionary? How well is it integrated with the other parts of the system?

   f. What support does the system provide for shared update? What type of locking is used? Can the system handle deadlock?

   g. What services does the system provide for backup and recovery? Does recovery consist only of copying a backup over the live database, or does the system support the use of a journal in the recovery process?

   h. What security features are provided by the system? Does it support passwords, encryption, and/or views? How easy is it for a user to bypass the security controls of the DBMS?

   i. What type of integrity support is present? What kinds of integrity constraints can be enforced?

   j. What types of support does it provide for replication and for distributing data.

   k. What are the system limitations with respect to the number of tables, columns, rows, and the number of files that can be open at the same time? What hardware limitations exist?

   l. How good are the manuals? How good is the on-line help facility, if there is one?

   m. What reputation does the vendor have for support of their products?

   n. How well does the system perform?

   o. How portable is the system?

   p. What is the cost of the DBMS, of additional hardware, and of support?

   q. What plans does the vendor have for further development of the system?

   r. This category includes any special requirements an organization might have that do not fit into any of the previous categories.

11. DBA has primary responsibility for the DBMS once it has been selected. DBA installs the DBMS, makes any changes to its configuration when they are required, determines whether it is appropriate to install a new version of the DBMS when it becomes available, and, if a decision is made to install a new DBMS, coordinates the installation.

13. The answer depends on the DBMS you selected.

CHAPTER 9 — ADVANCED TOPICS

1. A distributed database is one in which the data is physically stored at more than one site. A distributed database management system is a database management system capable of managing a distributed database.

3. The local site is the one at which the user is currently operating. A remote site is any other site in the network.

5. Replication is the storing of the same data item at more than one site in the network. It is done to speed access to the data. The benefit is that users at each of the sites where the replicated data is stored can access the data more efficiently than they could if the data were stored only at some remote site. The main problem concerns update: when replicated data is updated, all copies of the data around the network must be updated.

7. Data fragmentation is the dividing of a logical object, like the collection of all records of a given type, among the various locations in a network. Its main purpose is to place data at the site where it is most often accessed.

9. a. Since each location can keep its own data, greater local control can be exercised over it.

    b. In a well-designed distributed system, capacity can often be increased at only one site rather than for the whole database. Capacity can be further increased through the addition of new sites to the network.

    c. Other users can continue their processing even though a site on the network is unavailable. In a centralized system, no users can continue processing if the database is unavailable.

    d. Data available locally can be retrieved much more efficiently than data stored on a remote, centralized system.

11. Local deadlock means two users at the same site are in deadlock. Global deadlock means two users at different sites are in deadlock.

13. The complete data dictionary may be stored at a single site. A complete copy of the data dictionary may be stored at every site. The entries in the dictionary may be distributed among the sites in the network (possibly with replication).

15. In the physical-level design process, in addition to all the usual factors, communication time must be considered in the choice of an optimum design.

17. A file server returns entire files to workstations on a network, whereas, in a client/server system, the server only returns the necessary data.

19. Client/server systems should possess the following features: support for SQL; a central data dictionary; optimization to provide maximum performance; support for data integrity; support for logical transactions; support for shared update; support for security; and support for backup and recover.

21. A stored procedure is a special file containing a collection of SQL statements that will be executed frequently. The statements in a stored procedure are compiled and optimized, enabling the stored procedure to execute as efficiently and as rapidly as possible.

23. A data warehouse is a subject-oriented, time-variant, nonvolatile collection of data in support of management's decision-making process.

25. A multidimensional database contains a central fact table, which consists of many rows containing consolidated and summarized data, and several dimension tables, each of which contains a single-part primary key that serves as an index into the fact table and contains other fields associated with that primary key value. The fact table has a multipart primary key, each part of which is a foreign key to the surrounding dimension tables.

27. OLAP systems should follow the following twelve rules: users should be able to view data in a multidimensional way; the location of OLAP software should be transparent to users; the location of data should be transparent to users; the size and complexity of the warehouse should not affect performance; the server portion of the OLAP software should allow the use of different types of clients; each data dimension should have the same structural and operational capabilities; nulls should be handled correctly and efficiently; OLAP should provide secure, concurrent access; users should be able to perform the same operations across any number of dimensions; users should not need to use special interfaces to make their requests; users should be able to report data results any way they want; OLAP software should allow at least 15 data dimensions and an unlimited number of summary levels.

29. In an object-oriented system, encapsulation is the characteristic that the details about the data and its procedures are hidden from the users of a database without affecting their ability to access the data and use the procedures.

31. When one class is a subclass of another, it inherits the structure of the class as well as the methods that apply to the class. The benefit to this is that we only need to define the structure or methods that were not inherited from the class.

33. Organizations are using the Internet and the Web increasingly to provide information from their databases to customers, suppliers, and others. At the same time, customers and other external entities use the Internet and the Web to directly update an organization's internal databases.

GLOSSARY

■

Alias An alternate name for a table; can be used within a query.

Alternate key A candidate key that was not chosen to be the primary key.

Archive *see data archive*.

Attribute A property of an entity.

■

Background The permanent part of a screen form, that is, the part that does not change from one transaction to the next. See also *foreground*.

Backup A copy of a database; used to recover the database when it has been damaged or destroyed.

Batch processing Processing of a transaction file, which contains a *batch* of records, to update a database or another file.

Binary large object (BLOB) A generic term for a special data type used by relational database management systems to store complex objects.

Binding The association of operations to actual program code in an object-oriented system.

Boyce-Codd Normal Form (BCNF) A relation is in Boyce-Codd normal form if it is in second normal form and the only determinants it contains are candidate keys; also called third normal form in this text.

■

Candidate key A minimal collection of attributes (columns) in a relation on which all attributes are functionally dependent but which has not necessarily been chosen as the *primary key*.

Calculated field A field whose value may be computed from other fields in the database.

Catalog A source of information on the types of entities, attributes, and relationships in a database.

Class The general structure of an object in an object-oriented system.

Client/server system A networked system in which a special site on the network, called the *server* provides services to the other sites, called the *clients*. Clients send requests for the specific services they need. Software, often including a DBMS, running on the server then processes the request and sends only the appropriate data and other results back to the client.

Communications network A number of computers configured in such a way that data can be sent from any one computer in the network to any other.

Compound condition Two simple conditions combined with AND or OR.

Computed field A field whose value may be computed from other fields in the database.

Concatenation Combination of attributes. To say a key is a concatenation of two attributes, for example, means that a combination of values of both attributes is required to uniquely identify a given tuple.

Concurrent update Several updates taking place to the same file or database at almost the same time; also called *shared update*.

Condition A statement that can be either true or false. In queries, only records for which the statement is true will be included.

Coordinator In a distributed network, the site that directs the update process. Often, it is the site that initiates the transaction.

Data archive A place where historical corporate data is kept. Data that is no longer needed in the corporate database but must be retained for future needs is removed from the database and placed in the archive.

Data definition language A language that is used to communicate the structure of a database to the database management system.

Data dictionary A tool that is used to store descriptions of the entities, attributes, relationships, programs, and so on, that are associated with an organization's database.

Data fragmentation The process of dividing a logical object, such as the collection of records of a certain type, among various locations in a distributed database.

Data independence The property that allows the structure of the database to change without requiring changes in programs.

Data warehouse A data warehouse is a subject-oriented, integrated, time-variant, nonvolatile collection of data in support of management's decision-making process.

Database A structure that can house information about various types of entities and about the relationships among the entities.

Database administration (DBA) The individual or group that is responsible for the database.

Database administrator The individual who is responsible for the database, or the head of database administration.

Database design The process of determining the content and arrangement of data in a database in order to support some activity on behalf of a user or group of users.

Database Design Language (DBDL) A relational-like language that is used to represent the result of the database design process.

Database management system A software package that is designed to manipulate the data in a database on behalf of a user.

Database processing The type of processing in which the data is stored in a *database* and manipulated by *a DBMS*.

DBA See *database administration*. (Sometimes the acronym stands for database administrator).

DBDL See *database design language*.

DBMS See *database management system*.

Deadlock A state in which two or more users are each waiting to use resources that are held by the other(s).

Deadly embrace Another name for *deadlock*.

Defining query The query that is used to define the structure of a view.

Dependency diagram A diagram that indicates the dependencies among the attributes in a relation.

Determinant An attribute that determines at least one other attribute.

Dimension table A table in a data warehouse that contains a single-part primary key, serving as an index into the central fact table, and other fields associated with the primary key value.

Distributed database A database that is stored on computers at several sites of a computer network and in which users can access data at any site of the network.

Distributed database management system (DDBMS) A database management system that is capable of manipulating distributed databases.

DML See *data manipulation language.*

E-commerce Electronic commerce on the World Wide Web (Web).

Encapsulated The binding together of data and actions in an object-oriented system so that they are hidden from user view.

Encryption The transformation of data into another form, for the purpose of security, before it is stored in the database. The data is returned to its original form for any legitimate user who accesses the database.

Entity An object (person, place, or thing) of interest.

Entity integrity The rule that no attribute that participates in the primary key may accept null values.

Example In Query-by-Example an entry that represents a possible value in a field. Matching examples are used to join tables.

Extensible The capability of defining new data types in an object-oriented database management system.

Fact table The central table in a data warehouse that consists of many rows that contain consolidated and summarized data.

Field The smallest unit of data to which we assign a name; can be thought of as the columns in a table. For example, in a table for customers, the fields (columns) would include such things as the customer's number, the customer's name and address, and so on.

File Technically, a collection of bytes (characters) on a disk; could be data, a program, a document created by a word processor, and so on. Often refers to a data file, which is a structure used to store data about some entity. Such a file can be thought of as a table. The rows in such a table are called records, and the columns are called fields.

File server A networked system in which a special site on the network stores files for users at other sites. When a user needs a file, the file server sends the entire file to the user.

First Normal Form (1NF) A relation is in first normal form if it does not contain repeating groups. (Technically, this is part of the definition of a relation.).

Foreground The portion of a screen form that changes from one transaction to the next, that is, the portion of the form into which the user enters data and/or data is displayed. See also *background*.

Foreign key An attribute (or collection of attributes) in a relation whose value is required either to match the value of a primary key in another relation or to be null.

Form A screen object you use to maintain, view, and print records from a database.

Fragmentation transparency The property that users do not need to be aware of any data fragmentation (splitting of data) that has taken place in a distributed database.

Fully relational The expression used to refer to a DBMS in which users perceive data as tables, which supports all the operations of the *relational algebra* and which supports *entity* and *referential integrity*.

Functionally dependent Attribute B is functionally dependent on attribute A (or on a collection of attributes) if a value for A determines a single value for B at any one time.

Functionally determine Attribute A functionally determines attribute B if B is *functionally dependent* on A.

Global deadlock Deadlock in a distributed database that cannot be detected solely at any individual site.

Growing phase A phase during an update in which new locks are acquired but no locks are released.

Help facility A facility through which users can receive on-line assistance.

Heterogeneous DDBMS A distributed DBMS in which at least two of the local DBMSs are different from each other.

Homogeneous DDBMS A distributed DBMS in which all the local DBMSs are the same.

Index A file that relates key values to records that contain those key values.

Information level of database design The step during *database design* in which the goal is to create a clean, DBMS-independent design that will support user requirements.

Inheritance The property that a subclass inherits the structure of the class as well as the methods.

Integrity A database has integrity if all *integrity constraints* that have been established for it are currently met.

Integrity constraint A condition that data within a database must satisfy; also, a condition that indicates the types of processing that may or may not take place.

Integrity rules See *entity integrity* and *referential integrity*.

Intranet The use of Internet and Web software tools on an internal network.

■

Join In the *relational algebra,* the operation in which two tables are connected on the basis of common data.

Join column The column on which two tables will be joined. *See join.*

Journal A record of all changes in the database; also called a *log.* Used to recover a database that has been damaged or destroyed.

■

Key Field that will be used for sorting.

■

LAN See *local area network.*

Local Area Network (LAN) A configuration of several computers that are all linked together in a limited geographic area; allows users to share a variety of resources.

Local deadlock Deadlock that can be detected totally at one site in a distributed system.

Local site From a user's perspective, the site in a distributed system at which the user is working.

Location transparency The property that means users do not need to be aware of the location of data in a distributed database.

Lock A device that prevents other users from accessing a portion of a database.

Locking The process of placing a lock on a portion of a database, which prevents other users from accessing that portion.

Log A record of all changes in the database; also called a *journal.* Used to recover a database that has been damaged or destroyed.

■

Major sort key When sorting on two fields, the more important field.

Many-to-many relationship A relationship between two entities in which each occurrence of each entity is related to many occurrences of the other entity.

Mapping The process of creating an initial *physical-level design.*

Menu-driven A style of program in which the user selects an action from a list (called a menu) of available options that are displayed on the screen.

Message A request to execute a method.

Method An action defined for an object (class).

Minimally relational A DBMS in which users perceive data as tables and which supports at least the SELECT, PROJECT, and JOIN operations of the *relational algebra* without requiring any predefined access paths.

Minor sort key When sorting on two fields, the less important field.

Multidimensional database The overall structure of the tables in a data warehouse.

Natural language A language in which users communicate with the computer through the use of standard English questions and commands.

Nonkey attribute An attribute that is not part of the primary key.

Nonprocedural language A language in which the user specifies the task that is to be accomplished rather than the steps that are required to accomplish it.

Normal form See *first normal form, second normal form, third normal form,* and *Boyce-Codd Normal Form.*

Normalization Technically, the process of removing repeating groups to produce a *first normal form* relation. Sometimes refers to the process of creating a *third normal form* relation.

Null A special value meaning "unknown" or "not applicable."

Object A unit of data along with the actions that can take place on that data.

Object-oriented database management system (OODBMS) A DBMS in which data and the methods that operate on data are encapsulated into objects.

On-line analytical processing (OLAP) Software that is optimized to work efficiently with multidimensional databases in a data warehouse environment.

On-line transaction processing (OLTP) A system that processes a transaction by dealing with a small number of rows in a relational database in a highly structured, repetitive, and predetermined way.

One-to-many relationship A relationship between two entities in which each occurrence of the first entity is related to many occurrences of the second entity but each occurrence of the second entity is related to only one occurrence of the first entity.

One-to-one relationship A relationship between two entities in which each occurrence of the first entity is related to one occurrence of the second entity and each occurrence of the second entity is related to one occurrence of the first entity.

Operations One of the two components of a *data model;* the facilities given users of the DBMS to manipulate data within the database.

Optimizer The DBMS component that selects the best way to satisfy a query.

Partial dependency A dependency of an attribute on only a portion of the primary key.

Password A word that must be entered before a user can access certain computer resources.

Persistence The ability to have a program "remember" its data from one execution to the next.

Physical level of database design The step during *database design* in which a design for a given DBMS is produced from the final information-level design.

Primary copy In a distributed database with replicated data, the copy that must be updated in order for the update to be deemed complete.

Primary key A minimal collection of attributes (columns) in a relation on which all attributes are functionally dependent and which is chosen as the main direct-access vehicle to individual tuples (rows). See also *candidate key*.

Procedural language A language in which the user must specify the steps that are required for accomplishing a task instead of merely specifying the task itself.

QBE See *Query-by-Example*.

Qualify To indicate the table (relation) of which a given column (attribute) is a part by preceding the column name with the table name. For example, *CUSTOMER.ADDRESS* indicates the column named *ADDRESS* within the table named *CUSTOMER*.

Query A question, the answer to which is found in the database; also used to refer to a command in a *nonprocedural language* such as SQL that is used to obtain the answer to such a question.

Query-By-Example (QBE) A *data manipulation language* for relational databases in which users indicate the action to be taken by filling in portions of blank tables on the screen.

Query facility A facility that enables users to obtain information easily from the database.

Query language A language that is designed to permit users to obtain information easily from the database.

Record A collection of related fields; can be thought of as a row in a table.

Recovery The process of restoring a database that has been damaged or destroyed.

Redundancy Duplication of data.

Referential integrity The rule that if a relation A contains a *foreign key* that matches the primary key of another relation B, then the value of this foreign key must either match the value of the primary key for some row in relation B or be null.

Relation A two-dimensional table in which all entries are single-valued; each column has a distinct name; all the values in a column are values of the attribute that is identified by the column name, the order of columns is immaterial; each row is distinct; and the order of rows is immaterial.

Relational algebra A relational data manipulation language in which relations are created from existing relations through the use of a set of operations.

Relational database A collection of relations.

Relational model A *data model* in which the structure is the *table* or *relation*.

Relationally complete A term applied to any relational *data manipulation language* that can do whatever can be done through the use of the *relational algebra;* also applied to a DBMS that supplies such a data manipulation language.

Relationship An association between entities.

Remote site From a user's perspective, any site other than the one at which the user is working.

Repeating group Several entries at a single location in a table.

Replicas Duplicate versions of data that are stored at more than one site in a distributed database.

Replication Duplicating data at more than one site in a distributed database.

Replication transparency The property that users do not need to be aware of any replication that has taken place in a distributed database.

Roll back The process of undoing changes that have been made to a database.

Save A backup copy.

Second Normal Form (2NF) A relation is in second normal form if it is in first normal form and no nonkey attribute is dependent on only a portion of the primary key.

Secondary key An attribute or collection of attributes that is of interest for retrieval purposes (and that is not already designated as some other type of key).

Security The protection of the database against unauthorized access.

Shared update Several updates taking place to the same file or database at almost the same time; also called *concurrent update*.

Shrinking phase A phase during an update in which all locks are released and no new locks are acquired.

Simple condition A condition that involves only single field and a single value.

SQL See *Structured Query Language.*

Star-join schema A multidimensional database whose conceptual shape resembles a star.

Stored procedure A file containing a collection of SQL statements that are available for future use.

Structure One of the two components of a *data model:* the manner in which the system structures data or, at least, the manner in which the users perceive that the data is structured.

Structured Query Language (SQL) A very popular relational *data definition and manipulation language* that is used in many relational DBMSs.

Subquery In SQL, a query that is contained within another query.

Switchboard A special form used to provide controlled access to the data, forms, reports, and other content of a database.

Synchronization The periodic exchange by a DBMS of all updated data between two databases in a replica set.

Table In the database environment, another name for a relation.

Tabular A type of DBMS in which users perceive data as tables but which does not furnish any of the other characteristics of a relational DBMS.

Third Normal Form (3NF) A relation is in third normal form if it is in second normal form and if the only determinants it contains are candidate keys. (Technically, this is the definition of *Boyce-Codd Normal Form,* but in this text the two are used synonymously.).

Trigger An action that will take place automatically when an associated database operation takes place.

Tuning The process of altering a database design in order to improve performance.

Tuple The formal name for a row in a table.

Two-phase commit An approach to the commit process in distributed systems in which there are two phases. In the first phase, each site is instructed to prepare to commit and must indicate whether the commit will be possible. After each site has responded, the second phase begins: If every site has replied in the affirmative, all sites must commit. If any site has replied in the negative, all sites must abort the transaction.

Two-phase locking An approach to locking in which there are two phases: a growing phase, in which new locks are acquired but no locks are released, and a shrinking phase, in which all locks are released and no new locks are acquired.

Union A combination of two tables consisting of all records that are in either table.

Union-compatible Two tables are union-compatible if they have the same number of fields and if their corresponding fields have identical data types.

Unnormalized relation A structure that satisfies the properties required to be a relation with one exception: repeating groups are allowed; that is, the entries in the table do not have to be single-valued.

Update anomaly An update problem that can occur in a database as a result of a faulty design.

User view The view of data that is necessary to support the operations of a particular user.

View An application program's or an individual user's picture of the database.

Wild card A symbol that can be used in place of an unknown character or group of characters in a *query*.

Index